Poetry and Repression

REVISIONISM FROM BLAKE TO STEVENS

Harold Bloom

This reinterpretation of the full sweep of English and American romantic poetry expands Harold Bloom's recent theoretical speculations. Emphasizing practical criticism, the book offers close readings of poems of Blake, Wordsworth, Shelley, Keats, Tennyson, Browning, Whitman, Yeats, and Stevens. It also reviews the crucial ideas of Emerson, Nietzsche, and in particular Freud, whose psychoanalytic theory of repression and defense Bloom undertakes to revise for purposes of literary criticism.

In his theory of poetic influence as defensive revisionism, Bloom offers a fully defined alternative to the principal modes of contemporary criticism — to the "Freudian literary criticism" that he insists is neither Freudian nor literary criticism; to the "deconstructions" of Jacques Derrida and Paul de Man; to the still-current American New Criticism based upon the rhetorical theories of I. A. Richards; and to various structuralist and archetypal approaches. More than any other writer on poetry today, Harold Bloom strives to avoid reductionism. He returns the reader to the poems themselves, not just as linguistic entities but as intentions of their shapers' will-to-power — power over history, over other poems, and over the poets' own selves.

As a fuller and more general study than Bloom's recent books, *Poetry and Repression* contributes importantly to ideas about literary history, working out a dialectic of the way poetic tradition emerges from the processes of revisionism and canon-formation. The book will be of compelling and provocative interest to teachers and students. To a wider audience its greatest appeal will lie in the intensity and depth of the feeling for poetry that animates every page Harold Bloom writes.

Poetry and Repression

Poetry and Repression

Revisionism from Blake to Stevens

Harold Bloom

New Haven and London, Yale University Press

1976

Library of Congress catalog card number: 75-18165
International standard book number: 0-300-01923-8

Designed by John O. C. McCrillis
and set in Baskerville type by Achorn Graphic Services,
Hudson, Massachusetts.
Printed in the United States of America by
Alpine Press Inc., South Braintree, Mass.

Published in Great Britain, Europe, and Africa by
Yale University Press, Ltd., London.
Distributed in Latin America by Kaiman & Polon,
Inc., New York City; in India by UBS Publishers'
Distributors Pvt., Ltd., Delhi; in Japan by John
Weatherhill, Inc., Tokyo.

For

Archie Randolph Ammons

O earth, how like to heaven, if not preferred
More justly, seat worthier of gods as built
With second thoughts, reforming what was old!
For what god after better worse would build?

Paradise Lost

The past and present wilt—I have fill'd them, emptied
  them,
And proceed to fill my next fold of the future.

Song of Myself

Contents

1. Poetry, Revisionism, Repression   1

2. Blake and Revisionism   28

3. Wordsworth and the Scene of Instruction   52

4. Shelley and His Precursors   83

5. Keats: Romance Revised   112

6. Tennyson: In the Shadow of Keats   143

7. Browning: Good Moments and Ruined Quests   175

8. Yeats, Gnosticism, and the Sacred Void   205

9. Emerson and Whitman: The American Sublime   235

10. Wallace Stevens: The Transcendental Strain   267

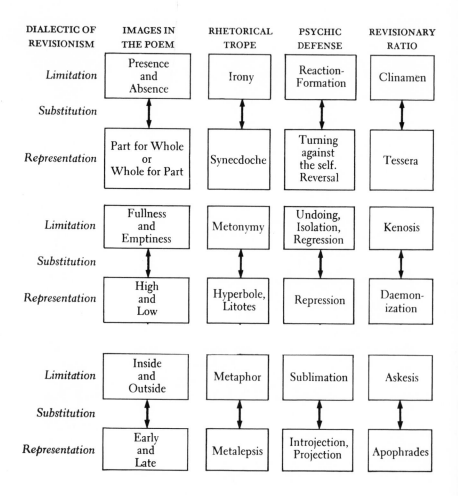

DIALECTIC OF REVISIONISM	IMAGES IN THE POEM	RHETORICAL TROPE	PSYCHIC DEFENSE	REVISIONARY RATIO
Limitation	Presence and Absence	Irony	Reaction-Formation	Clinamen
Substitution				
Representation	Part for Whole or Whole for Part	Synecdoche	Turning against the self. Reversal	Tessera
Limitation	Fullness and Emptiness	Metonymy	Undoing, Isolation, Regression	Kenosis
Substitution				
Representation	High and Low	Hyperbole, Litotes	Repression	Daemonization
Limitation	Inside and Outside	Metaphor	Sublimation	Askesis
Substitution				
Representation	Early and Late	Metalepsis	Introjection, Projection	Apophrades

1

Poetry, Revisionism, Repression

Jacques Derrida asks a central question in his essay on Freud and the Scene of Writing: "What is a text, and what must the psyche be if it can be represented by a text?" My narrower concern with poetry prompts the contrary question: "What is a psyche, and what must a text be if it can be represented by a psyche?" Both Derrida's question and my own require exploration of three terms: "psyche," "text," "represented."

"Psyche" is ultimately from the Indo-European root *bhes*, meaning "to breathe," and possibly was imitative in its origins. "Text" goes back to the root *teks*, meaning "to weave," and also "to fabricate." "Represent" has as its root *es*: "to be." My question thus can be rephrased: "What is a breath, and what must a weaving or a fabrication be so as to come into being again as a breath?"

In the context of post-Enlightenment poetry, a breath is at once a *word*, and a *stance* for uttering that word, a word and a stance *of one's own*. In this context, a weaving or a fabrication is what we call a poem, and its function is to represent, to bring back into being again, an individual stance and word. The poem, as text, is represented or seconded by what psychoanalysis calls the psyche. But the text *is* rhetoric, and as a persuasive system of tropes can be carried into being again only by another system of tropes. Rhetoric can be seconded only by rhetoric, for all that rhetoric can *intend* is more rhetoric. If a text and a psyche can be represented by one another, this can be done only because each is a departure from proper meaning. Figuration turns out to be our only link between breathing and making.

The strong word and stance issue only from a strict will, a will that dares the error of reading all of reality as a text, and all prior texts as openings for its own totalizing and unique interpretations. Strong poets present themselves as looking for truth *in the world*, searching in reality and in tradition, but such a stance, as Nietzsche said, remains under the mastery of desire, of instinctual drives. So, in effect, the strong poet wants pleasure and not truth; he wants what Nietzsche named as "the belief in truth and the pleasurable effects of this belief." No strong poet can admit that Nietzsche was accurate in this insight, and no critic need fear that any strong poet will accept and so be hurt by demystification. The concern of this book, as of my earlier studies in poetic misprision, is only with strong poets, which in this series of chapters is exemplified by the major sequence of High Romantic British and American poets: Blake, Wordsworth, Shelley, Keats, Tennyson, Browning, Yeats, Emerson, Whitman, and Stevens, but also throughout by two of the strongest poets in the European Romantic tradition: Nietzsche and Freud. By "poet" I therefore do not mean only versewriter, as the instance of Emerson also should make clear.

A poetic "text," as I interpret it, is not a gathering of signs on a page, but is a psychic battlefield upon which authentic forces struggle for the only victory worth winning, the divinating triumph over oblivion, or as Milton sang it:

> Attir'd with Stars, we shall for ever sit,
> Triumphing over Death, and Chance, and thee O Time.

Few notions are more difficult to dispel than the "commonsensical" one that a poetic text is self-contained, that it has an ascertainable meaning or meanings without reference to other poetic texts. Something in nearly every reader wants to say: "*Here* is a poem and *there* is a meaning, and I am reasonably certain that the two can be brought together." Unfortunately, poems are not things but only words that refer to other words, and *those* words refer to still other words, and so on, into the densely overpopulated world of literary language. Any poem is an inter-poem, and any reading of a poem is an inter-reading. A poem is not writing, but *rewriting*, and though a strong poem is a fresh start, such a start is a starting-again.

In some sense, literary criticism has known always this reliance of texts upon texts, but the knowing changed (or should have changed) after Vico, who uncovered the genuine scandal of poetic origins, in the complex defensive trope or troping defense he called "divination." Poetry began, according to Vico, out of the ignorance and mortal fear of the gentile giants, who sought to ward off danger and death through interpreting the auguries, through divination: "Their poetic wisdom began with this poetic metaphysics . . . and they were called theological poets . . . and were properly called divine in the sense of diviners, from *divinari*, to divine or predict." These were the giants or poets before the Flood, for Vico a crucial image of two modes of encroachment always threatening the human mind, a divine deluge and a natural engulfment. Edward Said eloquently interprets Vico's own influence-anxieties:

These threatening encroachments are described by Vico as the result of a divinely willed flood, which I take to be an image for the inner crisis of self-knowledge that each man must face at the very beginning of any conscious undertaking. The analogy, in Vico's *Autobiography*, of the universal flood is the prolonged personal crisis of self-alienation from full philosophic knowledge and self-knowledge that Vico faces until the publication of his major work, the *New Science*. His minor successes with his orations, his poems, his treatises, reveal bits of the truth to him, but he is always striving with great effort to come literally into his own.

Said's commentary illuminates the remarkable passage in Vico's early *On the Study Methods of Our Time*, where Vico suddenly appears to be the precursor of Artaud, arguing that the great masterpieces of anterior art must be destroyed, if any great works are still to be performed. Or, if great art is to be retained, let it be for "the benefit of lesser minds," while men of "surpassing genius, should put the masterpieces of their art out of their sight, and strive with the greatest minds to appropriate the secret of nature's grandest creation." Vico's primary precursor was Descartes, whom he repudiated in favor of Bacon as a more distant and antithetical precursor, but it could be argued that Vico's *New Science* as a "severe poem" is a strong misprision of Descartes.

Language for Vico, particularly poetic language, is always and necessarily a revision of previous language. Vico, so far as I know, inaugurated a crucial insight that most critics still refuse to assimilate, which is that every poet is belated, that every poem is an instance of what Freud called *Nachträglichkeit* or "retroactive meaningfulness." Any poet (meaning even Homer, if we could know enough about his precursors) is in the position of being "after the Event," in terms of literary language. His art is necessarily an *aftering,* and so at best he strives for a selection, through repression, out of the traces of the language of poetry; that is, he represses some of the traces, and remembers others. This remembering is a misprision, or creative misreading, but no matter how strong a misprision, it cannot achieve an autonomy of meaning, or a meaning *fully* present, that is, free from all literary context. Even the strongest poet must take up his stance *within* literary language. If he stands *outside* it, then he cannot begin to write poetry. For poetry lives always under the shadow of poetry. The caveman who traced the outline of an animal upon the rock always retraced a precursor's outline.

The curse of an increased belatedness, a dangerously self-conscious belatedness, is that creative envy becomes the ecstasy, the Sublime, of the sign-system of poetic language. But this is, from an altered perspective, a loss that can become a shadowed gain, the blessing achieved by the latecomer poet as a wrestling Jacob, who cannot let the great depart finally, without receiving a new name all his own. Nothing is won for the reader we all need to become if this wrestling with the dead is idealized by criticism. The enormous distinction of Vico, among all critical theorists, is that he idealized least. Vico understood, as almost no one has since, that the link between poetry and pagan theology was as close as the war between poetry and Hebrew-Christian theology was perpetual. In Vico's absolute distinction between gentile and Jew, the gentile is linked both to poetry and history, through the revisionary medium of language, while the Jew (and subsequently the Christian) is linked to a sacred origin transcending language, and so has no relation to human history or to the arts. We only know what we ourselves have made, according to Vico, and so his science excludes all knowledge of the true God, who can be left to the Church and its theologians. The happy consequence, for Vico, is that the world of the indefinite, the world of ambivalent and uncertain images, which is the universe of poetry, becomes identical with our fallen state of being in the body. To be in the body, according to Vico, is to suffer a condition in which we are ignorant of causation and of origins, yet still we are very much in quest of origins. Vico's insight is that poetry is born of our ignorance of causes, and we can extend Vico by observing that if any poet knows too well what causes his poem, then he cannot write it, or at least will write it badly. He must repress the causes, including the precursor-poems, but such forgetting, as this book will show, itself is a condition of a particular exaggeration of style or hyperbolical figuration that tradition has called the Sublime.

2

How does one read a strong poem? How does one write a strong poem? What makes a poem strong? There is a precarious identity between the Over-reader and the Over-poet, both of them perhaps forms of the Over-man, as prophesied by Nietzsche's Zarathustra. Strong poetry is a paradox, resembling nothing so much as Durkheim on Marxism, or Karl Kraus on Freudianism. Durkheim said that socialism was not a sociology or miniature science, but rather a cry of grief; not so much a scientific formulation of social facts, as itself a social fact. Following the aphorism of Kraus, that psychoanalysis itself was the disease for which it purported to be the cure, we can say that psychoanalysis is more a psychic fact than a formulation of psychic facts. Similarly, the reading of strong poetry is just as much a poetic fact as is the writing of such poetry. Strong poetry is strong only by virtue of a kind of textual usurpation that is analogous to what Marxism encompasses as its social usurpation or Freudianism as its psychic usurpation. A strong poem does not *formulate* poetic facts any more than strong reading or criticism formulates them, for a strong reading *is* the only poetic fact, the only revenge against time that endures, that is successful in canonizing one text as opposed to a rival text.

There is no textual authority without an act of imposition, a declaration of property that is made figuratively rather than properly or literally. For the ultimate question a strong reading asks of a poem is: Why? Why should it have been written? Why must we read it, out of all the too many other poems available? Who does the poet think he is, anyway? Why is his poem?

By defining poetic strength as usurpation or imposition, I am offending against civility, against the social conventions of literary scholarship and criticism. But poetry, when it aspires to strength, is necessarily a competitive mode, indeed an obsessive mode, because poetic strength involves a self-representation that is reached only through trespass, through crossing a daemonic threshold. Again, resorting to Vico gives the best insight available for the nature and necessity of the strong poet's self-proclamation.

Vico says that "the true God" founded the Jewish religion "on the prohibition of the divination on which all the gentile nations arose." A strong poet, for Vico or for us, is precisely like a gentile nation; he must divine or invent himself, and so attempt the impossibility of *originating himself*. Poetry has an origin in the body's ideas of itself, a Vichian notion that is authentically difficult, at least for me. Since poetry, unlike the Jewish religion, does not go back to a truly divine origin, poetry is always at work *imagining its own origin*, or telling a persuasive lie about itself, to itself. Poetic strength ensues when such lying persuades the reader that his own origin has been reimagined by the poem. Persuasion, in a poem, is the work of rhetoric, and again Vico is the best of guides, for he convincingly relates the origins of rhetoric to the origins of what he calls poetic logic, or what I would call poetic misprision.

Angus Fletcher, writing on *The Magic Flute*, observes that: "To begin is always uncertain, nextdoor to chaos. To begin requires that, uncertainly, we bid farewell to some thing, some one, some where, some time. Beginning is still ending." Fletcher, by emphasizing the uncertainty of a beginning, follows Vico's idea of the indefiniteness of all secular origins. But this indefiniteness, because it is made by man, can be interpreted by man. Vico says that "ignorance, the mother of wonder, made everything wonderful to men who were ignorant of everything." From this followed a poetic logic or language "not . . . in accord with the nature of the things it dealt with . . . but . . . a

fantastic speech making use of physical substances en-
dowed with life and most of them imagined to be divine."
For Vico, then, the trope comes from ignorance. Vico's
profundity as a philosopher of rhetoric, beyond all others
ancient and modern except for his true son, Kenneth
Burke, is that he views tropes as defenses. Against what?
Initially, against their own origins in ignorance, and so
against the powerlessness of man in relation to the world:

... man in his ignorance makes himself the rule of the universe, for in the examples cited he has made of himself an
entire world. So that, as rational metaphysics teaches that man
becomes all things by understanding them, this imaginative
metaphysics shows that man becomes all things by *not* understanding them; and perhaps the latter proposition is truer than
the former, for when man understands he extends his mind
and takes in the things, but when he does not understand he
makes the things out of himself and becomes them by transforming himself into them.

Vico is asking a crucial question, which could be interpreted reductively as, What is a poetic image, or what
is a rhetorical trope, or what is a psychic defense? Vico's
answer can be read as a formula: poetic image, trope,
defense are all forms of a ratio between human ignorance
making things out of itself, and human self-identification
moving to transform us into the things we have made.
When the human ignorance is the trespass of a poetic
repression of anteriority, and the transforming movement is a new poem, then the ratio measures a rewriting
or an act of revision. As poetic image, the ratio is a
phenomenal masking of the mind taking in the world of
things, which is Vico's misprision of the Cartesian relationship between mind and the *res extensa*. An image is
necessarily an imitation, and its coverings or maskings in
poetic language necessarily center in certain fixed areas:
presence and absence, partness and wholeness, fullness
and emptiness, height and depth, insideness and outside-

ness, earliness and lateness. Why these? Because they are
the inevitable categories of our makings and our becom-
ings, or as inevitable as such categories can be, within the
fixities and limits of space and time. As trope, the ratio between ignorance and identification takes us back to the realization, by Vico, that the first
language of the gentiles was not a "giving of names to
things according to the nature of each," unlike the sacred
Hebrew of Adam, but rather was fantastic and figurative.
In the beginning was the trope, is in effect Vico's formula
for pagan poetry. Kenneth Burke, the Vico of our century, gives us a formula for why rhetoric rises:

> In pure identification there would be no strife. Likewise,
> there would be no strife in absolute separateness, since oppo-
> nents can join battle only through a mediatory ground that
> makes their communication possible, thus providing the first
> condition necessary for their interchange of blows. But put
> identification and division ambiguously together, so that you
> cannot know for certain just where one ends and the other
> begins, and you have the characteristic invitation to rhetoric.
> Here is a major reason why rhetoric, according to Aristotle,
> "proves opposites."

Vico saw rhetoric as being defensive; Burke tends to
emphasize what he calls the realistic function of rhetoric:
"the use of language as a symbolic means of inducing
cooperation in beings that by nature respond to symbols."
But Vico, compared to Burke, is more of a magical for-
malist, like his own primitives, his "theological poets."
Vico's giants divinate so as to defend against death, and
they divinate through the turns of figurative language. As
a ratio between ignorance and identification, a psychic
defense in Vichian terms is not significantly different
from the Freudian notion of defense. Freud's
"mechanisms" of defense are directed toward Vico's "ignorance," which in Freud is "instinct" or "drive." For
Freud and Vico alike the "source" of all our drives is the

body, and defense is finally against drive itself. For though defense takes instinct as its object, defense becomes contaminated by instinct, and so becomes compulsive and at least partly repressed, which rhetorically means hyperbolical or Sublime.

A specific defense is for Freud an operation, but for Vico a trope. It is worth noting that the root-meaning of our word "defense" is "to strike or hurt," and that "gun" and "defense" are from the same root, just as it is interesting to remember that *tropos* meaning originally "turn, way, manner" appears also in the name *Atropos* and in the word "entropy." The trope-as-defense or ratio between ignorance and identification might be called at once a warding-off by turning and yet also a way of striking or manner of hurting. Combining Vico and Freud teaches us that the origin of any defense is its stance towards death, just as the origin of any trope is its stance towards proper meaning. Where the psychic defense and the rhetorical trope take the same particular phenomenal maskings in poetic images, there we might speak of the ultimate ratio between ignorance and identification as expressing itself in a somber formula: death is the most proper or literal of meanings, and literal meaning partakes of death.

Talbot Donaldson, commenting upon Chaucer's *Nun's Priest's Tale,* speaks of rhetoric as "a powerful weapon of survival in a vast and alien universe," a mode of satisfying our need for security. For a strong poet in particular, rhetoric is also what Nietzsche saw it as being, a mode of interpretation that is the will's revulsion against time, the will's revenge, its vindication against the necessity of passing away. Pragmatically, a trope's revenge is against an earlier trope, just as defenses tend to become operations against one another. We can define a strong poet as one who will not tolerate words that intervene between him and the Word, or precursors standing between him and the Muse. But that means the strong poet in effect takes up the stance of the Gnostic, ancestor of all major Western revisionists.

3

What does the Gnostic *know*? These are the injunctions of the Gnostic adept Monoimus, who sounds rather like Emerson:

Abandon the search for God and the creation. . . . Look for him by taking *yourself* as the starting point. Learn who it is who *within you* makes everything his own and says, "*My* god, *my* mind, *my* thought, *my* soul, *my* body." Learn the sources of sorrow, joy, love, hate. Learn how it happens that one watches without willing, rests without willing, becomes angry without willing, loves without willing. If you search these matters you will find him *in yourself.*

What the Gnostic knows is his own subjectivity, and in that self-consciousness he seeks his own freedom, which he calls "salvation" but which pragmatically seems to be freedom from the anxiety of being influenced by the Jewish God, or Biblical Law, or nature. The Gnostics, by temperament, were akin both to Vico's magic primitives and to post-Enlightenment poets; their quarrel with the words dividing them from their own Word was essentially the quarrel of any belated creator with his precursor. Their rebellion against religious tradition as a process of supposedly benign transmission became the prophecy of all subsequent quarrels with poetic tradition. R. M. Grant, in his *Gnosticism and Early Christianity*, remarks of the proto-Gnostic yet still Jewish *Prayer of Joseph* that it "represents an attempt to supplant an archangel of the older apocalyptic by a new archangel who makes himself known by a new revelation." But Gnostics, as Grant indicates, go beyond apocalyptic thought, and abandon Judaism (and Christianity) by denying the goodness and true divinity of the Creator god, as well as the law of Moses and the vision of the Resurrection.

Part of the deep relevance of Gnosticism to any theory
of poetic misprision is due to the attempt of Simon Magus
to revise Homer as well as the Bible, as in this Simonian
misreading of the *Iliad*, where Virgil's stationing of Helen
is ascribed to Homer, an error wholly typical of all strong
misinterpretation:

> She who at that time was with the Greeks and Trojans was
> the same who dwelt above before creation. . . . She is the one
> who now is with me; for her sake I descended. She waited for
> my coming; for she is the Thought called Helen in Homer. So
> Homer has to describe her as having stood on the tower and
> signaling with a torch to the Greeks the plot against the Phry-
> gians. Through its shining he signified the light's display from
> above. . . . As the Phrygians by dragging in the wooden horse
> ignorantly brought on their own destruction, so the gentiles,
> the men apart from my gnosis, produce perdition for them-
> selves.

Simon is writing his own poem, and calling it Homer,
and his peculiar mixture in this passage of Homer, Virgil,
the Bible, and his own Gnosis amounts to a revisionary
freedom of interpretation, one so free that it transgresses
all limits and becomes its own creation. Christianity has
given Simon a bad name, but in a later time he might
have achieved distinction as a truly audacious strong poet,
akin to Yeats.

Valentinus, who came after Simon, has been compared
to Heidegger by Hans Jonas, and I myself have found the
Valentinian speculation to be rather more useful for poetic theory than the Heideggerian. Something of that usefulness I attempt to demonstrate in the chapter on Yeats
in this book; here I want to cite only a single Valentinian
passage, for its view of the Demiurge is precisely the view
taken of a strong precursor poet by a strong ephebe or
latecomer poet:

> When the Demiurge further wanted to imitate also the
> boundless, eternal, infinite and timeless nature of [the original

eight Aeons in the Pleroma], but could not express their immutable eternity, being as he was a fruit of defect, he embodied their eternity in times, epochs, and great numbers of years, under the delusion that by the quantity of times he could represent their infinity. Thus truth escaped him and he followed the lie. Therefore he shall pass away when the times are fulfilled.

This is a misprision-by-parody of Plato, as Plotinus eloquently charged in his *Second Ennead IX,* "Against the Gnostics; or, Against Those that Affirm the Creator of the Cosmos and the Cosmos Itself to be Evil." Hans Jonas observes the specific parody of the *Timaeus* 37C ff:

When the father and creator saw the creature which he had made moving and living, the created image of the eternal gods, he rejoiced, and in his joy determined to make the copy still more like the original, and as this was an eternal living being, he sought to make the universe eternal, so far as might be. Now the nature of the ideal being was everlasting, but to bestow this attribute in its fullness upon a creature was impossible. Wherefore he resolved to have a moving image of eternity, and when he set in order the heaven, he made this image eternal but moving according to number, while eternity itself rests in unity, and this image we call time.

The Demiurge of Valentinus lies against eternity, and so, against the Demiurge, Valentinus lies against time. Where the Platonic model suggests a benign transmission (though with loss) through imitation, the Gnostic model insists upon a doubly malign misinterpretation, and a transmission through catastrophe. Either way, the belated creator achieves the uniqueness of his own consciousness through a kind of fall, but these kinds are very different, the Platonic model positing time as a necessity, the Valentinian misprision condemning time as a lie. While the major traditions of poetic interpretation have followed Platonic and/or Aristotelian models, I think that the major traditions of post-Enlightenment poetry have tended more to the Gnostic stance of misprision. The Valentinian doctrine of creation could serve my own revisionist purpose, which is to adopt an interpretative model closer to the stance and language of "modern" or post-Enlightenment poetry than the philosophically oriented models have proved to be. But, again like the poets, so many of whom have been implicitly Gnostic while explicitly even more occult, I turn to the medieval system of Old Testament interpretation known as Kabbalah, particularly the doctrines of Isaac Luria. Kabbalah, demystified, is a unique blend of Gnostic and Neoplatonic elements, of a self-conscious subjectivity founded upon a revisionist view of creation, combined with a rational but rhetorically extreme dialectic of creativity. My turn to a Kabbalistic model, particularly to a Lurianic and "regressive" scheme of creation, may seem rather eccentric, but the readings offered in this book should demonstrate the usefulness of the Lurianic dialectics for poetic interpretation.

The quest for interpretative models is a necessary obsession for the reader who would be strong, since to refuse models explicitly is only to accept other models, however unknowingly. All reading is translation, and all attempts to communicate a reading seem to court reduction, perhaps inevitably. The proper use of any critical paradigm ought to lessen the dangers of reduction, yet clearly most paradigms are, in themselves, dangerously reductive. Negative theology, even where it verges upon theosophy, rather than the reasoning through negation of Continental philosophy, or structuralist linguistics, seems to me the likeliest "discipline" for revisionary literary critics to raid in their incessant quest after further metaphors for the act of reading. But so extreme is the situation of strong poetry in the post-Enlightenment, so nearly identical is it with the anxiety of influence, that it requires as interpretative model the most dialectical and negative of theologies that can be found. Kabbalah pro-

vides not only a dialectic of creation astonishingly close
to revisionist poetics, but also a conceptual rhetoric
ingeniously oriented towards defense.

Kabbalah, though the very word means "tradition" (in
the particular sense of "reception") goes well beyond orthodox tradition in its attempt to *restore* primal meanings
to the Bible. Kabbalah is necessarily a massive misprision
of both Bible and Talmud, and the initial sense in which
it accurately was "tradition" is the unintentionally ironic
one that means Neoplatonic and Gnostic traditions, rather than Jewish ones. The cosmology of Kabbalah, as
Gershom Scholem definitively observes, is Neoplatonic.
Scholem locates the originality in a "new religious impulse," yet understandably has difficulty in defining such
an impulse. He distinguishes Kabbalistic theories of the
emanation of the *sefirot*, from Neoplatonic systems, by
noting that, in the latter, the stages of emanation "are not
conceived as processes within the Godhead." Yet he
grants that certain Gnosticisms also concentrated on the
life within the Godhead, and we can notice the same
emphasis in the analysis of the Valentinian Speculation by
Hans Jonas: "The distinguishing principle . . . is the attempt to place the origin of darkness, and thereby of the
dualistic rift of being, *within* the godhead itself." Jonas
adds that the Valentinian vision relies on "terms of divine
error" and this *is* the distinction between Gnosticism and
Kabbalah, for Kabbalah declines to impute error to the
Godhead.

Earlier Kabbalah from its origins until Luria's older
contemporary Cordovero, saw creation as an outgoing or
egressive process. Luria's startling originality was to revise
the *Zohar*'s dialectics of creation into an ingoing or regressive process, a creation by contraction, destruction, and
subsequent restitution. This Lurianic story of creation-
by-catastrophe is a genuine dialectic or dialectical process
by the ordeal of the toughest-minded account of dialectic
I know, the one set forth by the philosopher Karl Popper

in his powerful collection, *Conjectures and Refutations: The Growth of Scientific Knowledge,* which has a decisive essay, "What Is Dialectic?" in which neither Hegel nor Marx passes the Popperian test.

The Lurianic story of creation begins with an act of self-limitation on God's part that finds its aesthetic equivalent in any new poet's initial rhetoric of limitation, that is, in his acts of re-seeing what his precursors had seen before him. These re-seeings are translations of desires into verbal acts, instances of substantive thinking, and tend to be expressed by a nominal style, and by an imagery that stresses states of absence, of emptiness, and of estrangement or "outsideness." In the language of psychoanalysis, these modes of aesthetic limitation can be called different degrees of sublimation, as I will explain in this chapter's last section. Lurianic *zimzum* or divine contraction, the first step in the dialectic of creation, can be called God's sublimation of Himself, or at least of His own Presence. God begins creation by taking a step inside Himself, by voiding His own Presence. This *zimzum,* considered rhetorically, is a composite trope, commencing as an irony for the creative act, since it says "withdrawal" yet means the opposite, which is absolute "concentration." Making begins with a regression, a holding-in of the Divine breath, which is also, curiously, a kind of digression.

Even so, the strong poems of the post-Enlightenment, from Blake through Stevens, begin with the parabasis of rhetorical irony. But the psychic defense concealed in the irony is the initial defense that Freud called reaction-formation, the overt attitude that opposes itself directly to a repressed wish, by a rigidity that expresses the opposite of the instinct it battles. The Kabbalistic contraction/withdrawal is both trope and defense, and in seeking an initial term for it I have settled upon the Epicurean-Lucretian *clinamen,* naturalized as a critical term long before me, by Coleridge in his *Aids to Reflection.* The *clinamen* or "swerve" is the trope-as-misreading, irony as a dialectical alternation of images of presence and absence, or the beginnings of the defensive process. Writing on *The Magic Flute,* Angus Fletcher ventures some very useful observations upon irony as an aesthetic limitation:

> Irony is merely a darkened awareness of that possibility of change, of transformation, which in its fixed philosophic definition is the "crossing over" of dialectic process. But we can never say too often that irony implies the potential defeat of action, defeat at the hands of introspection, self-consciousness, etc., modes of thought which sap the body and even the mind itself of its apparent motivation.

Kenneth Burke notes that dialectic irony provides us with a kind of technical equivalent for the doctrine of original sin, which for a strong new poem is simply a sin of transgression *against origins.* The Lurianic dialectic follows its initial irony of Divine contraction, or image of limitation, with a process it calls the breaking-of-the-vessels, which in poetic terms is the principle of rhetorical substitution, or in psychic terms is the metamorphic element in all defenses, their tendency to turn into one another, even as tropes tend to mix into one another. What follows in the later or regressive Kabbalah is called *tikkun* or "restitution" and is symbolic representation. Here again, Coleridge can be our guide, as he identified Symbol with the trope of synecdoche, just as Freud located the defense of turning-against-the-self, or masochistic reversal, within a thinking-by-synecdoche. Here, seeking for a broader term to hold together synecdoche and reversal within the part/whole image, I have followed Mallarmé and· Lacan by using the word *tessera,* not in its modern meaning as a mosaic-building unit, but in its ancient, mystery-cult meaning of an antithetical completion, the device of recognition that fits together the broken parts of a vessel, to make a whole again.

There is an opening movement of *clinamen* to *tessera,* in most significant poems of our era, that is, of the last three

centuries. I am aware that such a statement, between its
home-made terminology and its apparent arbitrariness, is
rather outrageous, but I offer it as merely descriptive and
as a useful mapping of how the reading of poems begins.
By "reading" I intend to mean the work both of poet and
of critic, who themselves move from dialectic irony to
synecdochal representation as they confront the text before them. The movement is from a troubled awareness
of dearth, of signification having wandered away and
gotten lost, to an even more troubled awareness that the
self represents only part of a mutilated or broken whole,
whether in relation to what it believes itself once to have
been, or still somehow hopes to become.

    Clinamen is a swerve or step inside, and so is a move-
ment of internalization, just as *tessera* is necessarily an
antithetical completion that necessarily fails to complete,
and so is less than a full externalization. That is reason
enough for strong modern poems passing into a middle
movement, where as terms-for-mapping I have employed
kenosis, St. Paul's word for Christ's "humbling" or
emptying-out of his own divinity, and *daemonization,*
founded upon the ancient notion of the daemonic as the
intervening stage between the human and the divine.
Kenosis subsumes the trope of metonymy, the imagistic
reduction from a prior fullness to a later emptiness, and
the three parallel Freudian defenses of regression, undoing, and isolating, all of them repetitive and compulsive
movements of the psyche.

    Daemonization, which usually marks the climax or Sub-
lime crisis point of the strong poem, subsumes the principal Freudian defense, repression, the very active defense that produces or accumulates much of what Freud
calls the Unconscious. As trope, poetic repression tends to
appear as an exaggerated representation, the overthrow
called hyperbole, with characteristic imagery of great
heights and abysmal depths. Metonymy, as a reification
by contiguity, can be called an extension of irony, just as

hyperbole extends synecdoche. But both extremes lack finality, as their psychic equivalents hint, since the reductiveness of metonymy is only the linguistic version of the hopelessly entropic backward movements of the regressing, undoing, and isolating psyche. The metonymizer is a compulsive cataloger, and the contents of the poetic self never can be wholly emptied out. Similarly, there is no end to repression in strong poetry, as again I will indicate in the last section of this chapter. The dialectics of revisionism compel the strong poem into a final movement of ratios, one that sets space against time, space as a metaphor of limitation and time as a restituting metalepsis or transumption, a trope that murders all previous tropes.

I take the name, *askesis*, for the revisionary ratio that subsumes metaphor, the defense of sublimation, and the dualistic imagery of inside consciousness against outside nature, from Walter Pater, who himself took it from pre-Socratic usage. Pater said of *askesis* (which he spelled *ascesis*) that in a stylistic context it equalled "self-restraint, a skillful economy of means," and in his usually subtle play on etymological meaning, he hinted at the athlete's self-discipline. Even more subtly, Pater was attempting to refine the Romantic legacy of Coleridge, with its preference for mind/nature metaphors over all other figurations. To Pater belongs the distinction of noting that the secularized epiphany, the "privileged" or good moment of Romantic tradition, was the ultimate and precarious form of this inside/outside metaphor. The third and final dialectical movement of modern strong poems tends to begin with such a sublimating metaphor, but again this is another limitation of meaning, another achieved dearth or realization of wandering signification. In the final breaking-of-the-vessels of Romantic figuration, an extraordinary substitution takes place, for which I have proposed the name *apophrades*, the unlucky days, dismal, when the Athenian dead return to reinhabit their former

houses, and ritualistically and momentarily drive the living out of doors.

Defensively, this poetic final movement is frequently a
balance between introjection (or identification) and projection (or casting-out the forbidden). Imagistically, the
balance is between earliness and belatedness, and there
are very few strong poems that do not attempt, somehow,
to conclude by introjecting an earliness and projecting the
affliction of belatedness. The trope involved is the unset-
tling one anciently called metalepsis or transumption, the
only trope-reversing trope, since it substitutes one word
for another in earlier figurations. Angus Fletcher follows
Quintilian in describing transumption as a process "in
which commonly the poet goes from one word to another
that sounds like it, to yet another, thus developing a chain
of auditory associations getting the poem from one image
to another more remote image." Kenneth Burke, commenting upon my *A Map of Misreading*, sees daemonic
hyperbole and transumption as heightened versions of
synecdoche, representations related to Plato's transcen-
dentalized eros:

> The *Phaedrus* takes us from seed in the sense of sheer sperm
> to the heights of the Socratic erotic, as transcendentally em-
> bodied in the idea of doctrinal insemination. And similarly, via
> hyperbole and metalepsis, we'd advance from an ephebe's
> sheer *physical* release to a poetically ejaculatory analogue.

Metalepsis or transumption thus becomes a total, final
act of taking up a poetic stance in relation to anteriority,
particularly to the anteriority of poetic language, which
means primarily the loved-and-feared poems of the precursors. Properly accomplished, this stance figuratively
produces the illusion of having fathered one's own
fathers, which is the greatest illusion, the one that Vico
called "divination," or that we could call poetic immortality.

What is the critic's defense for so systematic a mapping

of the poet's defenses? Burke, in the preface to his first book, *Counter-Statement,* said that his set-piece, his "Lexicon Rhetoricae," was "frankly intended as a machine— machine for criticism, however, not for poetry," since poetry "is always beyond the last formula." I too offer a "machine for criticism," though I sometimes fear that poetry itself increasingly has become the last formula. Modern poetry, as Richard Rorty sums it up, lives under a triple curse: (1) Hegel's prophecy that any future will be transcended automatically by a future future, (2) Marx's prophecy of the end of all individual enterprise, (3) Freud's prophetic analysis of the entropic drive beyond the Pleasure Principle, an analysis uneasily akin to Nietzsche's vision of the death of Man, a vision elaborated by Foucault, Deleuze, and other recent speculators. As Rorty says: "Who can see himself as caught in a dialectical moment, enmeshed in a family romance, parasitic upon the last stages of capitalism, yet still in competition with the mighty dead?" The only answer I know is that the strongest artists, but only the strongest, can prevail even in this entrapment of dialectics. They prevail by reattaining the Sublime, though a greatly altered Sublime, and so I will conclude this chapter by a brief speculation upon that fresh Sublime, and its dependence upon poetic equivalents of repression.

4

The grandfathers of the Sublime are Homer and the Bible, but in English, Milton is the severe father of the Sublime mode. Erich Auerbach said that "the *Divine Comedy* is the first and in certain respects the only European poem comparable in rank and quality to the sublime poetry of antiquity," a judgment that seems to exclude *Paradise Lost* from Europe. I suppose that Dante's superiority over Milton, insofar as it exists, best might be justified by Auerbach's beautiful observations upon Dante's personal involvement in his own Sublime:

Dante . . . is not only the narrator; he is at the same time the suffering hero. As the protagonist of his poem which, far greater in scope than the Homeric epics, encompasses all the sufferings and passions, all the joys and blessings of human existence, he himself is involved in all the movements of his immense action. . . . it is he himself who, held fast in the depths of hell, awaits the savior in a moment of extreme peril. What he relates, accordingly, is not a mere happening, but something that happens to him. He is not outside, contemplating, admiring, and describing the sublime. He is in it, at a definite point in the scene of action, threatened and hard pressed; he can only feel and describe what is present to him at this particular place, and what presents itself is the divine aid he has been awaiting.

Elsewhere in the same book (*Literary Language and Its Public in Late Latin Antiquity and in the Middle Ages*), Auerbach sets Petrarch above even Dante in one respect, which I believe is also the one in which the English line that goes from Spenser through Milton on to Wordsworth surpassed even Petrarch:

The Italians learned to control the devices of rhetoric and gradually to rid them of their coldness and obtrusive pedantry. In this respect Petrarch's Italian is markedly superior even to Dante's, for a feeling for the limits of expressibility had become second nature to Petrarch and accounts in good part for his formal clarity, while Dante had to struggle for these acquisitions and had far greater difficulty in maintaining them in the face of his far greater and more profound undertaking. With Petrarch lyrical subjectivism achieved perfection for the first time since antiquity, not impaired but, quite on the contrary, enriched by the motif of Christian anguish that always accompanies it. For it was this motif that gave lyrical subjectivism its dialectical character and the poignancy of its emotional appeal.

The dialectical character of lyrical subjectivism is indeed my subject, and is what I attempt to map through my interplay of revisionary ratios. Auerbach, in the same book, says of Vico that "In the rhetorical figures of the schools he saw vestiges of the original, concrete, and sensuous thinking of men who believed that in employing words and concepts they were seizing hold of things themselves." Auerbach is thus in Vico's tradition when he praises Dante for being *in* his own Sublime, as though the Sublime were not so much a word or concept but somehow was the thing itself, or Dante was one with his own severe poem. The lyrical subjectivism of Petrarch knows more clearly its distance from the thing itself, its reliance upon words apart from things. Perhaps this is why John Freccero so persuasively can nominate Petrarch as the first strong instance in Western poetry of the anxiety of influence, an anxiety induced by the greatness of Dante. Petrarch, like Spenser and Milton after him, suffers several dialectical anguishes, besides the anguish of attempting to reconcile poetry and religion.

Milton does stand outside his own Sublime; his astonishing invention was to place Satan inside the Sublime, as even a momentary comparison of the Satans of Dante and Milton will show. I am an unreconstructed Romantic when I read *Paradise Lost*; I continue to be less surprised by sin than I am surprised by Satan. If I can recognize the Sublime in poetry, then I find it in Satan, in what he is, says, does; and more powerfully even in what he is not, does not say, and cannot do. Milton's Satan is his own worst enemy, but that is his strength, not his weakness, in a dualizing era when the self can become strong only by battling itself in others, and others in itself. Satan is a great rhetorician, and nearly as strong a poet as Milton himself, but more important he is Milton's central way through to the Sublime. As such, Satan prophesies the post-Enlightenment crisis-poem, which has become our modern Sublime.

I find that my map of misprision with its dialectic of limitation/substitution/representation, and its three pairs of ratios, alternating with one another, works well enough

for the pattern of Satan's major soliloquies, possibly because these are among the ancestors of the crisis-of-
poetic-vision poem, by way of the eighteenth-century Sublime ode. Satan's hyperbolical rhetoric is wonderfully
described by a theoretician of the Sublime, Martin Price,
in a passage which tries only to explicate Longinus, but
which nevertheless conveys the force of Satan's characteristic imagery:

> One finds, then, a conception of passion that transcends
> material objects, that moves through the sensible universe in
> search of its grandest forms and yet can never find outward
> grandeur adequate to its inherent vision and its capacities of
> devotion. The intensity of the soul's passions is measured by
> the immensity of its objects. The immensity is, at its extreme,
> quite literally a boundlessness, a surpassing of measurable ex-
> tension.

The hyperbole or intensified exaggeration that such
boundlessness demands exacts a psychic price. To "ex-
aggerate" etymologically means "to pile up, to heap," and
the function of the Sublime is to heap us, as Moby Dick
makes Ahab cry out "He heaps me!" Precisely here I
locate the difference between the strong poets and Freud,
since what Freud calls "repression" is, in the greater
poets, the imagination of a Counter-Sublime. By attempting to show the poetic ascendancy of "repression" over
"sublimation" I intend no revision of the Freudian trope
of "the Unconscious," but rather I deny the usefulness of
the Unconscious, as opposed to repression, as a literary
term. Freud, in the context of poetic interpretation, is
only another strong poet, though the strongest of modern poets, stronger even than Schopenhauer, Emerson,
Nietzsche, Marx, and Browning; far stronger than Valéry, Rilke, Yeats, Stevens. A critic, "using" Freud, does
nothing different in kind from "using" Milton or Valéry.
If the critic chooses to employ Freud reductively, as a
supposed scientist, whatever that is, then the critic forgets

that tropes or defenses are primarily figures of willed falsification rather than figures of unwilled knowledge. There is willed knowing, but that process does not produce poems. Whatever the criticism of poetry that I urge is, and whether it proves to be, as I hope, a necessary error, or just another useless mistake, it has nothing in common with anything now miscalled "Freudian literary criticism." To say that a poem's true subject is its repression of the precursor poem is not to say that the later poem reduces to the process of that repression. On a strict Freudian view, a good poem is a sublimation, and not a repression. Like any work of substitution that replaces the gratification of prohibited instincts, the poem, as viewed by the Freudians, may contain antithetical effects but not unintended or counterintended effects. In the Freudian valorization of sublimation, the survival of those effects would be flaws in the poem. But poems are actually stronger when their counterintended effects battle most incessantly against their overt intentions.

Imagination, as Vico understood and Freud did not, is the faculty of self-preservation, and so the proper use of Freud, for the literary critic, is not so to apply Freud (or even revise Freud) as to arrive at an Oedipal interpretation of poetic history. I find such to be the usual misunderstanding that my own work provokes. In studying poetry we are not studying the mind, nor the Unconscious, even if there is an unconscious. We are studying a kind of labor that has its own latent principles, principles that can be uncovered and then taught systematically. Freud's lifework is a severe poem, and its own latent principles are more useful to us, as critics, than its manifest principles, which frequently call for interpretation as the misprisions of Schopenhauer and Nietzsche that they are, despite their own intentions.

Poems are not psyches, nor things, nor are they renewable archetypes in a verbal universe, nor are they architectonic units of balanced stresses. They are defensive processes in constant change, which is to say that poems themselves are *acts of reading.* A poem is, as Thomas Frosch says, a fierce, proleptic debate *with itself,* as well as with precursor poems. Or, a poem is a dance of substitutions, a constant breaking-of-the-vessels, as one limitation undoes a representation, only to be restituted in its turn by a fresh representation. Every strong poem, at least since Petrarch, has known implicitly what Nietzsche taught us to know explicitly: that there is only interpretation, and that every interpretation answers an earlier interpretation, and then must yield to a later one.

I conclude by returning to the poetic equivalent of repression, to the Sublime or the Counter-Sublime of a belated *daemonization,* because the enigma of poetic authority can be resolved only in the context of repression. Geoffrey Hartman, in *The Fate of Reading,* calls the poetic will "sublimated compulsion." I myself would call it "repressed freedom." Freud, expounding repression, was compelled to posit a "primal repression," a purely hypothetical first phase of repression, in which the very idea representing a repressed instinct itself was denied any entrance into consciousness. Though the French Freudians courageously have tried to expound this splendidly outrageous notion, their efforts have left it in utter darkness. To explain repression at all, Freud overtly had to create a myth of an archaic fixation, as though he were saying: "In the beginning was repression, even before there was any drive to be repressed or any consciousness to be defended by repression." If this is science, then so is the Valentinian Speculation, and so is Lurianic Kabbalah, and so is Ferenczi's *Thalassa,* and perhaps all of them are. But clearly they are also something else, poems that commence by defensive processes, and that keep going through an elaboration of those processes.

A primal fixation or repression, as I have tried to show

in *A Map of Misreading,* takes us back not to the Freudian
Primal Scene of the Oedipus Complex, nor to the Freudian Primal History Scene of *Totem and Taboo,* nor to
Derrida's Scene of Writing, but to the most poetically
primal of scenes, the Scene of Instruction, a six-phased
scene that strong poems must will to overcome, by repressing their own freedom into the patterns of a revisionary
misinterpretation. Thomas Frosch's lucid summary is
more admirably concise than I have been able to be, and
so I borrow it here:

. . . a Primal Scene of Instruction [is] a model for the unavoid-
able imposition of influence. The Scene—really a complete play,
or process—has six stages, through which the ephebe emerges:
election (seizure by the precursor's power); covenant (a basic
agreement of poetic vision between precursor and ephebe); the
choice of a rival inspiration (e.g., Wordsworth's Nature vs.
Milton's Muse); the self-presentation of the ephebe as a new
incarnation of the "Poetical Character"; the ephebe's interpretation of the precursor; and the ephebe's revision of the
precursor. Each of these stages then becomes a level of interpretation in the reading of the ephebe's poem.

To this, I would add now only the formula that a poem
both takes its origin in a Scene of Instruction and finds its
necessary aim or purpose there as well. It is only by
repressing creative "freedom," through the initial fixation
of influence, that a person can be reborn as a poet. And
only by revising that repression can a poet become and
remain strong. Poetry, revisionism, and repression verge
upon a melancholy identity, an identity that is broken
afresh by every new strong poem, and mended afresh by
the same poem.

2

Blake and Revisionism

What happens to a poem after it has succeeded in clearing a space for itself? As the poem itself begins to be misread, both by other poems and by criticism, is it distorted in the same way or differently than it has been distorted by itself, through its own activity in misreading others? Clearly its meanings do change drastically between the time that it first wrestles its way into strength, and the later time that follows its canonization. What kinds of misreading does canonization bring about? Or, to start further back, why call the canonization of texts a necessary misreading of texts?

What is canonization, in a purely secular context, and why ought criticism to talk about it? Criticism in fact hardly has talked about canon-formation, at least for quite a while now, and the process is a troublesome one, and so not easy to discuss. Canon-formation, in the West, began in the creation of Scripture, when the rabbis accepted certain texts and rejected others, so as to arrive at last at the library of thirty-nine books now commonly referred to as the Old Testament. The rabbis were no more unanimous than any other body of literary critics, and some of the disputes about canonization were not settled for several generations. The three main divisions of the Hebrew Bible—the Law, the Prophets, the Writings or Wisdom literature—represent three stages of canon-formation. It is likely that the Law was canonized by about 400 B.C., the Prophets by about 100 B.C., the Writings not until A.D. 90.

"Canon" as a word goes back to a Greek word for a measuring rule, which in Latin acquired the additional meaning of "model." In English we use it to mean a church code, a secular law, a standard or criterion, or a part of the Catholic Mass, or as a musical synonym for a kind of fugue, or in printing for a size of type. But we also use it for authoritative lists of works, sacred or secular, by one author or by many. The Greek work *kanon* was of Semitic origin, and it is difficult to distinguish between its original meanings of "reed" or "pipe," and "measuring rod." Canon-formation or canonization is a richly suggestive word for a process of classic-formation in poetic tradition, because it associates notions of music and of standards.

But before considering poetic canon-formation, I want to go back to the biblical process of canonization. Samuel Sandmel makes the useful observation that before a text was canonized, it could be copied with inattention, as you or I tend to copy. But, he adds: "Once a writing became canonical, it was copied with such relentless fidelity that even the inherited mistakes and the omissions and the telescoping were retained." The late Edmund Wilson, perhaps not understanding the indirect descent of academic textual scholars from these pious copyists, complained bitterly at its modern continuance, but we can attain a critical realization about how a copying-canonization fosters misreading, of a peculiarly uninteresting, weak, and unproductive kind. A canonical reading, like a canonical copying, attempts to stop the mind by making a text redundantly identical with itself, so as to produce a total presence, an unalterable meaning. So many texts, so many meanings—might be the motto of weak canonization. But there is also strong canonization, and it is more dangerous, whether carried on by the Academy of Ezra, the Church, the universities, or most of all by strong critics from Dr. Samuel Johnson to the present day. Though my own texts-for-reading in this chapter will be two famous lyrics by Blake, *London* and *The Tyger,* I will try to illustrate the ways in which strong canonization misreads by a religious example, before I turn to Blake. But before I come to my religious example, I want to say something about the transition from religious to secular canon-formation.

Whether in religion or in poetry, or (as I suspect) everywhere else as well, memory is a crucial mode of thought, as Hannah Arendt remarks in the context of political philosophy. We can make a more drastic assertion; in poetry memory is always the most important mode of thought, despite Blake's passionate insistences upon the contrary view. The reason why most strong post-Enlightenment poems end with schemes of transumption or metaleptic reversals, with defensive patterns of projection and/or introjection, with imagery of earliness and/or belatedness, in short with the revisionary ratio I have called the *apophrades* or Return of the Dead, is that, particularly in poems, the past, like the future, is always a force, and indeed, in poems, the future's force is directed to driving the poem back into the past, no matter what the poet is trying to do.

Hannah Arendt tells us that political thought as a tradition goes from Plato to Marx, and ends there. I suppose we could say that moral psychology as a tradition goes from Plato to Freud and ends there. But poetry as a tradition has no Marx or Freud (though Wordsworth came closest to that end-stop position) because you cannot break the tradition without ceasing to write poetry, in the sense that the tradition from Homer to Goethe defines poetry, and Wordsworth's best poetry paradoxically breaks the tradition only to extend it, but at the high cost of narrowing and internalizing the tradition, so that all subsequent attempts to get beyond Wordsworth have failed. Blake was a much less original poet than Wordsworth, as I think we are only beginning to understand. Despite his surface innovations, Blake is closer to

Spenser and to Milton than he is to Wordsworth, and far closer than Wordsworth is to Spenser and Milton. Wordsworth imposed himself upon the canon; Blake, though a major intellectual revisionist, was more imposed upon *by* the canon than modern Blake scholarship is willing to accept or admit. I return to the process of canonic imposition. E. R. Curtius sums it up by saying: "Canon formation in literature must always proceed to a selection of classics." But Curtius, so far as I can tell, hardly distinguishes between religious and secular canon-formation. A secular tradition presumably is open to intruders of genius, rather more readily than a religious tradition, and surely this difference is the crucial one between revisionism and heresy. Revisionism alters *stance*; heresy alters *balance*. A secular canon stands differently, after it subsumes a great revisionist, as British poetry manifested a different relation between the poet and the poem, after Wordsworth. But a religious canon is thrown out of balance by a great heretic, and cannot subsume him unless it is willing to be a different religion, as Lutheranism and Calvinism were very different religions than Catholicism. Joachim of Flora or Eckhart could not become canonical texts, but in the secular canon Blake has been legitimatized. What this has done to Blake is now my concern, a concern I want to illuminate first by one large instance of the reading peculiarities brought about through religious canonization. The book *Koheleth* or Ecclesiastes is, rather astonishingly, a canonical work, part of Scripture. The book Ecclesiasticus, or *The Wisdom of Jesus the Son of Sirach* was not taken into the canon, and is part of the Old Testament Apocrypha.

As literary works, they both are magnificent; in the King James version, it would be difficult to choose between them for rhetorical power, but Ecclesiastes is far stronger in the original. Their peculiar fascination for my purposes is that they exist in a relation of precursor and

ephebe, with Koheleth or Ecclesiastes, written about 250
B.C., being the clearly dominant influence upon Ben
Sirach or Ecclesiasticus, written about 200 B.C. By a
splendid irony, the canonical Koheleth is a highly problematic text in regard to normative Judaism, while the
uncanonical Ben Sirach is explicitly and unquestionably
orthodox, a monument to normative Judaism.

Koheleth derives from the Hebrew word *kahal,* meaning "the community" or "the congregation." The Greek
"Ecclesiastes," meaning a member of the *ecclesia* or as-
sembly of citizens, is not a very exact equivalent. Neither
word, Hebrew or Greek, means "the Preacher," which is a
famous mistranslation for Koheleth. Tradition identifies
Koheleth with Solomon, a beautiful but false idea. Like
his imitator, Ben Sirach, Koheleth worked in the literary
genre of Wisdom Literature, a vast genre in the ancient
Near East. "Instruction" is a synonym for "Wisdom" in
this sense, and may be a better modern translation for
Hokmah, which really meant: "How to live, what to do,"
but was also used as a synonym for poetry and song,
which were not distinguished from Instruction.

Robert Gordis, in the most widely accepted modern
study of Koheleth, shows that Koheleth was a·teacher in
one of the Wisdom academies in third-century B.C.
Jerusalem, teaching aristocratic youth, in a quasi-secular
way. His ambiance was anything but prophetic, and his
highly individual vision of life and religion was much
closer to what we would call skeptical humanism than it
was to the central traditions of Judaism. God, for
Koheleth, is the Being who made us and rules over us,
but Koheleth has nothing more to say about Him. God is
there at our beginning and at our end; in between what
matters is our happiness. How did *this* book become canonized?

Not without a struggle, is part of the answer. The two
great interpretative schools of the rabbis Hillel and
Shammai fought a long spiritual war over Koheleth, and
the Hillelites did not win a final victory until A.D. 90 when

the Council of Jamnia (Jabneh) closed out Scripture by affirming that Koheleth was part of the canon. The school of Shammai sensibly asserted that the book was self-contradictory, merely literary, not inspired by God, and was marked plainly by skepticism towards the Torah. The Hillelites insisted that the book was by Solomon (though surely even they knew this was a pious fiction), and pointed to certain passages in the book that were traditionally Torah-oriented. What was the motive of the Hillelites? Theologically, they were liberals, and presumably Koheleth helped them to achieve more daring and open interpretations of the Law. Yet the deeper motive, as with the great Rabbi Akiba's passion for the *Song of Songs,* seems to have been what we call literary or aesthetic esteem. Koheleth was, rhetorically and conceptually, too good a book to lose. Though both a belated and an audacious work, it was taken permanently into Scripture. I myself am a mere amateur at biblical scholarship, yet I want to go further in expressing the misreading of this canonization, for as I read it, Koheleth is a revisionist poem, a strong misprision of Torah, which suffered the happy irony of being absorbed by the precursor against whom it had rebelled, however ambivalently. Koheleth 3:14 echoes Deuteronomy 4:2 and 13:1 in a revisionist way, so as to change the emphasis from the Law's splendor to human powerlessness. It echoes passages in Kings, Samuel, and Leviticus, so as to undo the moral point from a categorical insistence upon righteousness as a divine commandment to the skeptical view that moral error is inevitable and even necessary but that righteousness is always more humanly sensible if only you can achieve it. Robert Gordis insightfully remarks that Koheleth refers only to Torah and to Wisdom Scripture, and wholly ignores the canonical prophets, as nothing could be more antithetical to his own vision than Isaiah and Ezekiel.

Let us contrast to Koheleth his eloquent and more traditionally pious ephebe, Ben Sirach, who about a half-century later seems to have followed much the same pro-

fession, teaching pragmatic Wisdom, of a literary kind, at
an upper-class academy in Jerusalem. Ben Sirach can be
described as the Lionel Trilling of his day, even as his
precursor, Koheleth, seems a figure not wholly unlike
Walter Pater or even Matthew Arnold, in Arnold's more
skeptical moments, though I hasten to add that Arnold
was hardly in Koheleth's class as poet or intellect. Ben
Sirach, by a charming but not unexpected antithetical
irony, echoes or alludes constantly to Koheleth, but always canonically misreading Koheleth into a Shammai-
like high Pharisaic orthodoxy. Wherever Koheleth urges
the necessity of pleasure, Ben Sirach invokes the principle
of echoing Koheleth while urging restraint, but in the
vocabulary of his precursor. Robert Gordis observes that
wherever Koheleth is literal in his meaning, Ben Sirach
interprets him as being figurative. Any close comparison
of the texts of Ecclesiastes and Ecclesiasticus will confirm
the analysis that Gordis makes.

Let me sum up this rather intricate excursus upon
Koheleth and the book of Jesus Ben Sirach. The revisionist work, through canonization, is misread by being
overfigurated by the canonically informed reader. The
derivative, orthodox work, left uncanonized because of its
belatedness, is misread by being overliteralized by those
who come after it, ourselves included.

I turn to two texts of Blake, two famous *Songs of Experience: London* and *The Tyger*. How are we to read these
two revisionist lyrics that Blake intended us to canonize,
that indeed now are part of the canon of British poetry?
What kinds of misreadings are these poems now certain
to demand? *London* is a revisionist text with regard to the
book of the prophet Ezekiel; *The Tyger* is a revisionist text
with regard to the Book of Job, and also in relation to
Paradise Lost.

Here is the precursor-text for Blake's *London*, chapter 9
of the Book of Ezekiel:

He cried also in mine ears with a loud voice, saying, "Cause them that have charge over the city to draw near, even every man with his destroying weapon in his hand."

And, behold, six men came from the way of the higher gate, which lieth toward the north, and every man a slaughter weapon in his hand; and one man among them was clothed with linen, with a writer's inkhorn by his side: and they went in, and stood beside the brasen altar.

And the glory of the God of Israel was gone up from the cherub, whereupon he was, to the threshold of the house. And he called to the man clothed with linen, which had the writer's inkhorn by his side;

And the Lord said unto him, "Go through the midst of the city, through the midst of Jerusalem, and set a mark upon the foreheads of the men that sigh and that cry for all the abominations that be done in the midst thereof."

And to the others he said in mine hearing, "Go ye after him through the city, and smite: let not your eye spare, neither have ye pity:

Slay utterly old and young, both maids, and little children, and women: but come not near any man upon whom is the mark; and begin at my sanctuary." Then they began at the ancient men which were before the house.

And he said unto them, "Defile the house, and fill the courts with the slain: go ye forth." And they went forth, and slew in the city.

And it came to pass, while they were slaying them, and I was left, that I fell upon my face, and cried, and said, "Ah Lord God! wilt thou destroy all the residue of Israel in thy pouring out of thy fury upon Jerusalem?"

Then said he unto me, "The iniquity of the house of Israel and Judah is exceeding great, and the land is full of blood, and the city full of perverseness: for they say, 'The Lord hath forsaken the earth, and the Lord seeth not.'

"And as for me also, mine eye shall not spare, neither will I have pity, but I will recompense their way upon their head."

And, behold, the man clothed with linen, which had the inkhorn by his side, reported the matter, saying, "I have done as thou hast commanded me."

Chapter 8 of Ezekiel ends with God's warning that he will punish the people of Jerusalem for their sins. Chapter 9 is Ezekiel's prophetic vision of the punishment being carried out, despite the prophet's attempt at intercession on behalf of a saving remnant. The crucial verse for Blake's *London* is clearly the fourth one, which gives Blake not only the central image of his poem but even the rhyme of "cry" and "sigh":

. . . And he called to the man clothed with linen, which had the writer's inkhorn by his side;

And the Lord said unto him: "Go through the midst of the city, through the midst of Jerusalem, and set a mark upon the foreheads of the men that sigh and that cry for all the abominations that be done in the midst thereof."

This mark is given to the saving remnant of Jerusalem, who alone are to be spared destruction. The Hebrew word for "mark" used here is *taw*, which is the name also of the letter *t*, the last letter of the Hebrew alphabet, even as zed (z) is last in ours, or omega is last in the Greek alphabet. Traditional commentary on Ezekiel interpreted this to mean that the *taw* set upon the forehead of the righteous would be written in ink and signify *tichyeh*, "you shall live," but the *taw* upon the forehead of the wicked would be written in blood and would signify *tamuth*, "you shall die."

The intertextual relationship between Ezekiel and Blake here is quite unmistakable, even though it also has been quite unnoticed, except by myself, in my role as what Blake denounced as a "Satan's Watch-Fiend." How is Blake revising Ezekiel?

Not, so far as I can tell, by his initial equation of London = Jerusalem, which means that from the start all received readings of this poem, including my own, are wholly mistaken in seeing Blake's poem primarily as a protest against repression, whether societal or individual. That is, all received readings have said or intimated that in the poem *London*, Blake presents himself as a prophet or prophetic figure, akin to Ezekiel, with the people of London only roughly akin to those of Ezekiel's Jerusalem, in that they are shown as suffering beneath the counter-revolutionary oppression of the regime of William Pitt. On this view the people, however culpable for weakness or lack of will, are the righteous, and only the State and State Church of Pitt are the wicked. From this, a number of other interpretations necessarily follow throughout the poem, down to the famous lines about the harlot and the new-born infant at the poem's close.

I shall demonstrate, with the aid of what I call "antithetical criticism," that all such interpretations are weak, unproductive, canonical misreadings, quite alien to the spirit of Blake's strong misreading or misprision of Ezekiel, and alien in any case to the letter of Blake's text, to the words, images, figurations of the strong poem, *London*.

Blake begins: "I wander thro' each charter'd street," and so we begin also, with that wandering and that chartering, in order to define that "I." Is it an Ezekiel-like prophet, or someone whose role and function are altogether different? To "wander" is to have no destination and no purpose. A biblical prophet may wander when he is cast out into the desert, when his voice becomes a voice in the wilderness, but he does not wander when he goes through the midst of the city, through the midst of Jerusalem the City of God. There, his inspired voice always has purpose, and his inspired feet always have destination. Blake knew all this, and knew it with a knowing beyond our knowing. When he begins by saying that he *wanders* in London, his Jerusalem, his City of God, then he begins also by saying "I am not Ezekiel, I am not a prophet, I am too fearful to be the prophet I ought to be, *I am hid*."

"Charter'd" is as crucial as "wander." The word is even richer with multiple significations and rhetorical ironies, in this context, than criticism so far has noticed. Here are the relevant shades-of-meaning: There is certainly a reference to London having been created originally as a city by a charter to that effect. As certainly, there is an ironic allusion to the celebrated political slogan: "the chartered rights of Englishmen." More subtly, as we will see, there is a reference to *writing*, because to be chartered is to be written, since a charter is a written grant from authority, or a document outlining a process of incorporation. In addition, there are the commercial notions of hiring, or leasing, indeed of binding or covenanting, always crucial in a prophetic context. Most important, I think, in this poem that turns upon a mark of salvation or destruction, is the accepted meaning that to be chartered is to be awarded a special privilege or a particular immunity, which is established by a written document. Finally, there is a meaning opposed to "wandering," which is charting or mapping, so as to preclude mere wandering. The streets of London are chartered, Blake says, and so he adds is the Thames, and we can surmise that for Blake, the adjective is primarily negative in its ironies, since his manuscript drafts show that he substituted the word "chartered" for the word "dirty" in both instances.

As is often the case with strong, antithetical poems that are highly condensed in their language, Blake's key-words in *London* are remarkably interrelated, as criticism again has failed to notice. Walter Pater, in his great essay on *Style*, urges that the strong poet, or "literary artist" as he puts it, "will be apt to restore not really obsolete or really worn-out words, but the finer edge of words still in use." Pater meant the restoration of etymological or original meaning, "the finer edge," and in this Pater was again a prophet of modern or belated poetry. But here Blake, who deeply influenced Pater, was already a pioneer. Let us return to "wander" which goes back to the root *wendh*, from which come also "turn," "weave," and "wind." I quote from Blake's *Auguries of Innocence*, notebook jottings clearly related to his *London*:

> The Whore & Gambler by the State
> Licencd build that Nations Fate
> The Harlots cry from Street to Street
> Shall weave Old Englands winding Sheet
> The Winners Shout the Losers Curse
> Dance before dead Englands Hearse
> Every Night & every Morn
> Some to Misery are Born

Contrast this to the final stanza of *London*:

> But most thro' midnight streets I hear
> How the youthful Harlots curse
> Blasts the new-born Infants tear
> And blights with plagues the Marriage hearse.

The harlot's cry or curse, a loser's curse, weaves a winding sheet for England and every marriage in England by blasting the infant's tear and by blighting with plagues. To weave is to wind is to wander is to turn is to blight and blast. Blight and blast what and how? The surprising answer is: voice, which of course is the prophet's one gift. Blake *wendhs* as the harlot *wendhs*, and both to the same result: the loss of human voice. For what is an "infant"? "Infant," "ban," and "prophet" all come from the same root, the Indo-European *Bha*, which is a root meaning to "speak." And "infant" means one incapable of speech; all the infant can do is weep. The Latin *fari* and the Greek *phanai* both mean "to speak," and "prophet" derives from them. A ban is a stated or spoken interdiction, which means that a ban *is* a curse, while to curse is to put something or someone under a ban. Ban and voice, in Blake's *London*, are natural synonyms and indeed we can say that the poem offers the following equation: every voice = a ban = a curse = weeping or a blasted tear. But the verbal network is even more intricate. The harlot's curse is not, as various interpreters have said, venereal disease, but is indeed what "curse" came to mean in the vernacular after Blake and still means now: menstruation, the natural cycle in the human female. Let us note the complexity of two more key words in the text: "mark" and "forg'd" in "mind-forg'd manacles." A "mark" is a boundary (or, as Blake said, a "Devourer" as opposed to a "Prolific"); it is also a visible trace, a sign in lieu of writing, and a grade of merit or demerit. To "forge" means to "fabricate" in both senses of "fabricate": to make, as a smith or poet makes, but also to counterfeit. The Indo-European root is *dhabh*, meaning "to fit together" and is related to the Hebrew *dabhar* for "word." "Mind-forg'd manacles" is a phrase deliberately evoking the Western metaphysical problem of dualism, since "manacles" for "hand-cuffs" involves *manus* or hand, and hence bodily act, which is at once made and yet feigned or counterfeited by the opposing principle of mind.

I have involved us in all of this verbal interrelation in order to suggest that Blake's *London* centers itself upon an opposition between *voice* and *writing*, by which I don't mean that somehow Jacques Derrida wrote the poem. No — the poem is precisely anti-Nietzschean, anti-Derridaean, and offers us a terrifying nostalgia for a lost prophetic *voice*, the voice of Ezekiel and religious logocentrism, which has been replaced by a demonic *visible trace*, by a mark, by the writing of the apocalyptic letter *taw*. With this as background, I am at last prepared to offer my own, antithetical, strong misreading of Blake's *London*, of which I will assert only that it is more adequate to the text than the weak misreadings now available to us.

I will commence by offering a very plain summary or paraphrase of what I judge to be the difference in meanings when we juxtapose Blake's *London* with its precursor-text in Ezekiel, chapter 9. Then I will proceed to an antithetical account of Blake's *London*, through a charting of its revisionary ratios, tropes, psychic defenses, and images.

In chapter 8 of Ezekiel, the prophet sits in his house of

exile in Babylon, surrounded by the elders of Judah. The Spirit of God raises him, and carries him "in the visions of God to Jerusalem," to the outraged Temple, where graven, idolatrous images of Asherah have been placed as substitutes for the Living God. A further and final vision of the *Merkabah,* God's triumphal chariot, is granted Ezekiel, after which four scenes of idolatry *within* the Temple are revealed to him. Chapter 8 concludes with a fierce warning from God:

> Therefore will I also deal in fury; Mine eye shall not spare, neither will I have pity; and though they cry in Mine ears with a loud voice, yet will I not hear them.

Chapter 9, which I have quoted already, mitigates this only for a small remnant. There are six angels of destruction, with only Gabriel (according to the Talmud) armed with the inkhorn that will spare the righteous. Unlike Gabriel, Blake does not necessarily set a mark, since his "mark in every face I meet," primarily is intransitive, meaning "remark" or "observe."

Blake begins *London* with a curious irony, more a scheme than a figure, or if a figure, then more a figure of thought than of speech. For he adopts the outcast role he called Rintrah, the John-the-Baptist or unheeded forerunner, in place of the prophetic vocation, but in the context of Ezekiel's Jerusalem as well as his own London. In the opening dialectic of presence and absence, precisely what is absent is prophetic direction and prophetic purpose; what is present are chartering and marks. So voice is absent, and only demonic writing is present. Blake's defensive reaction-formation to the call he cannot answer is to be a wanderer, and to mark passively rather than mark actively with the *taws* of righteousness and wickedness, life and death. But righteousness and wickedness are alike absent; present only are weakness and woe, neither of which merits a *taw,* whether of ink or of blood. The synecdoche of the universal human face represents Blake's turning against his

own self, for he also is weak and woeful, and not the
Ezekiel-like prophet he should be.

The litany of "every" becomes a weird metonymic reification, a regression in moving all men back to a state of
infancy, but also an isolation, as this is an "every" that
separates out rather than unifies people:

> In every cry of every Man,
> In every Infants cry of fear
> In every voice: in every ban
> The mind-forg'd manacles I hear.

"Every Man" includes the Londoner William Blake,
whose voice also must betray the clanking sound of "mind-
forg'd manacles," where the mind belongs to every man,
again including William Blake. An infant's cry of fear is
all-too-natural, for the infant is voiceless but for his fear and
hunger, which for him is a kind of fear. When the crucial
word "voice" enters the poem, it is put into a metonymic,
reductive series with "cry of fear" and "ban," with terror
and curse, fear and the threat of fear.

When Blake answers this reduction with a Sublime repressive hyperbole, it is governed by the same "I hear," as
spoken by a Jonah, a renegade prophet who never does
speak in his own poem, but only hears:

> I hear
> How the Chimney-sweepers cry
> Every blackning Church appalls,
> And the hapless Soldiers sigh,
> Runs in blood down Palace walls.

The chimney-sweepers' cry, as in the two Blakean songs
of the sweeps, is "Weep, weep," due to the cockney lisp of
the children, as they attempt to advertise their labor with a
voiced "sweep, sweep." The cry of weep helps blacken
further the perpetually blackening Church, possibly drap-
ing it in a pall through the mark of *taw* in a black ink, giving
it an edge over the royal palace, which receives the bloody

taw of destruction. The soldier's hapless sigh prefigures the curse of the harlot, as both are losers, in the term from *Auguries of Innocence*. But what about Blake's synaesthesia? How, even in Sublime representation, can you *hear* a Church being draped in a pall, and how can you *hear* a sigh running in blood down palace walls. The answer, I think, is given by our map of misreading. What Blake is repressing into this hyperbolical hearing-seeing is the visionary power of the *nabi*, the Hebrew prophet, and the running of the repressed voice *down* the repressive walls represents not only the soldier's hapless sigh, but the more powerful hapless sigh of the prophet who has repressed the voice that is great within us.

We come then to the final stanza, the most weakly misread of all. Here is the characteristic Romantic ending that follows a limiting metaphor by a representing transumption:

> But most thro' midnight streets I hear
> How the youthful Harlots curse
> Blasts the new-born Infants tear
> And blights with plagues the Marriage hearse.

I want to reject altogether the customary interpretation that makes "curse" here a variety of venereal infection, and that makes the infant's condition a prenatal blindness. Instead, I want to reaffirm my own earlier interpretation of the Harlot here as Blake's perpetually youthful Harlot, Nature, *not* the human female, but the natural element in the human, male or female.

The inside/outside perspectivism here gives us Blake as pent-up voice wandering still at midnight *through* the streets, and through that labyrinth he achieves another synaesthetic hearing-seeing, *how* another curse or ban or natural fact (menstruation) blasts or scatters another natural fact, the tearlessness of the new-born infant. For Blake every natural fact equals every other natural fact. The metalepsis that introjects the future here is one that

sees enormous plagues riding along in every marriage
coach, blighting life into death, as though every marriage
carries the *taw* of destruction. Remember again the
doggerel of *Auguries of Innocence*:

> The Harlots cry from street to street
> Shall weave Old Englands winding sheet
> The Winners Shout the Losers Curse
> Dance before dead Englands Hearse

If Old England is dead, then all her marriages are funer-
als. A cry that weaves a shroud is like a mark of *taw* or a ban
chartering weakness and woe. Blake's poem is not a protest,
not a prophetic outcry, not a vision of judgment. It is a
revisionist's self-condemnation, a Jonah's desperation at
knowing he is not an Ezekiel. We misread Blake's poem
when we regard it as prophecy, and see it as primarily
sympathy with the wretched of London, because we have
canonized the poem, and because we cannot bear to read a
canonical poem as being truly so altogether negative and
self-destructive a text.

Even as a revisionist strong poem, Blake's *London* is more
a deliberate parody of misprision than it is a revisionist text.
Blake's tonal complexities are uncanny, *unheimlich,* here
and elsewhere, and like Nietzsche Blake is something of a
parodist of world history. There is a grotesque element in
London, and what we take as Sublime hyperbole is actually
more the underthrow of litotes, the characteristic rhetorical
figure in grotesque representation. This parody is a clearer
strain in Blake's *The Tyger,* which I want to introduce more
by way of Nietzsche than by way of its origins in Job and
Milton.

Like Nietzsche, and like every other revisionist, Blake
desired always to keep origin and aim, source and purpose,
as far apart as possible. Nietzsche, if I understand him,
believed only in comic or preposterous schemes of transumption, in which a future laughter is introjected and a past
tragedy is projected. An aphorism in *Beyond Good and Evil*
says that we are

prepared as was no previous age for a Carnival in the grand style, for laughter and a high-spirited revelry, for transcendental flights of Sublime nonsense and an Aristophanes-like mockery of the universe. Perhaps this is where we shall yet discover the realm of our *invention*, that realm in which we also still can be original, say as parodists of world history and the clowns of God—perhaps, even if nothing else today has a future, our laughter may yet have a future.

We can observe here that a poem, in this view, must be a parody of a parody, just as a man is a parody of God. But Nietzschean repetition is even more bewildering, for any copy is both a parody of its original, yet also a self-parody. In terms of poetic misprision, this means that any poem is both a misreading of a precursor poem and, more crucially, a misreading of itself. Whether Nietzschean parody is universally applicable I do not know, but it illuminates poems of deliberately cyclic repetition like Blake's *The Tyger* or *The Mental Traveller* or *The Crystal Cabinet.*

Blake's Tyger has a pretty exact analogue in a Nietzschean tiger, a grand deconstructive tiger, in the curious text called *Truth and Falsehood in an Extra-Moral Sense:*

What indeed *does* man know about himself? Oh! that he could but once see himself complete, placed as it were in an illuminated glass case! Does not nature keep secret from him most things, even about his body . . . ? Nature threw away the key; and woe to the fateful curiosity which might be able for a moment to look out and down through a crevice in the chamber of consciousness and discover that man, indifferent to his own ignorance, is resting on the pitiless, the greedy, and insatiable, the murderous, and as it were, hanging in dreams on the back of a tiger. Whence, in the wide world, with this state of affairs, arises the impulse to truth?

Nietzsche's tiger is human mortality; our illusive day-to-day existence rests us, in dreams, as we ride the tiger who will be, who is our own death, a metaphorical embodiment of the unbearable truth that the pleasure-principle and the reality-principle are finally one.

Nietzsche's precursors were Goethe, Schopenhauer, Heine, and Wagner; Blake's were Milton and the Bible. Of all the thirty-nine books of the Old Testament, Job obsessed Blake most. The forerunners of Blake's Tyger are the Leviathan and Behemoth of Job, two horrible beasts who represent the God-ordained tyranny of nature over man, two beasts whose final name is human death, for to Blake nature *is* death.

God taunts Job by asking him if these great beasts will make a covenant with man? Rashi comments on Behemoth by saying: "prepared for the future," and the apocryphal apocalypses, Enoch and IV Ezra and Baruch, all say that Leviathan and Behemoth are parted only to come together one day, in the Judgment, when they will be the food of the Righteous. As God says of Leviathan, if none dare face him, then "Who is able to stand before Me?" Milton brings in the Leviathan (evidently a crocodile in Job) as a whale, but Melville's Moby Dick is closer to the beasts of Job, and to Blake's Tyger.

At this advanced date, I assert an exemption from having to argue against the usual run of merely trivial misreadings of *The Tyger.* I will oppose my antithetical reading to the received misreading of the earlier Bloom, in books like *The Visionary Company* and *Blake's Apocalypse,* or in the notes to *Romantic Poetry and Prose* in the Oxford Anthology. The fundamental principle for reading *The Tyger* is to realize that this is a dramatic lyric in which William Blake is not, cannot be the speaker. *The Tyger* is a Sublime or hyperbolical monologue, with little movement in its tropes or images. It is dominated by the single trope of repression, by an unconsciously purposeful forgetting, but this is not Blake's repression. The psychic area in which the whole poem centers is hysteria. What does it mean for a major lyric never to deviate from its own hysterical intensity?

The answer is that Blake, more even than Nietzsche, is a master of creative parody, and he is parodying a kind of greatness that he loves and admires, but vehemently does not wish to join. It is the greatness of William Cowper, and the other poets of the Burkean or Miltonic Sublime in the later eighteenth century. The two dominant images of the poem are both fearful—the burning or fire and the symmetry. Fire is the prime perspectivizing trope in all of Romanticism, as we will see again and again. It stands, most often, for discontinuity or for the possibility of, or desire towards discontinuity. Its opposite, the emblem of repetition or continuity, tends to be the inland sound of moving waters. These identifications may seem purely arbitrary now; I will vindicate them in later chapters.

What are we to make of "symmetry"? Symmetry is a one-to-one ratio, whether on opposite sides of a dividing line, or in relation to a center. A one-to-one ratio means that no revisionism has taken place; there has been no *clinamen*, no catastrophe-creation or breaking-of-the-vessels in the making of the Tyger. Like Leviathan and Behemoth, the Tyger is exactly what his creator meant him to be. But who is his creator? Does this poem set itself, for interpretation, in a relatively orthodox Genesis-Milton context, or in the context of some Gnosis? How fearful is the Tyger's maker? Or is it a canonical misreading that we allow this poem to set itself a genetic context for interpretation, at all?

By common consent of interpreters, *The Tyger* is made up of a series of increasingly rhetorical questions. The model for this series certainly is to be found in the Book of Job, where God confronts Job with crushingly rhetorical questions, all of them reducing to the cruelty of: Where were you, anyway, when I made everything? After all, Job's plea had been "Call Thou, and I will answer" (13:22), and God therefore relies upon a continuous irony as figure-of-thought. But the speaker of *The Tyger* is incapable of deliberate irony; every one of his tropes is, as I have noted already, an hyperbole. What is this profound repression defending against? What furnace is coming up, at last, against the will of this daemonizing speaker?

No speaker could be more determined to insist that ori-

gin and aim were the same impulse and the same event. We
can surmise that the unconsciously purposeful forgetting of
this poem's speaker is precisely that he himself, as an aim or
purpose, has been separated irreparably from his point of
origin. Confronting the Tyger, who represents his own
daemonic intensity, the form that is his own force, what Blake
would have called Vision or his own Imagination, the
dramatic speaker is desperately determined to identify
completely the Tyger's aim and purpose with the Tyger's
supposedly divine origins.

Yet it is not the speaker's text, but Blake's, and the meaning of the text rises parodistically and even with a wild
comedy out of the intertextual juxtapositions between the
text itself and texts by Cowper, by Milton, and the text cited
from Job.

First Cowper, from Book VI of *The Task:*

> The Lord of all, himself through all diffused,
> Sustains, and is the life of all that lives.
> Nature is but a name for an effect
> Whose cause is God. He feeds the secret fire
> By which the mighty process is maintained,
> Who sleeps not, is not weary; in whose sight
> Slow circling ages are as transient days,
> Whose work is without labour; whose designs
> No flaw deforms, no difficulty thwarts;

Here origin and purpose are one, without strain, anxiety,
or repression, or so it seems. Next Milton, from Book VII of
Paradise Lost, part of the most Sublime creation-scene in the
language:

> The grassy Clods now Calv'd, now half appear'd
> The Tawny Lion, pawing to get free
> His hinder parts, then springs as broke from Bonds,
> And Rampant shakes his Brinded mane; the Ounce,
> The Libbard, and the Tiger, as the Mole
> Rising, the crumbl'd Earth above them threw
> In Hillocks . . .

Milton shows rather less creative anxiety than the poet of Job, even allowing himself a transumption of a Lucretian allusion as if to indicate his own corrective confidence that God's origins and Milton's purposes are one and the same. Blake's speaker is not Blake, nor is he Milton, not even Blake's own Milton. He *is* Cowper or Job, or rather Cowper assimilated to Job, and both assimilated not to the strong poet or revisionist in Blake, but to Blake's own Spectre of Urthona, that is, the time-bound work-a-day ego, and not what Blake liked to call "the Real Man the Imagination."

I approach an antithetical formula. Blake's revisionism in *London* was to measure the ratios by which he fell short of Ezekiel. Blake's revisionism in *The Tyger* is to measure the ratio by which he surpasses Cowper and Job. Cowper's fearful ratio does not frighten Blake, whose entire dialectic depends upon separating origins, natural or natural religion's, from imaginative aims or revisionist purposes. Yet, in *London,* Blake shows himself knowingly incapable of separating prophetic voice as aim or purpose from the cry, curse, ban of natural voice as origin. We have underestimated Blake's complexities, and his own capacity for self-recognition. He is in no danger of falling into the repetition of the Bard confronting the Jobean Tyger. Yet, in the societal context in which a prophet must vindicate himself, Blake falls silent, and falls into the repetition of the wanderer who flees the burden of prophecy. There can no more be a mute prophet than there can be a mute, inglorious Milton. The prophet or *nabi* is precisely a *public orator,* and not a private mutterer or marker. The *nabi* never moans, as Blake did, "I am hid." Blake, who might have been more, by his own account was human—all too human—and gave in to natural fear. His belatedness, in the spiritual more than in the poetic sense, was a shadow that overcame him.

The Blake of *London* has become a canonical writer, unlike the Ben Sirach of Ecclesiasticus, but like Ecclesiasticus Blake gives us in *London* a text he lacks the authority to sustain. The Blake of *The Tyger*, like the Koheleth of Ec-

clesiastes, gives us a canonical text that tradition necessarily
has misread and goes on misreading. Revisionism or belated creation is a hard task, and exacts a very high price, a
price that meaning itself must pay for, by being emptied out
from a plenitude to a dearth.

I conclude with a final juxtaposition between the skeptical
Koheleth and the passionately certain Blake. Both Ecclesiastes and *The Tyger* are texts of conscious belatedness,
though *The Tyger* parodies and mocks its own condition of
belatedness. For the Tyger itself, as a Sublime representation, is a self-imposed blocking agent, what Blake called a
Spectre, and what Ezekiel and Blake called a Covering
Cherub. The guilt suffered by the speaker of Blake's *Tyger*
is also Cowper's guilt, and the guilt of a very un-Cowperian
figure, Milton's Satan. This is the guilt that Nietzsche, in his
Genealogy of Morals, called the "guilt of indebtedness." I
think that Blake meant something like this when he said in
Jerusalem that it was easier to forgive an enemy than it was to
forgive a friend. The speaker of *The Tyger* confronts a
burning, fearful symmetry that exists in a one-to-one ratio
with its Creator. Like Job confronting Leviathan and Behemoth, the Cowper-like bard confronts an unacceptable
surrogate for the divine Precursor, a surrogate who grants
him no priority, and who has authority over him insofar as
he is natural. Blake, in mocking a canonical kind of poem,
nevertheless is subsumed by the canonical traditions of
misreading, as any student of *The Tyger*'s interpretative
history could testify.

Where Blake's dramatic speaker is trapped in repetition,
Koheleth is a theorist of repetition, not far in spirit from the
Stoic Marcus Aurelius. "All words toil to weariness,"
Koheleth says early on in his book, and so he thinks that
fundamentally all the books have been written already.
Though he praises wisdom, Koheleth is weary of it. He too
might have said: "The flesh is sad alas, and I have read all
the books." But he adds: "For wisdom is a defense, even as
money is a defense," and the Hebrew translated here in the

King James version as "defense" is a word literally meaning "shadow." I end on that identification of the defense against influence with the metonymic trope of shade for wisdom or money, and for the forests of the night that frame the menace of the fire that meant a discontinuity from origins.

3

Wordsworth and the Scene of Instruction

I start with Nietzsche, as perhaps the least Wordsworthian of interpretative theorists. This is one of his notebook jottings, of 1855, urging a revisionary view of "memory":

One must revise one's ideas about *memory*: here lies the chief temptation to assume a "soul," which, outside time, reproduces, recognizes, etc. But that which is experienced lives on "in the memory"; I cannot help it if it "comes back," the will is inactive in this case, as in the coming of any thought. Something happens of which I become conscious: now something similar comes—who called it? roused it?

Nietzsche demystifies and desubjectivizes memory; Wordsworth so mystified memory as to make of it the one great myth of his antimythological poetry.

I set against both this demystification and this spiritualization the vast expansion of the concept of memory that took place in Freud. The empirical model for memory, before Freud, was an easy target for Nietzsche's deconstructive energies, since memory was seen as a mechanically causal process, based upon the association of ideas. One idea associated itself with another pretty much as the motion of one entity affected another. But here is the philosopher Stuart Hampshire's perceptive brief summary of the conceptual change that Freud accomplished:

For the simple machinery of the association of ideas, Freud substitutes complex activities of projection, introjection and identification in the solution of conflicts. The importance of this substitution, from the philosophical point of view, is just that these activities are represented as activities; and because they are so represented, the underlying motives of them can be investigated. Within this scheme, the question of "Why?"—the demand for an explanation in any particular case—does not call for a universally valid psychological law and a statement of initial conditions. Since these processes are represented as activities of mind, the question "Why" asks for a description of the situation or situations, and therefore of the given problem, to which these continuing activities were the solution adopted. The effect of the substitution of the active for the passive mood is that the subject is required to search in his memory for the past situation, as it survives in his mind, and to acknowledge or to disclaim its superimposition on the present.

One impulse that rises in me, as I read this lucid philosophical comment on Freud, is to remember Freud's remark that "The poets were there before me," since Hampshire's observation would be a perfectly commonplace and accurate enough description of the difference between a pre-Wordsworthian memory poem, like Gray's Eton Ode, and a poem like *Tintern Abbey*. The difference between Wordsworth and Freud is that while both greatly expanded the concept of memory, Wordsworth very nearly made it into a Kabbalistic hypostasis, a new *sefirah* or magical attribute of Divine Influence, while Freud set it overtly in the context of anxiety, repression, and defense. I revert to my analogical and antithetical principle; a composite trope and a composite defense are different faces of the same ratios of revision. "Memory," for Wordsworth, is a composite trope, and so in Wordsworth what is called memory, or treated as memory, is also a composite defense, a defense against time, decay, the loss of divinating power, and so finally a defense against death, whose other name is John Milton.

In *The Ego and the Id* (1927), Freud suggests as a model of our mental apparatus the vision of an organism floating in water. As the surface of this organism is molded, internally and externally, into differentiation, what results as a difference Freud called the "ego," the "ich." Beneath this surface, and going down to the depth of the organism, is what Freud called the "id," the *it*, a naming in which Freud ultimately followed Nietzsche. The model is complex and subtle, and I cannot give an adequate account of it here. But one feature of it is crucial as part of Freud's concept of memory. The ego is visualized as broadening out from a layer of memory-traces, called the preconscious. These memory-traces are defined as remnants of perceptions, and only through an accumulation of memory-traces is there a growth in consciousness.

A memory-trace is a very tricky notion, one that I myself do not understand, and while Freud doubtless understood it, he never explained it adequately. Freud's word is *Erinnerungsspur,* which could be interpreted psychologically *or* physiologically. Laplanche and Pontalis, the Lacanian authors of *The Language of Psychoanalysis,* do not help clarify this notion when they say that "memory-traces are deposited in different systems, and subsist permanently, but are only reactivated once they have been cathected," that is, invested with psychic energy. A trace that subsists permanently, while waiting for a heavy psychic investor to come along, is a vision of the mind that all great poetry, including Wordsworth's, refutes. Dr. Samuel Johnson, who darkly knew that the mind is above all a *ceaseless activity,* could have taught these current psychoanalytic linguistifiers a little more respect for the power of the mind over itself, as well as over nature and language. But Freud also, of course, knew what the great moral psychologists from Pascal and Montaigne to Dr. Johnson and Coleridge have known, which is that memory is active mind, always dangerous, always at work misreading the predicaments of consciousness. Here are Laplanche and Pontalis at their most hilarious, reducing

Freud to a kind of Chaplin or Buster Keaton of the memory-machine:

The memory-trace is simply a particular arrangement of facilitations [path-breakings], so organized that one route is followed in preference to another. The functioning of memory in this way might be compared to what is known as "memory" in the theory of cybernetic machines, which are built on the principle of binary oppositions.

Jacques Derrida, as usual, is a much more adequate and perceptive interpreter of the relation of memory to language in Freud. Derrida tells us that the psyche is a kind of text and that this text is constituted of what Derrida calls "written traces." Early Freud (1895) speaks of memory as if it is a composite trope rather like influence; memory is defined as "the capacity to be altered in a lasting way by events which occur only once." Derrida assimilates Freud to Nietzsche by finding "the real origin of memory and thus of the psyche in the difference between path-breakings" or sensory excitations as they encounter resistances in consciousness. What Derrida calls "the trace as memory" is the impalpable and invisible difference between two path-breaking forces impinging upon what becomes the individual mind. With Derrida's more complex and subtle Heideggerean notion of the *trace* proper, as opposed to Freud's memory-trace, I am not concerned here, because I wish to talk only about one text, Wordsworth's *Tintern Abbey,* and the intrusion of a concept of memory into the meaning of that poem. This concept is essentially Wordsworth's own, and can be illuminated by juxtaposition with Freud's, and with Derrida's brilliant exegesis of Freudian memory. But even the Wordsworthian concept of memory is very secondary to my aims in this discourse. I want to offer an antithetical reading of Wordsworth's *Tintern Abbey,* employing my map of misprision and some aspects of a larger scheme of

what I have called the Scene of Instruction in chapter 3
of *A Map of Misreading.* In that scheme the study of a
poem as misprision or a revisionary text is only the sixth
and final phase of a complex attempt at complete interpretation, in which a text is fully related to a precursor
text or texts.

I do not believe that Wordsworth meant this poem to
be "about" memory; I think he intended what he called
"restoration" to be the subject of the poem. He seems to
have wanted a far more positive, hopeful, even celebratory poem than the one he actually wrote. As with the
Intimations Ode, the poet desired to emphasize restitution,
compensation, gain rather than loss. But his revisionary
genius intended otherwise or, if we want to select Freudian terms, the defensive process of repression gave
Wordsworth a very different poem than the one he set
out to write. I am going to suggest that the Sublime
tropes or strong hyperboles of *Tintern Abbey* work to repress the still-haunting presence of Milton's texts, particularly of the invocations to Books III and VII of *Paradise
Lost.* Because of the preternatural strength of Wordsworth's unconsciously purposeful forgettings of Milton, the true subject of *Tintern Abbey* becomes memory
rather than spiritual or imaginative renovation. Indeed, I
will go so far as to argue not only that the meaning of
Tintern Abbey is in its relationship to Milton's invocations,
but that the poem becomes, despite itself, an invocation
of Milton. Memory deals with absence, and the crucial or
felt absence in *Tintern Abbey* is Milton's.

As with my antithetical account of Blake's *London,*
which uncovered an opposition in that poem between
prophetic voice and demonic writing, *Tintern Abbey* Kab-
balized will show some similar patterns of a struggle between voicing and marking, and between hearing and
seeing, a struggle in which visible traces usurp the hopeful murmur of prophetic voice. But Blake warred always
against the bodily eye, and overtly aspired towards the

status and function of the *nabi* or visionary orator. Wordsworth and Coleridge, as their better scholars have shown us, longed for a composite, originary sense that combined rather than opposed seeing and hearing. If memory-traces and their implicit metaphor of script usurp a greater dream in *Tintern Abbey*, then it is not so much the Hebraic dream of divine voice as it is the complex synaesthesia of a more culturally mixed idea of the poetic vocation. Thomas McFarland and M. H. Abrams have traced Coleridge's images of "A light in sound, a sound-like power in light" to the theosophist Boehme and the metaphysician Schelling, both of whom were aware of the more ultimate source of these images in Kabbalah. Like most Kabbalist images, these in turn go back to Neoplatonic speculative origins. Wordsworth's source for such images was invariably Coleridge, whose "conversation" poems provided an immediate model for *Tintern Abbey*. Yet we do not feel either Coleridge's presence or absence in the poem, for Coleridge induced in the much stronger Wordsworth no anxieties of poetic influence.

The joy of what they considered to be a fully active imagination expressed itself for both poets in a combined or synaesthetic sense of seeing-hearing. Wordsworth seems to have believed, quite literally, that he had retained this combined sense much later into childhood than most people do. The phenomenon is overtly an element in the *Intimations* Ode, and has little explicitly to do with *Tintern Abbey*. Yet *Tintern Abbey* is at once the most enigmatic and perhaps the most influential of modern poems. Among much else it begins that splendidly dismal tradition in which modern poems intend some merely ostensible subject, yet actually find their true subject in the anxiety of influence.

The most defiantly Wordsworthian of modern critics, Geoffrey Hartman, says that "in Wordsworth, it is always a sound or voice that must 'grow with thought,' as well as

a person. As if when voice broke, identity itself were in
danger of breaking." Hartman, commenting on the "Boy
of Winander" fragment, asserts a remarkable freedom
for Wordsworth from the burden of influence-anxiety.
Though Hartman, in my judgment, idealizes Wordsworth,
his formidable summary here is another antagonist that
must be met:

> Now the one kind of echo missing from Wordsworth's poet-
> ry, or very carefully used when used at all, is the echo we call a
> literary allusion. The literary echo, in Wordsworth, is "reduced"
> to experience by a "cure of the ground"; and when it does
> occur it is so internalized that it points to the *phenomenology* of
> literary allusion. This grounding of allusion in experience—in
> the personal and mortal experience of time—has an unex-
> pected result. Take away the play of allusion, the comforting
> ground of literary-historical texture, and you place the burden
> of responsiveness directly on the reader.

My first response to this is to marvel at the miracle of a
cure of the ground so thorough that "literary-historical
texture" has disappeared. Hazlitt spoke what he knew to
be a relative truth when he said of Wordsworth's poetry
that in it we *seem* to begin anew on a *tabula rasa* of poetry.
Hazlitt's relativism has become Hartman's absolutism, but
then Hartman loves Wordsworth more than Hazlitt did,
but then again Hazlitt had the mixed blessing of knowing
Wordsworth   personally.   Hartman's   true   point   is
Wordsworth's characteristic *internalization* of allusion. Internalization is at once the great Wordsworthian resource
and the great Wordsworthian disaster, and it is never
enough to praise Wordsworth for a process in which he
was indeed, as Keats saw, the great poetic inventor and,
as Keats also saw, the great poetic villain; indeed as much
a hero-villain, I would say, as his true precursor, Milton's
Satan. In *The Borderers*, Milton's Satan is Oswald, but
elsewhere in Wordsworth he becomes a much subtler and
finer figure, the Solitary of *The Excursion*, and even finer,

the really dangerous element in Wordsworth's own poetic ego, or what Blake would have called Wordsworth's own Spectre of Urthona, the anxiety-principle that usurps voice in all the great poems, and substitutes for voice various memorial inscriptions, various traces of a Miltonic anteriority.

Something richer and more mature in Wordsworth wins out over even this spectral blocking-agent in *The Prelude*, but I am uncertain as to who wins in the greatest and most influential of Wordsworth's shorter poems, the grand triad of *Resolution and Independence,* the *Intimations of Immortality* Ode, and *Tintern Abbey.* I myself love *Tintern Abbey* more than any other poem by Wordsworth, but the love is increasingly an uneasy one. I do not see how any poem could do more or do better; it dwarfs Yeats or Stevens when they write in the same mode. I suspect that *Tintern Abbey* is *the* modern poem proper, and that most good poems written in English since *Tintern Abbey* inescapably repeat, rewrite, or revise it. If there is something radically wrong with it, something radically self-deceptive, then this radical wrongness at last will not be seen as belonging to *Tintern Abbey* alone.

The language of *Tintern Abbey* centers upon the interplay of hearing and of seeing. To "hear" goes back to an Indo-European root (*ken*) which means to pay attention, watch, observe, beware, guard against, as well as to listen. To "see" goes back to a root (*sekw*) that means to perceive. *To hear is thus also, etymologically, to see, but to see is not necessarily to hear.* This etymological oddity holds, in a Kabbalistic kernel, the deepest anxiety of Wordsworth's poem, which is an anxiety about Wordsworth's relation to his precursor-of-precursors, that mortal god, John Milton. Of all Milton's poetic descendants, including even Blake, Wordsworth was the strongest, so strong indeed that we must face a dark truth. Wordsworth's greatest poem, *The Prelude,* was finished, in its essentials, a hundred and seventy years ago, and no subsequent poetry written in English can sustain a close comparison with it, no matter what fashionable criticism tries to tell us to the contrary. There is an Emersonian law of compensation in literary history as there is in any other history, including the life of each individual. Nietzsche and Emerson, more than any other theorists, understood that other artists must pay the price for too overwhelming an artist. Wordsworth, like Milton, both enriches and destroys his sons and daughters. Wordsworth is a less dramatic destroyer, because of the program of internalization that he carried out, but he may have been the greater Tamerlane of the two.

Let me reduce my own hyperboles, which seem to have been rather unacceptable to my own profession, the scholars of poetic tradition. The problem of surpassing Wordsworth is the fairly absurd one of going beyond Wordsworth in the process of internalization. But what, in a poem, is internalization? I will compare two passages of poetry, and then ask which of these has gone further in the quest towards internalizing what we still like to call the imagination.

Here is the first:

> I am still completely happy.
> My resolve to win further I have
> Thrown out, and am charged by the thrill
> Of the sun coming up. Birds and trees, houses,
> These are but the stations for the new sign of being
> In me that is to close late, long
> After the sun has set and darkness come
> To the surrounding fields and hills.
> But if breath could kill, then there would not be
> Such an easy time of it, with men locked back there
> In the smokestacks and corruption of the city.
> Now as my questioning but admiring gaze expands
> To magnificent outposts, I am not so much at home
> With these memorabilia of vision as on a tour

Of my remotest properties, and the eidolon
Sinks into the effective "being" of each thing,
Stump or shrub, and they carry me inside
On motionless explorations of how dense a thing can be,
How light, and these are finished before they have begun
Leaving me refreshed and somehow younger.

This is the opening of John Ashbery's beautiful *Evening in the Country*, one of the most distinguished descendants of *Tintern Abbey*. Contrast it to the ancestral passage:

> . . . that blessed mood
> In which the burthen of the mystery,
> In which the heavy and the weary weight
> Of all this unintelligible world,
> Is lightened:—that serene and blessed mood,
> In which the affections gently lead us on,—
> Until, the breath of this corporeal frame
> And even the motion of our human blood
> Almost suspended, we are laid asleep
> In body, and become a living soul:
> While with an eye made quiet by the power
> Of harmony, and the deep power of joy,
> We see into the life of things

I will revisit these lines later, as I attempt a full reading of the poem. Here I am concerned only with the poetry of the growing inner self. Whose poetic self is more inner, Ashbery's or Wordsworth's? Both poets are experiencing a blessed mood that is at work repairing a previous distress, and both poets are seeing into the life of things. But are there still things for them to see into? Can we distinguish, whether in Wordsworth, or Emerson, or in all of their mixed progeny, between internalization and solipsism? It is palpable, to me, that there is a touch more externality to the world of things in Ashbery's lines than there is in Wordsworth's. In Wordsworth's supreme moments, as in Emerson's, things become transparent,

and the inner self expands until it introjects not less than
everything, space and time included. At least Ashbery still
knows and says "how dense a thing can be," however
motionless or quiet the exploring eye of the poet may
have become.

No one is going to manage, ever, to accomplish the
delightful absurdity of writing the *history* of the perpetually growing inner self. This helps one to see why the
phrase "the history of poetry" is, at best, an oxymoron. If
a friend came to me and declared that he was about to
embark upon a history of consciousness, then I would
weep for him. But it *is* possible to write the more limited
history of a few changes in historical psychology, which is
what the Dutch psychiatrist J. H. Van den Berg admirably accomplished in a book called *Metabletica,* translated
into English under the title of *The Changing Nature of
Man.* It is also possible to work out some, at least, of the
relationship between philosophy's struggles with the idea
of solipsism, and literature's rather more desperate
struggles with the same notion. A disputable but provocative book by a British literary scholar, A. D. Nuttall, has
attempted just this, quite recently, under the title of *A
Common Sky: Philosophy and the Literary Imagination.* Van
den Berg does not discuss Wordsworth, but he centers
upon Rousseau and upon Freud, both of them relevant to
any account of Wordsworthian internalization. Nuttall
does not like Wordsworth, whom he oddly compounds
with Nietzsche, because to Nuttall the Wordsworthian
innerness is essentially a solipsism. Here is a cento of
Nuttall on Wordsworth:

Wordsworth remains a philosophically inarticulate member
of the school of Locke....

    ... Wordsworth is plainly bewildered. He is afraid that his
insights are merely projections, hopes that they are telling him
about external reality. But the important thing is that, whatever
the final decision ... the categories of his thought are Lockian.
But Wordsworth, unlike Locke, has a distinctive psychology, a

peculiar cast to his mind, and is therefore afraid, as Locke was not, that his ideas are not truly representative of the world. . . .
    . . . It was almost inevitable that the slow progress of subjective isolation should have, as one of its psychological consequences, a compensatory obsession with the objective condition. The poet, inhabiting an increasingly mental world, grows hungry for "thinghood." For the Cartesian rationalist, articulate thought is the foundation of our confidence in reality. For Wordsworth one suspects that articulate thought and reality are in some way inimical to one another. This may partly be traced to Wordsworth's own strange spiritual development in which articulateness was attained at the very time when his grip on the object became infirm.

I think that Nuttall, in these comments, has mixed up two closely related but still separate states: highly self-conscious extreme subjectivity, and solipsistic fear that there is nothing beyond the subject. He is correct in observing Wordsworth's curious nostalgia for the object, which after all became the tradition that led from Wordsworth to Ruskin to Pater to Proust to Beckett, and also from Wordsworth to Emerson to Whitman to Stevens to Hart Crane to Ashbery. But this nostalgia for nature, this sense of the estrangement of things, finds a more convincing explanation in Van den Berg's formulations, who distinguishes the historical changes that caused the inner self to expand so alarmingly. Here is a rather full cento of passages from Van den Berg:

The theory of repression . . . is closely related to the thesis that there is sense in everything, which in turn implies that everything is past and there is nothing new. . . .
    . . . The factualization of our understanding—the impoverishment of things to a uniform substantiality—and the disposal of everything that is not identical with this substantiality into the "inner self" are both parts of one occurrence. The inner self became necessary when contacts were devaluated. . . .
    . . . A pure landscape, not just a backdrop for human actions:

nature, nature as the middle ages did not know it, an exterior
nature closed within itself and self-sufficient, an exterior from
which the human element has, in principle, been removed
entirely. It is things-in-their-farewell, and therefore is as moving as a farewell of our dearest. . . .

. . . The inner self, which in Rousseau's time was a simple,
soberly filled, airy space, has become ever more crowded. Permanent residents have even been admitted; at first, only the
parents, who could not stand being outside any longer, required shelter, finally it was the entire ancestry. . . . The inner
life was like a haunted house. But what else could it be? It
contained everything. Everything extraneous had been put into
it. The entire history of mankind had to be the history of the
individual. Everything that had previously belonged to everybody, everything that had been collective property and had
existed in the world in which everyone lived, had to be contained by the individual. It could not be expected that things
would be quiet in the inner self.

. . . Almost unnoticed—for everybody was watching the inner
self—the landscape changed. It became estranged, and con-
sequently it became visible. . . .

. . . the estrangement of things . . . brought Romanticism to
ecstasy.

These passages are the background to Van den Berg's
formidable critique of Freud, for Freud is viewed as the
prophet of the complete inner self and the completely
estranged exterior:

Ultimately the enigma of grief is the libido's inclination toward exterior things. What prompts the libido to leave the
inner self? In 1914 Freud asked himself this question—the
essential question of his psychology, and the essential question
of the psychology of the twentieth century. His answer ended
the process of interiorization. It is: the libido leaves the inner
self when the inner self has become too full. In order to
prevent it from being torn, the I has to aim itself on objects
outside the self; [Freud]: ". . . ultimately man must begin to

love in order not to get ill." So that is what it is. Objects are of importance only in an extreme urgency. Human beings, too. The grief over their death is the sighing of a too-far distended covering, the groaning of an overfilled self.

It is clear to me that Van den Berg's analysis, rather than Nuttall's, is precisely relevant to Wordsworthian internalization, including what Hartman calls the internalizing of the phenomenology of literary allusion. Nuttall sees Wordsworth as another victim of the hidden solipsism inherent in British empiricism from Locke onwards. Thus, the key-formula of British literary solipsism would be the most celebrated sentence in Locke's *Essay Concerning Human Understanding:*

Since the mind, in all its thoughts and reasonings, hath no other immediate object but its own ideas, which it alone knows or can contemplate, it is evident that our knowledge is only conversant about them.

There are poets who followed Locke, and perhaps an aspect of Wordsworth did, but this is to discount entirely the Coleridgean element in Wordsworth's vision of the imagination. Wordsworth's mind asserted, *contra* Locke and Nuttall, that it had also an immediate object in nature, or rather an answering subject in nature. But I think it correct nevertheless to say of Wordsworth what Van den Berg says of Rousseau, that the love of that answering subject, nature, is a love that distances and estranges nature. Internalization and estrangement are humanly one and the same process.

I turn to the text of *Tintern Abbey,* and to the interpretation of the poem as a Scene of Instruction. I begin with the last phase of this scene, the application to *Tintern Abbey* of my map of misprision, in order to uncover the pattern of revisionism in the poem, to trace the network of ratios, tropes, defenses, and images that are the final consequences of Wordsworth's struggle with Milton.

Let us map *Tintern Abbey* together. The poem consists

of five verse-paragraphs, of which the first three (lines 1–57) form a single movement that alternates the ratios of *clinamen* and *tessera*. The fourth verse-paragraph is the second movement (lines 58–111) and goes from the ratio of *kenosis* to a *daemonization* that brings in the Sublime. The fifth and final verse paragraph is the third and last movement (lines 112–159), and alternates the ratios of *askesis* and *apophrades*. To abandon my own esoteric shorthand, lines 1–57 shuttle back and forth between dialectical images of presence and absence and representing images of parts and wholes. Lines 58–111 alternate images of fullness and emptiness, of gain and loss, with images of height and depth. Finally lines 112–159 move from inside/outside juxtapositions of the self and nature to an interplay of images of earliness and lateness. This is of course merely a very rough revisionary pattern, but it is there all right, in *Tintern Abbey* as in hundreds of good poems afterwards, down to the present day. What is unique to each poem is the peculiar balance between tropes and defenses in these ratio-structures or patterns-of-images. It will be seen that in *Tintern Abbey* the intricate dance of substitutions between tropes and defenses of limitation and of representation exposes the problematics of the Wordsworthian motives for so thoroughly internalizing literary allusion as to give the effect of the first thoroughly original stylistic breakthrough in British poetry since Milton's *Penseroso*. But the price of this breakthrough is considerable, and can be traced up the interpretative ladder of a scene or scheme of Instruction.

In *A Map of Misreading*, I cited Kierkegaard as the Theorist of the Scene of Instruction, this being the Kierkegaard of the *Philosophical Fragments*. Perhaps I should have cited earlier Kierkegaard, particularly the remarkable brief essay in volume 1 of *Either/Or* called "The Rotation Method." In some sense, Wordsworth's *Tintern Abbey* is a "rotation method," and it may be illuminating to interpret Wordsworth's opening lines with a few Kierkegaardian excerpts firmly in mind:

My method does not consist in change of field, but resembles the true rotation method in changing the crop and the mode of cultivation. Here we have at once the principle of limitation, the only saving principle in the world. The more you limit yourself, the more fertile you become in invention. . . .

The more resourceful in changing the mode of cultivation one can be, the better; but every particular change will always come under the general categories of *remembering* and *forgetting*. Life in its entirety moves in these two currents, and hence it is essential to have them under control. It is impossible to live artistically before one has made up one's mind to abandon hope; for hope precludes self-limitation. . . . Hope was one of the dubious gifts of Prometheus; instead of giving men the foreknowledge of the immortals, he gave them hope.

To forget—all men wish to forget, and when something unpleasant happens, they always say: Oh, that one might forget! But forgetting is an art that must be practiced beforehand. The ability to forget is conditioned upon the method of remembering. . . . The more poetically one remembers, the more easily one forgets; for remembering poetically is really only another expression for forgetting. . . .

. . . Forgetting is the true expression for an ideal process of assimilation by which the experience is reduced to a sounding-board for the soul's own music. Nature is great because it has forgotten that it was chaos; but this thought is subject to revival at any time. . . .

. . . Forgetting and remembering are thus identical arts.

We cannot apply Kierkegaard to the opening of *Tintern Abbey*, or Van den Berg to its close, without de-idealizing our view of this great poem. Wordsworthian criticism at its best has overidealized *Tintern Abbey*. To this day I would judge the account of *Tintern Abbey* in Hartman's early book, *The Unmediated Vision*, the strongest reading the poem has received, but it is a canonical reading, and an apocalyptically idealizing one. The experience that Wordsworth had five years before writing *Tintern Abbey* is indeed, as Kierkegaard said, "reduced to a sounding-

board for the soul's own music," but Hartman follows
Wordsworth's own idealization of his supposed ex-
perience. Who is right, Kierkegaard or Wordsworth?
Shall we believe the poet in his own self-presentation?

Wordsworth's title for the poem is deceptively casual,
or rather this immensely ambitious poem is deceptively
left untitled, since the title proper is the throw-away,
Lines. But the generations of readers who have canonized
the poem have given it the mistitle that has stuck, *Tintern
Abbey,* which is not even the place of the poem's composi-
tion and vision, but gratuitously happens to be the
nearest landmark. The place *does* matter, at least to
Wordsworth, and so does the time:

> Five years have passed; five summers, with the length
> Of five long winters! and again I hear
> These waters, rolling from their mountain-springs
> With a soft inland murmur. —Once again
> Do I behold these steep and lofty cliffs,
> That on a wild secluded scene impress
> Thoughts of more deep seclusion; and connect
> The landscape with the quiet of the sky.
> The day is come when I again repose
> Here, under this dark sycamore, and view
> These plots of cottage-ground, these orchard-tufts,
> Which at this season, with their unripe fruits,
> Are clad in one green hue, and lose themselves
> 'Mid groves and copses. Once again I see
> These hedge-rows, hardly hedge-rows, little lines
> Of sportive wood run wild: these pastoral farms,
> Green to the very door; and wreaths of smoke
> Sent up, in silence, from among the trees!
> With some uncertain notice, as might seem
> Of vagrant dwellers in the houseless woods,
> Or of some Hermit's cave, where by his fire
> The Hermit sits alone.

That exclamation point in the middle of line 2 indicates

surprise that it should have been as long as five years
since the poet's last visit, a surprise that must indicate an
overwhelming sense of the past recaptured, of everything
at first being or at least seeming much the same as it had
been. Every interpreter has noted, surely correctly, the
importance of the more comprehensive sense, hearing,
having the primacy over sight, here at the outset of the
poem. Wordsworth does not commence talking about the
renewal of vision in any literal sense. Once again he hears
these waters, with their murmur that to his ears oddly
marks them as inland. Wordsworth attached a lame note
to this "inland murmur" as to just how many miles in
along the Wye you could still hear the sea. But his
literalism misinterprets his own figuration, and his "soft
murmur" prophesies his own *Intimations* Ode:

> Hence in a season of calm weather
> Though inland far we be,
> Our Souls have sight of that immortal sea
> Which brought us hither,
> Can in a moment travel thither,
> And see the children sport upon the shore,
> And hear the mighty waters rolling evermore.

Though twenty-eight years inland from his birth,
Wordsworth hears again the particular intimation of his
own immortality that he first heard five years before on
the banks of the Wye. This is what the opening figuration
of *Tintern Abbey* means, but hardly what it says, for the
poem's opening *illusio* speaks of an absence in order to
image a hoped-for presence. Rhetorically, Wordsworth
emphasizes the length of the five years that have gone by,
but his meaning is not in how long the absence of the
"soft inland murmur" has been felt, but how vividly the
presence of the hearing is revived. Psychologically, the
phenomenon is the primary defense of reaction-
formation, the opposition of a particular self-limitation to
a repressed desire by manifesting the opposite of the

desire. The desire repressed here is the ultimate, divinating desire to live forever, and the reaction-formation is the awareness, breaking through repression, of the passage of five long winters, despite the renewal of hearing and subsequently of vision.

Hartman and others have written usefully of the reciprocity that is renewed in the opening passage between Wordsworth's mind and the presence of nature. I want to emphasize instead the transition throughout the poem's first movement, up through line 57, from the initial reaction-formation or rhetorical irony to a psychic turning-against-the-self on Wordsworth's part, which as a figural representation is a remarkable instance of thinking-by-synecdoche. In line 42 of the poem, Wordsworth suddenly switches from "I" and "me" to "us" and "we." He is the part, and all people capable of imaginative experience become the whole. This plural subject is sustained until the magnificent "We see into the life of things" in line 49, after which in lines 50–57, Wordsworth is back to "I" and "me," to being a solitary or mutilated part of an universal whole, and a note of the vicissitudes of instinct, of psychic reversal, enters into the text again. This passage into and out of the universal is determined, in my interpretation, by the poem's largely hidden, revisionary struggle with two great precursor-texts, the invocations to Books III and VII of *Paradise Lost*. I want now to review the first fifty-seven lines of *Tintern Abbey* in the particular context of poetic misprision, of Wordsworth's relation to Milton, which centers upon the curiously placed figuration of the Hermit.

Hartman relates the Hermit of *Tintern Abbey* to the Leech Gatherer of *Resolution and Independence* and both to the vision and voice of St. John in Revelation. I would use Hartman's own description of the Hermit to suggest a more radical and poetically dangerous identification, in which the Hermit stands, through the fixation of a primal repression, for the blind contemplative Milton of the

great invocations. Here is Hartman's account of the
Hermit:

> The Hermit of *Tintern Abbey* is an image of transcendence: he
> sits fixed by his fire, the symbol, probably, for the pure or
> imageless vision. . . .
> . . . the Hermit appears, fixed near his fire, freed in his
> perception from the forms of the external world, a relic of
> eternity and prophet of the immortal sea's return.

Milton's presentation of himself, in his maturity, is certainly not as a Hermit, I would admit. But the Miltonic
Solitary or *Penseroso*, the true start for Wordsworth as
Pilgrim and Wanderer, appears at the close of *Il Penseroso*
as a Hermit. This Hermit first *hears* an immortal music
and only then has a vision of heaven. But the dialectic of
Milton's presence and absence begins earlier in *Tintern
Abbey* than in the epiphany of the Hermit, and continues
long after the vision of the Hermit has faded.

Hartman does not view the traces, hidden and visible,
of Milton in *Tintern Abbey* as evidence of Wordsworth's
anxiety, but rather of his strength. Hartman does not
overestimate the strength, for it is indeed beyond estima-
tion, but he discounts the anxiety that pervades the poem,
an anxiety that mixes worries about imaginative priority
with more overt worries about the continuity of imagination between the younger and the older Wordsworth. But
to discount the anxiety of influence is to commit oneself
to the idealizing process that is canonization, and that
leads to canonical misreading, so that strong readers become weaker than they need be. Here is Leslie Brisman,
very much in Hartman's tradition, writing of the
Milton-Wordsworth influence-relation in his sensitive and
brilliant book, *Milton's Poetry of Choice and Its Romantic
Heirs:*

> Throughout *The Prelude*, Wordsworth labors to create mo-
> ments where an arrest of time at the "uncreated" opens into a

sense of the re-created, of imaginative alternatives imagined
anew. . . . But in expressing a longing for a voice like that of
nature, Wordsworth achieves a moment of voice: "Spring
returns,— / I saw the Spring return." Appealing for poetic voice
in the invocation to *Paradise Lost,* Book III, Milton also expressed the failure of voice when he acknowledged that the
seasons return, "but not to me returns / Day." Wordsworth
cannot be said to echo Milton—"spring" is just the word for
which Milton could not at that moment find voice. But
Wordsworth has the power of sight, the power of relationship
with nature, and can gather from that relationship the voice
with which to proclaim, and rest on the claim, "Spring
returns,— / I saw the Spring return." The return of the word
"Spring" makes poetry participate in the renewal, taking on the
authority of the natural world.

This seems to me a beautiful idealism, but sadly
counter to the truths and sorrows of poetic misprision,
and particularly to the sorrowful truth of Wordsworth's
deep anxieties as to whether his power of relationship
with nature can compensate him for his failures to rise to
as much as he could have risen of Milton's more antithetical visionary power. For Wordsworth as well as Milton knows that poetry cannot take on the authority of the
natural world, but must assault the supposed priority of
the natural object over the trope. The old paradoxes of
poetic influence are at work here; Brisman shows us
Wordsworth consciously, overtly alluding to the Invocation of Book III. I will proceed now to show Wordsworth
unconsciously, repressively alluding to the same invocation in *Tintern Abbey,* with this repression in turn leading
to a greater, more daemonic, precisely Sublime repressive
alluding to the invocation to Book VII of *Paradise Lost.*

Book III of *Paradise Lost* begins by hailing the Holy
Light. Milton speaks of himself as revisiting the Light,
and of hearing again the "warbling flow" of Divine waters. But Milton is like the nightingale, and sings darkling.
Seasons return, but not to Milton, for the Day does not

return. Milton therefore prays to the "Celestial light" to purge and disperse all mist from his mind, that he may see and tell of invisible things. Lines 9–18 of *Tintern Abbey* are a misprision or reversed epiphany of this Miltonic passage, and are resumed in the opening lines of the *Intimations* Ode, where the "Celestial light" is absent though all the glories of nature are present. For Wordsworth, unlike Milton, "the day is come," and the season is seasonally bestowing its fruits to the seeing eyes. The mist that Milton prays be purged from his mind is sent up, to Wordsworth's sight, from the fire of the Hermit's cave. And if all this transposition seems far-fetched, then examine the very strangely phrased opening of the poem's very next verse-paragraph:

> These beauteous forms,
> Through a long absence, have not been to me
> As is a landscape to a blind man's eye:

Need we question who this blind man is?

Let us, for now, pass rapidly over the great second movement of the poem (lines 58–111), concentrating in it only upon the major interplay between tropes and defenses. There are a series of metonymic reductions—thought half-extinguished to gleams, recognitions to dimness and faintness, joys and raptures to aches and dizziness. This emptying-out psychically is less a regression or even an undoing than it is an isolation—the reduction from fullness to emptiness is a loss of context. The enormous restitution for this loss is in the magnificent series of hyperboles that dominate lines 93–111.

> And I have felt
> A presence that disturbs me with the joy
> Of elevated thoughts; a sense sublime
> Of something far more deeply interfused,
> Whose dwelling is the light of setting suns,
> And the round ocean and the living air,
> And the blue sky, and in the mind of man:

A motion and a spirit, that impels
All thinking things, all objects of all thought,
And rolls through all things. Therefore am I still
A lover of the meadows and the woods,
And mountains; and of all that we behold
From this green earth; of all the mighty world
Of eye, and ear,—both what they half create
And what perceive; well pleased to recognize
In nature and the language of the sense
The anchor of my purest thoughts, the nurse,
The guide, the guardian of my heart, and soul
Of all my moral being.

If an antithetical criticism of poetry is in any way useful, then it must illuminate this major instance of the
Sublime. If the Sublime depends upon repression, as I
insist it does, then where shall we find repression in these
remarkably expressive and emphatic lines? How can
there be meaningful repression where so much emerges,
where it seems surely that Wordsworth must be having
his whole say, must be bringing his whole soul into activity?

I would reply to these questions by indicating how
problematic this passage is, and how deeply a repressed
element is at work in it. Despite the hyperbolic language,
Wordsworth makes only a measured assertion of the
power of his mind over the universe of sense, and also
over language. The hyperboles make it difficult for us to
realize, at first, how guarded the passage is. The poet's
thoughts are touched to sublimity by a presence that
dwells in nature and in the mind, but is identified with
neither. The monistic presence is clearly more allied to
Hebrew than to Greek thought, but this pervasive motion
and spirit is not identified with the Hebrew-Christian
ruach, or breath-of-Jehovah. And though this presence/
motion/spirit appears to be monistic in its aims, the poet
stops well short of asserting that it reconciles subject and
object. It impels both, it rolls both through things and

through the poet's mind, but it does not abolish the differences between them. Nor is the poet's reaction to the spirit what we might expect, for instead of declaring his love for or worship of the spirit, he proclaims instead the continuity of his love for natural sights and sounds. Having invoked directly his eye and his ear, he makes, even more surprisingly, a deep reservation about his own perpetual powers, or rather an almost hyperbolical admission of limitation. The mighty world of eye and ear is not a balance of creation and of perception, but of half-creation and full-perception. Having acknowledged such a shading of imagination, it is no surprise that Wordsworth should then be happy to recognize anchor, nurse, guide, and guardian in powers not his own—in nature and the language of the self.

What *is* being repressed here is Wordsworth's extraordinary pride in the strength of his own imaginings, his preternatural self-reliance, as we find it, say, in the verse "Prospectus" to *The Excursion* or in Book XIV of *The Prelude*. An unconsciously purposeful forgetting is at work in the depths of Wordsworth's own spirit, and what it forgets is a ferocity of autonomy and strength unequalled in British poetry since Milton. Are these the accents of one whose eye and ear only half-create?

> For I must tread on shadowy ground, must sink
> Deep—and, aloft ascending, breathe in worlds
> To which the heaven of heavens is but a veil.
> All strength—all terror, single or in bands,
> That ever was put forth in personal form—
> Jehovah—with his thunder, and the choir
> Of shouting Angels, and the empyreal thrones—
> I pass them unalarmed. Not Chaos, not
> The darkest pit of lowest Erebus,
> Nor aught of blinder vacancy, scooped out
> By help of dreams—can breed such fear and awe
> As fall upon us often when we look

Into our Minds, into the Mind of Man—
My haunt, and the main region of my song.

That is Wordsworth, taking on Jehovah and Milton
together, only a few months before writing *Tintern Abbey.*
That is not a poet whose eye and ear "half-create." *Power*
is being repressed in *Tintern Abbey,* a power so antithetical
that it could tear the poet loose from nature, and take
him into a world of his own, restituting him for the
defense of self-isolation by isolating him yet more sublimely. Wordsworth defends himself against his own
strength through repression, and like all strong poets he
learns to call that repression the Sublime.

What are we to do with the phrase "half-create"? Can
we keep memory out of it? I think not. For you cannot
have repression without *remembering to forget,* and the
price of repression in *Tintern Abbey* is that memory largely
usurps the role of subject in the poem. But memory of
what? I return to an earlier formula in this discourse—
there is a struggle in *Tintern Abbey* between voicing and
marking, in which Wordsworth wants to rely upon voice
and the memory of voice, and somewhat fears relying
upon sight and the memory of sight. There is a hidden
but quite definite *fear of writing* in *Tintern Abbey*, or
perhaps rather a fear of being delivered up to a potential
fear of writing.

It is in Dorothy's voice that Wordsworth first recaptures
his own former language, and only then does he read his
own lost ecstasies in the shooting lights of her wild eyes.
All through the poem, the poet says he is being *taught*,
indeed he explicitly affirms that he has returned to a
Scene of Instruction. But it becomes clearer as the poem
proceeds that he wants to be taught or retaught primarily
through the ear (as the later Milton was), though he
knows that this is not really possible, since the eye is the
most despotic of our senses. *And Nature will not stop writing,* though he would prefer her to keep to oral composi-
tion. For consider the vocabulary of the poem: it opens

with a murmur, but then nature begins to write when the cliffs *impress* thoughts upon the scene, and when they connect landscape and sky. Whatever the source of the Hermit's fire, the silent wreaths of smoke are also a writing, and so are the beauteous forms that have been held as memory-traces. Wordsworth, like his scholarly disciple, Hartman, prefers the after-image to the spoken-trace, but his own poem keeps forcing him to read nature and not just to hear her. The world is not intelligible without writing, not even the natural world, and this is a sorrow to Wordsworth. Though his eye is chastened and made quiet by a power of sound, he still is constrained to say not that he *hears* the life of things, but that he *sees* into them. This pattern persists throughout the poem; the gleams and dim recognitions are visual, and when he does *look* on nature, in his mature phase, he *hears* loss, however beautifully, in "the still, sad music of humanity." But I have taken us now to the last dialectical movement of the poem, an alternation between metaphor and transumption, and I want to pause to brood on image-patterns before returning to the opposition between sight and sound.

The surprisingly beautiful passage from lines 134 through 146 juxtaposes nature as a benign *outside* force with Dorothy as a benign *inside* presence, but as always with the perspectivism of metaphor, Nature and Dorothy are taken further apart rather than being brought closer together by the juxtaposition. But the remarkable metaleptic reversals of lateness for earliness and earliness for lateness, which follow, give a much more powerful and convincing rhetorical illusion:

>   nor, perchance—
> If I should be where I no more can hear
> Thy voice, nor catch from thy wild eyes these gleams
> Of past existence—wilt thou then forget
> That on the banks of this delightful stream
> We stood together . . .

Those gleams are technically the metonymy of a metonymy—they trope upon an earlier trope in the poem, and so work as a trope-reversing trope. This allows Wordsworth a proleptic representation of his own death, and also of a kind of survival through the surrogate of Dorothy. I do not think this is literal death, despite Wordsworth's apparent intention, but the figural and much-feared death of the poetic imagination. The power of Miltonic transumption is worked again; defensively, Wordsworth introjects the past, projects the future except as a world for Dorothy, and utterly destroys the present moment, the living time in which he no longer stands. His gain in all this troping or defending is palpable; it is crucial to consider his loss, which will bring us back to memory, to writing opposing voicing, and at last to Milton again, and with Milton to the poem's full-scale staging of a Scene of Instruction.

Wordsworth's wishful prophecy for his sister would make her mind "a mansion for all lovely forms" and her memory "a dwelling-place / For all sweet sounds and harmonies." Because of the direct contrast the poet enforces between an earlier phase of "wild ecstasies" and a supposedly more "mature" one of "sober coloring" of the close of the *Intimations* Ode, there is something about that "mansion" and that "dwelling-place" that makes the reader a little uneasy. The mansion is a touch like a museum, and the dwelling-place a kind of tape- or record-library. But, setting this uneasiness aside, a curious preference seems to be shown here for "memory", over the "mind," since the preferred sensory impressions are harbored in "memory." Wordsworth of course, unlike Blake, made no sharp distinction between memory and poetry as modes of thought, but we must question still why *Tintern Abbey,* as a poem, ends with so emphatic an emphasis upon memory. Three times Wordsworth repeats his anxious exhortation to his sister, whom he loved and was always to love far more intensely than anyone else (with of course the single exception, always, of himself):

> oh! then,
> If solitude, or fear, or pain, or grief,
> Should be thy portion, with what healing thoughts
> Of tender joy wilt thou remember me,
> And these my exhortations! Nor, perchance—
> If I should be where I no more can hear
> Thy voice, nor catch from thy wild eyes these gleams
> Of past existence—wilt thou then forget
> That on the banks of this delightful stream
> We stood together; and that I, so long
> A worshipper of Nature, hither came
> Unwearied in that service: rather say
> With warmer love—oh! with far deeper zeal
> Of holier love. Nor wilt thou then forget,
> That after many wanderings, many years
> Of absence, these steep woods and lofty cliffs,
> And this green pastoral landscape, were to me
> More dear, both for themselves and for thy sake!

I think we learn in time, however much we love this poem, that we must read the last line with four words added: "More dear, both for themselves and for thy sake, and for my sake!" I am not attacking this superb poem, but I wish to acknowledge two very different readings or misreadings of the poem, the powerfully revisionist or deconstructive one implied by Paul de Man, in which the whole poem is an *aporia,* an "uncertain notice" like the smoke sent up among the trees, or the powerfully canonical one, in which Keats pioneered and which culminates in Hartman's *The Unmediated Vision.* Is *Tintern Abbey* an *aporia,* or is it the prolepsis of a dark passage, a major internalization of Milton's *agon* with tradition? Or is it, as an antithetical reading or misreading would seem to tell us, a very great visionary lie, not as much a myth of memory as it is a utilization of memory as a lie against time? Actually or potentially, these are all strong misreadings, and they may not differ from one another as much as they would like to, though clearly they also cannot be

reconciled. Which of the three readings/misreadings
would cost us too much of the poem's strength? Or to say it
in more Nietzschean terms, of these three errors, these
three composite tropes, which is the most necessary error?

Why, mine of course, though of the three it is the one I
like the least, because it increases the problematics-of-loss
in the poem. Memory, in *Tintern Abbey,* attempts to become a trope and/or defense that overcomes time, which
means that memory, going bad, would fall into the realm
of paranoia, but working properly would project or spit-
out Wordsworth's fears of the future. I think we must
praise Wordsworth, almost always, as a poet so strong
that he does make his defenses work, a strength in which
we could contrast him, most favorably, to a poet like Eliot,
whose *Gerontion* is a curious compound of *Tintern Abbey*
gone bad, and one of *Tintern Abbey*'s stronger descendants, Tennyson's *Tithonus.* Eliot is a poet whose poems,
with some exceptions, tend to become weaker rather than
stronger, the more provocatively they trope, defensively,
against the burden of anteriority. Wordsworth also deforms himself, or rather his poem-as-self, but in him the
deformation has a power so immense that after one
hundred and seventy-five years it has not stopped surprising us.

Why is Wordsworth so afraid of time in *Tintern Abbey*?
Surely it *is* time that is the hidden reference in the enigmatic: "more like a man / Flying from something that
he dreads than one / Who sought the thing he loved." Yet
Wordsworth's dread of mortality impresses us because
more than any poet's, at least since the Milton of *Lycidas,*
it seems to turn upon the magnificent, primal poetic urge
for *divination,* in the complex sense best defined by Vico,
the poet's apotropaic concern for his own immortality.
Milton and Wordsworth alike feared premature death,
"premature" meaning before their great epics had been
written.

On an antithetical reading, *Tintern Abbey* is a Scene of

Instruction in which the poet brings a Sublime response to a place or state of heightened demand, but the genius of the state counts for more than the genius of place, which means that Milton counts for more than nature does, both here and in *The Prelude*. It is Milton whose hidden presence in the poem makes the heightened demand that forces Wordsworth into the profoundly ambivalent defensive trope of memory. Renovation, or "tranquil restoration" as the text terms it, is only a mystification, a mask for the real concern of the poem. The Hermit is the synecdoche for Milton's hiddenness, and so for Milton's triumphant blindness towards anteriority. To see the writing or marking of nature is to see prophetically one's own absence or imaginative death. To see the "uncertain notice" of the Hermit's presence is to be disturbed into sublimity by way of repressing the mighty force of remembering Milton's sublimity, particularly in the Creation of *Paradise Lost*, Book VII, which haunts every Wordsworthian account of the subject- and object-worlds approaching one another again.

Wordsworth, where he is most self-deceiving, remains so strong that the self-deception finally does not matter. For no other poet since Milton holds Milton off so triumphantly, without even always knowing that he is engaged in a wrestling-match. The greatness of *Tintern Abbey*, no matter what the necessity is or is not of any particular strong misreading of it, is assured by its paradoxical triumph over its own hidden subject of memory. *Our* memory of the poem, any of our memories, is finally not a memory of nature's marking nor of Milton's writing, but of *hearing again*, with Wordsworth, "these waters, rolling from their mountain-springs / With a soft inland murmur." Though he was far inland, too far really from the oceanic autonomy he craved, his literally incredible strength of misprision rescued him, nearly intact, from a Scene of Instruction that had destroyed Collins, and partly malformed Blake. It is the peculiar and ex-

travagant greatness of Wordsworth that only he
supplanted Milton as the tutelary genius of the Scene of
Instruction, and it is the scandal of modern poetry that
no one, not even Yeats or Stevens, in turn has supplanted
Wordsworth. The Hermit of *Tintern Abbey* is Milton, but
the Hermit in *Notes toward a Supreme Fiction* is William
Wordsworth, even if Wallace Stevens repressed his memory of who it was:

> That sends us back to the first idea, the quick
> Of this invention; and yet so poisonous
>
> Are the ravishments of truth, so fatal to
> The truth itself, the first idea becomes
> The hermit in a poet's metaphors,
>
> Who comes and goes and comes and goes all day.

4

Shelley and His Precursors

I open as I will close, with the transumptive image proper, the *Merkabah,* which Milton called the Chariot of Paternal Deity. This Divine Chariot had a long prehistory in poetic texts both sacred and secular before it reached Shelley. It came to Shelley through the sequence that goes from Ezekiel to the Revelation of St. John to Dante, and onwards in English to Milton. Shelley did not know Blake's poetry, but I want to trace also the movement of this image from Milton through Gray to Blake, in order to contrast the image in Shelley and in Blake. Since I have been resorting to Kabbalistic conceptual images as paradigms for antithetical interpretation, I want also to make some observations upon the esoteric traditions of the Merkabah, though Shelley himself knew nothing of them.

The tradition of the Merkabah or Divine Throne in motion as a Chariot begins with the extraordinary first chapter of the Book of the Prophet Ezekiel, where the word *Merkabah* does not occur. As a word, *Merkabah* is first found in the Bible in I Chronicles 28:18, where we find also the origin of the emblem of the Covering Cherub:

And for the altar of incense refined gold by weight; and gold for the pattern of the chariot of the cherubims, that spread out their wings, and covered the ark of the covenant of the LORD.

The anxiety of visual representation was of course

acute among the ancient Jews. Thorleif Boman is correct in emphasizing that whereas Greek literature describes the appearances of all man-made artifacts, the Bible instead substitutes origin and process for appearance, by describing every appearance through an account showing how the thing was made. It is all the more remarkable that just one visual representation was allowed for the Jews, and this was always that of the images of the cherubim, as they flanked the enclosure containing the tablets of the Law, in the ark of the Covenant. The crucial act of poetic revisionism performed by Ezekiel was to assimilate this one visual representation that had escaped prohibition, to Isaiah's vision of God:

> In the year that king Uzziah died I saw the LORD sitting upon a throne high and lifted up, and His train filled the temple. Above him stood the Seraphim . . .

Blake, in a poem like *The Tyger,* follows the Hebraic pattern (as we have seen) by having his speaker describe not so much what confronts him, but the supposed process by which the beast was produced, the origins of the Tyger. Ezekiel also describes the heavenly chariot, the Cherubim and the Enthroned Divinity in motion, but he is curiously less Hebraic than Blake is, by his emphasizing so intensely the iconic aspects of the vision he confronts. When the Book of Ezekiel was accepted into the canon, the great image of the Merkabah was canonized also, which meant that it had to be misread canonically. Long before Kabbalah came into existence, a series of esoteric interpretations of the Merkabah had come into being, to be preserved in Talmud and in Midrash. The orthodox or canonical interpretation that gradually separated itself out from esoteric tradition culminated in the *Guide for the Perplexed* of Maimonides (III,7). Maimonides, with the saving caution of canonical misprision, explained that the closing clause of chapter 1 of Ezekiel was to be interpreted as meaning just the opposite of what esoteric teachings had asserted it meant. Verse 28 reads: "This was the appearance of the likeness of the glory of the LORD," upon which Maimonides commented: "*The glory of the LORD* is different from *the LORD* Himself. All the figures in this vision refer to the glory of the LORD, that is, to the chariot, and not to Him Who rides upon the chariot; for God cannot be compared to anything." By a single interpretative act, Maimonides had undone the esoteric element in Ezekiel and had insisted that the chariot was *not* a trope for God. This brilliant defense against esoteric interpretation can be said to have worked in one sense, and not at all in another. But both these senses can be deferred until we have seen further transformations in the image.

Ezekiel emphasizes what he calls the "Wheels and their Work":

Now as I beheld the living creatures, behold one wheel upon the earth by the living creatures, with his four faces.

The appearance of the wheels and their work was like unto the colour of a beryl: and they four had one likeness: and their appearance and their work was as it were a wheel in the middle of a wheel.

When they went, they went upon their four sides: and they turned not when they went.

As for their rings, they were so high that they were dreadful; and their rings were full of eyes round about them four.

And when the living creatures went, the wheels went by them: and when the living creatures were lifted up from the earth, the wheels were lifted up.

Whithersoever the spirit was to go, they went, thither was their spirit to go; and the wheels were lifted up over against them: for the spirit of the living creature was in the wheels.

When those went, these went; and when those stood, these stood; and when those were lifted up from the earth, the wheels were lifted up over against them: for the spirit of the living creature was in the wheels.

And the likeness of the firmament upon the heads of the living creature was as the colour of the terrible crystal, stretched forth over their heads above.

And under the firmament were their wings straight, the one toward the other: every one had two, which covered on this side, and every one had two, which covered on that side, their bodies.

And when they went, I heard the noise of their wings like the noise of great waters, as the voice of the Almighty, the voice of speech, as the noise of an host: when they stood, they let down their wings.

And there was a voice from the firmament that was over their heads, when they stood, and had let down their wings.

And above the firmament that was over their heads was the likeness of a throne, as the appearance of a sapphire stone: and upon the likeness of the throne was the likeness as the appearance of a man above it.

And I saw as the colour of amber, as the appearance of fire round about within it, from the appearance of his loins even upward, and from the appearance of his loins even downward, I saw as it were the appearance of fire, and it had brightness round about.

As the appearance of the bow that is in the cloud in the day of rain, so was the appearance of the brightness round about. This was the appearance of the likeness of the glory of the LORD. And when I saw it, I fell upon my face, and I heard a voice of one that spake.

[Ezekiel 1:15–28]

There is one wheel to each four-faced being. The rabbinical commentators identified the wheel with the angel Sandalphon, while the Book of Enoch called the wheels another order of angels, who like the Cherubim and Seraphim attended God. There is a rich confusion, much exploited by the Kabbalists, in calling the Merkabah "the wheels and their work," so that chariot and angels scarcely can be distinguished, and there is an even richer confusion, despite Maimonides and his tradition of canonical interpretation, between God and the Merkabah. We can say that there are three major biblical tropes for God, and these are voice, fire, and chariot, or respectively a metonymy, a metaphor, and a transumption or metaleptic reversal. Voice, not being an image, was favored by canonical traditions of interpretation, while fire and, much more strikingly, the chariot, became the prime images for Jewish Gnosticism and later for Kabbalism. Orthodox or Talmudic Haggadah made an inevitable connection between the two images, by warning that any expounder of the Merkabah would find himself surrounded by flame from heaven. Though Kabbalah tended to substitute meditation upon the more abstract *sefirot* for meditation upon the chariot, there are curious amalgamations of *sefirot* and the chariot in Kabbalistic writings. The Kabbalistic tendency to compound or, in rare cases, identify *sefirot* with "the wheels and their work" helped stimulate the Christian Kabbalah, because of the crucial revision of Ezekiel carried out in the last book of the Christian Bible, the Revelation of St. John the Divine, where in chapter 4:6 a vision is recorded of an enthroned man, Christ, surrounded by the four-faced Cherubim of Ezekiel:

And before the throne there was a sea of glass like unto crystal: and in the midst of the throne, and round about the throne were four beasts full of eyes before and behind.

What is the canonical mode of interpretation that connects the visions of Ezekiel and of Revelation, and subsequently both of these to the vision of Dante? *Figura*, as expounded by Erich Auerbach, Austin Farrer, A. C. Charity, is certainly the accurate answer. Auerbach traced the change in meaning of *figura*, from its original use as "form" through "model," "copy," "dream image," and trope or rhetorical figure until Tertullian and other Christian writers after him began to use it as a figure of

things to come. So Tertullian sees Joshua, the minister of
Moses, as a *figura* of whom Jesus Christ was the fulfillment, Joshua and Jesus being the same name. As Auerbach says, "*figura* is something real and historical which
announces something else that is also real and historical."

In our terms, we might say that to the ephebe or later
poet, the precursor is the *figura*, and the ephebe is the
fulfillment, but that would be to share the later poet's
self-idealization. Instead, the following can be stated as a
basic principle of poetic misprision: *No later poet can be the
fulfillment of any earlier poet.* He can be the reversal of the
precursor, or the deformation of the precursor, but
whatever he is, *to revise is not to fulfill.* Unlike *figura*, poetic
misprision must be seen as the troping or erroring it is.
But so, of course, *contra* Auerbach and Tertullian, is
figura, and it is surely time to see that *figura* was always a
revisionary mode, and so a lie against time. The Old
Testament is far too strong, as poetry, to be fulfilled by its
revisionary descendant, the self-proclaimed New Testament. "New" means "Early" here and "Old" means
"Late," and precisely what the New Testament lacks in
regard to the Old is a transumptive stance, which is why
the New Testament is a weak poem. *Figura* is supposed to
work by making Joshua late and Jesus perpetually early.
This works well enough for Joshua and Jesus, since the
prior figure is less central, but would have had more
difficulty if Moses had been taken as the *figura*. The
entire point of the theory of *figura* must be that the
second term or fulfillment is the truth, and the first term
or *figura* only a shadowy type of the truth. Here is Auerbach's definitive formulation:

> Figural interpretation establishes a connection between two
> events or persons, the first of which signifies not only itself but
> also the second, while the second encompasses or fulfills the
> first.

Auerbach cites the historical Virgil as a *figura* of Dante's

Virgil: "The historical Virgil is 'fulfilled' by the dweller in limbo, the companion of the great poets of antiquity." The distance between *figura* and transumption, we might say, is shown by observing that the historical Rousseau is most certainly *not* "fulfilled" by the Rousseau of *The Triumph of Life,* a notion of fulfillment utterly alien to Shelley. But we may wonder whether the idea of *figura* was ever more than a pious self-deception. Is Ezekiel's chariot-vision a *figura* of the vision of St. John? Unless one believes in Revelation, then there is no doubt whatsoever which is the stronger text. The more complex case is when we compare Ezekiel with Dante's Triumphal Chariot of the Church, for here the texts are equally strong. In Canto XXIX of the *Purgatorio,* Dante explicitly refers his chariot to Ezekiel's as well as to John's, but his chariot is unique in bearing his Beatrice, rather than an enthroned version of God. Singleton, in his commentary, remarks suggestively that this is:

. . . the kind of two-wheeled chariot used by the ancient Romans in war and in triumphal processions. As will become evident in the symbolism of the procession, this chariot represents the Church. But it is also, in this instance, a triumphal chariot, and as such it is strangely empty! Whose triumph is this?

As Singleton suggests, Dante is being superbly audacious, for if Ezekiel's Enthroned Man is the *figura,* then Beatrice is the fulfillment, the truth of which the Bible's most crucial permitted image of God is only a shadowy type. In our terms, Dante is on the threshold that Milton, with even greater audacity, will cross when a very Miltonic Christ is shown riding the Chariot of Paternal Deity at the climax of the War in Heaven in Book VI. As the great master, indeed the inventor of transumptive allusion, Milton fittingly transumes Dante as well as all other relevant non-biblical precursors in the chariot-vision.

. . . forth rush'd with whirl-wind sound
The Chariot of Paternal Deitie,
Flashing thick flames, Wheele within Wheele, undrawn,
It self instinct with Spirit, but convoyd
By four Cherubic shapes, four Faces each
Had wondrous, as with Starrs thir bodies all
And Wings were set with Eyes, with Eyes the Wheels
Of Beril, and careering Fires between;
Over thir heads a chrystal Firmament,
Whereon a Saphir Throne, inlaid with pure
Amber, and colours of the showrie Arch.
Hee in Celestial Panoplie all armd
Of radiant *Urim,* work divinely wrought,
Ascended, at his right hand Victorie.

[VI, 749–62]

The scheme of transumption, as I have demonstrated in *A Map of Misreading,* demands a juxtaposition of three times; a true one that was and will be (here, Ezekiel, Revelation, and Milton himself); a less true one that never was (here, Virgil, Dante, Petrarch); and the present moment, which is emptied out of everything but the experiential darkness against which the poet-prophet struggles (here, the allusion, noted by Verity, in the imagery of lines 840–41, to Milton's pamphlet war against "the proud resistance of carnall, and false doctors"). It is illuminating to juxtapose to Milton's vision of Christ in the Chariot of Wrath, Milton's vision of his own "Zeale" as polemicist in his *An Apology Against a Pamphlet:*

Zeale whose substance is ethereal, arming in compleat diamond ascends his fiery Chariot drawn with two blazing Meteors figur'd like beasts, but of a higher breed than any the Zodiack yields, resembling two of those four which *Ezechiel* and *S. John* saw, the one visag'd like a Lion to expresse power, high autority and indignation, the other of count'nance like a man to cast derision and scorne upon perverse and fraudulent seducers; with these the invincible warriour Zeale shaking loosely the slack reins drives over the heads of Scarlet Prelats, and such as are insolent to maintaine traditions, bruising their stiffe necks under his flaming wheels. Thus did the true Prophets of old combat with the false; Thus Christ himselfe the fountaine of meeknesse found acrimony enough to be still galling and vexing the Prelaticall Pharisees.

Though this transumption to the present is subtly covert, it is there nevertheless, and hints at one aspect of Milton himself, his "Zeale" for the truth, riding in the chariot with his Christ. More even than Dante, Milton has made the *figura* of the chariot in Ezekiel or Revelation a touch questionable. There is no biblical *figura* that Milton is fulfilling; he has mounted Christ in the Merkabah, made the throne-world into a war machine, and sent Christ out to battle as a larger version of his own self-image as Puritan polemicist burning through the ranks of the bishops and the presbyters. If this is *figura*, then the Milton who was Cromwell's Latin Secretary is the only *figura* involved, which is to overturn the Christian notion entirely. The true interpreter of what Milton has done in his chariot-vision is Gray, in the magnificent misprision of his Pindaric ode, *The Progress of Poesy,* where the starting point of Milton's appearance is an allusion to the Christ of Book VI, line 771: "Hee on the wings of Cherub rode sublime." What Milton discreetly hinted at, Gray makes overt, and so Milton himself dares the Lucretian adventure into the abyss:

> Nor second he, that rode sublime
> Upon the seraph-wings of Ecstasy,
> The secrets of the abyss to spy.
> He passed the flaming bounds of place and time:
> The living throne, the sapphire-blaze,
> Where angels tremble while they gaze,
> He saw; but blasted with excess of light,
> Closed his eyes in endless night.

Like certain sages in esoteric tradition, this Milton compensates frighteningly for his daring, but Gray's emphasis is on Milton's own language, since Milton's blindness here echoes his own "Dark with excessive bright" (*Paradise Lost,* III, 380). It is certainly to Gray's vision of Milton that Blake refers, when Blake dares to see himself, in succession to Milton, ascending the chariot in the introductory quatrains to his own poem, *Milton:*

> Bring me my Bow of burning gold:
> Bring me my Arrows of desire:
> Bring me my Spear: O clouds unfold!
> Bring me my Chariot of fire!

The emphasis is on "my," as Blake moves to be the Enthroned Poet riding the chariot that is at once drawn by, and constituted of, the Four Zoas, the "living creatures" of Ezekiel and Revelation.

We are ready, before passing on to Shelley's transformations of the chariot, to surmise the meaning of the chariot as a trope of transumption. The image of the Merkabah is one whose reappearances, to men, are troped necessarily by metalepsis, for each fresh epiphany of the chariot is a belatedness made early again. The chariot, whether in Ezekiel, Revelation, Dante, or Milton, moves always in a time that is never present, a time that restores *in illo tempore,* in *that* time, the realm of "there was a time when." The chariot is a metonymy of a metonymy for God, which meant that Maimonides, as he secretly knew, was making a deliberately canonical misreading when he remarked that God "cannot be compared to anything." As a metalepsis for God, the chariot uniquely succeeds in breaking continuity, in substituting itself for nature.

I will illustrate this last observation by returning to the biblical metaphor of the fire of God, and juxtaposing it to the chariot. The fire of God, in the Merkabah mystics and later in the Kabbalists, is Gnostic metaphor and very different from the rather matter-of-fact flame out of which the voice of God emerges. Since Jehovah infinitely transcends the whole of His creation, He disdains any ostentatious or cosmic fires. After all, compared to the Greeks or any other ancient people, the biblical Hebrews were not much interested in the four elements, fire included. God's major fire is His descent upon Mount Sinai, which produces a version of a fair-sized earthquake, but nothing really extraordinary or preternatural. In the calling of Moses, it *is* preternatural that the bush is not consumed, but very little is made of the fire itself. I think that, following Freud, we can speak of the Hebraic image of fire as a sublimation, as a perspectivizing metaphor, that suggests God's respect for the nature He has made. It is not from normative Judaism or from orthodox Christianity, but again from Stoicism, Platonism, Gnosticism, and Kabbalism that the more interesting images of fire in poetic and Romantic tradition derive. But I will defer further discussion of the contrast between the image of fire as metaphor, and of the chariot as transumption, until we confront these images in Shelley.

We have been tracing the Chariot as the image of transumption, and particularly as a poetic ratio transforming the visionary's belatedness into an earliness, from its biblical and esoteric origins through poetic tradition down to Shelley. In his twentieth year, Shelley composed his first attempt at a major poem, *Queen Mab,* a revised fragment of which he salvaged under the title, *The Daemon of the World,* in the *Alastor* volume of 1816, four years after *Queen Mab* was finished. The Daemon descends in Shelley's version of the Merkabah:

> The chariot of the Daemon of the World
>> Descends in silent power:
> Its shape reposed within: slight as some cloud
> That catches but the palest tinge of day
>> When evening yields to night,
> Bright as that fibrous woof when stars indue
>> Its transitory robe.

Four shapeless shadows bright and beautiful
Draw that strange car of glory, reins of light
Check their unearthly speed; they stop and fold
  Their wings of braided air.

About all that Shelley has done, or could do, this early
on, is to appropriate the Miltonic chariot, and give it not
to Paternal Deity, but to a spirit of rebellion. In *Prometheus Unbound*, the actual attempt at transuming Milton
and Milton's sources is made, and though it does not
succeed entirely in capturing the image away from canonical tradition, the attempt is formidable:

I see a chariot like that thinnest boat,
In which the Mother of the Months is borne
By ebbing light into her western cave,
When she upsprings from interlunar dreams;
O'er which is curved an orblike canopy
Of gentle darkness, and the hills and woods,
Distinctly seen through that dusk aery veil,
Regard like shapes in an enchanter's glass;
Its wheels are solid clouds, azure and gold,
Such as the genii of the thunderstorm
Pile on the floor of the illumined sea
When the sun rushes under it; they roll
And move and grow as with an inward wind;
Within it sits a wingèd infant, white
Its countenance, like the whiteness of bright snow,
Its plumes are as feathers of sunny frost,
Its limbs gleam white, through the wind-flowing folds
Of its white robe, woof of ethereal pearl.
Its hair is white, the brightness of white light
Scattered in strings; yet its two eyes are heavens
Of liquid darkness, which the Deity
Within seems pouring, as a storm is poured
From jaggèd clouds, out of their snowy lashes,
Tempering the cold and radiant air around,
With fire that is not brightness; in its hand

It sways a quivering moonbeam, from whose point
A guiding power directs the chariot's prow
Over its wheelèd clouds, which as they roll
Over the grass, and flowers, and waves, wake sounds,
Sweet as a singing rain of silver dew.

[IV, 206–35]

I have written several commentaries on this vision of
Ione, and of the related, more magnificent vision of
Panthea that follows it directly. My commentaries have
been canonical, not in the sense that I can assert necessarily that they were more definitive as canonical misreadings than those of other Shelley critics (though like all
interpreters I aspired, and aspire, to strength) but canonical in that they organized themselves around the
assumption that Shelley was in the canon of major poetry
in English, and so a vital element of meaning in him had
to come out of his counterpointing his vision of myth-
making against his own reception of tradition. That now
seems to me too idealizing and optimistic a view of Shelley's, or any poet's, relation to a strong tradition. Poets no
more fulfill one another than the New Testament fulfills
the Old. It is this carry-over from the tradition of figural
interpretation of Scripture to secular literature that has
allowed a curious overspiritualization of texts canonized
by poetic tradition. Since poets also idealize themselves,
and their relations to other poets, there is already an
excessive self-regard in poetic and critical tradition. Modern theories of mutually benign relations between tradition and individual talent, including those of T. S. Eliot
and of Northrop Frye, have added their idealizations, so
that it becomes an enormous labor to clear away all of this
noble obfuscation.

I note the observation made by Milton-scholarship that
Christ ascends the Chariot of Paternal Deity at the exact,
numerological midpoint of the first edition of *Paradise
Lost*. Shelley was wary of origins, in an almost Nietzschean

way, and he had no patience whatsoever with midpoints, but he had the apocalyptic temperament, as Blake did, and so he was obsessed with the last things. In *Prometheus Unbound,* Shelley attempted a humanistic apocalypse, which may be an oxymoron. To overcome this seeming contradiction, Shelley resorted to his version of the image of the Merkabah, doubtless hoping to redeem the crudity of his early vision of the chariot in *The Daemon of the World.* The visions of Ione and Panthea are meant to humanize the visions of Ezekiel, Revelation, Dante, and Milton. Do they succeed in this extraordinarily difficult aim, or do they collapse back into their orthodox origins? Who controls the meanings in Shelley's courageous attempts to reverse, correct, and "fulfill" tradition?

I return to my earlier attack upon the theory of *figura* as expounded by Auerbach; Shelley, like Blake, seems to seek a use of *figura* against *figura,* but I would argue that no reversal in such a use can be a true reversal, but all too easily itself can be reversed back into its original. I have argued already that Milton seems to have understood this, and that in his schemes of allusion in *Paradise Lost* he replaced *figura* by transumption—not a fulfillment or even a reversed fulfillment of tradition, but a true subversion of tradition that enforced Milton's own earliness while troping tradition into belatedness. I will argue now that Shelley learned this Miltonic lesson only *after* he had completed *Prometheus Unbound.* In *The Triumph of Life,* the Merkabah itself becomes a transumption of transumption, but in *Prometheus Unbound* Milton overcomes his revisionist.

Contrast to Panthea's vision (*Prometheus Unbound,* Act IV, lines 236–318) its Miltonic source in *Paradise Lost,* Book V, lines 618–27. God has proclaimed His Son and challenged any recalcitrant angels to disobey this proclamation, and then be cast out. The speech is powerfully provocative, so much so that Empson properly says that God Himself caused all the trouble by being so pugnacious in the first place. A celebratory dance of angels follows, which Milton compares to the Platonic dance of the spheres:

> That day, as other solemn days, they spent
> In song and dance about the sacred Hill,
> Mystical dance, which yonder starry Sphere
> Of Planets and of fixt in all her Wheels
> Resembles nearest, mazes intricate,
> Eccentric, intervolv'd, yet regular
> Then most, when most irregular they seem:
> And in thir motions harmony Divine
> So smooths her charming tones, that God's own ear
> Listens delighted . . .

Does Shelley surmount the peculiar strength of this anterior vision, with its astonishing transumptive victory over Plato's *Timaeus,* a victory accomplished by assimilating Plato's cosmic dance to the Ezekiel and Revelation chariots? Panthea's vision gives us, not a dance that is most regular where it seems most irregular, or a dance that Platonically returns upon itself, but rather a dance that "with the force of self-destroying swiftness," is grinding all substance into the ethereal, into light and air. The Shelleyan question is not: "How can we tell the dancer from the dance?" but "How soon can the dance consume the dancer?" Yet the speed that Shelley relies upon for the orb to be self-destructive is itself the Platonic and Miltonic return of a divine motion upon itself, and Shelley's apocalypse of the physical universe is thus accomplished only through the oddity of identifying the whole of reality with the Miltonic dance of angels, and also with the Miltonic chariot. It is only through becoming more divine, meaning more Miltonic, that nature will undo herself. The sacred dance is sped up by Shelley to a quasi-Dionysiac or Orphic frenzy, but the figuration remains Milton's blend of Plato and the Bible, rather than a trope of Shelley's own invention. Shelley's intended defense is his characteristic and magnificent speed in and at the process of rhetorical substitution, but the defense is a desperate one, and Milton triumphs over his revisionist, because it is Milton's transumptive trope that gives coherence to Shelley's image, rather than the reverse. Milton remains *early,* and Shelley, thrusting towards finality, achieves only a superb *belatedness,* a sense that he has come too late into the poetic cosmos to do more than agree with a structure it has bequeathed him, however much he desires to hasten that legacy into a glorious sublimation. Milton captures and overturns Plato; Shelley is *captured* by Milton, and avoids being overturned only by sending the mythic machinery up into the aethereal as rapidly as he can.

In *The Triumph of Life,* his apparently unfinished last poem, and certainly his greatest achievement, Shelley struggles more with Wordsworth than with Milton, and the struggle is in one sense more successful, in that *The Triumph of Life* manages to transume the *Intimations* Ode in the way earlier Wordsworthian poems by Shelley could not, as a comparison of the *Triumph* with the *Hymn to Intellectual Beauty* would show. But Wordsworth is a dangerous opponent to take on, and we will see that Shelley's victory is equivocal. What he gains from Wordsworth, Shelley loses to time or to language, both of which become more problematic in the *Triumph* than they are in Wordsworth. It is as though a casting-out of Wordsworthian nature demands a compensation, a price exacted both by poetic history and by poetic language.

I turn now to the proof text for this critical discourse, *The Triumph of Life,* one of the crucial antithetical texts in the language. The title itself redefines what "antithetical" means for us, since in isolation the phrase, "The Triumph of Life," seems a victory for the natural man or woman, but in context the Shelleyan phrase means "The pageant or celebratory procession of Death-in-Life over

the Imagination," or indeed the triumph of what is antithetical in us.

On the model of our map of misprision, *The Triumph of
Life* divides as meaningfully as does its precursor, the
Intimations Ode, despite the technical status of the
Triumph as a supposedly "unfinished" poem. But there
are, of course, no "unfinished" strong poems; there are
only stronger and weaker poems. The idea of a "finished"
poem itself depends upon the absurd, hidden notion that
reifies poems from relationships into entities. As a poem
is not even so much a relationship between entities, as it is
a relationship between relationships, or a Peircean Idea
of Thirdness, we can say that no relationship between
relationships can ever be finished *or* unfinished except
quite arbitrarily. A monad presumably can be finished;
perhaps a dyad can be left unfinished; but a modern
poem is a triad, which is why it begins in a dialectical
alternation of presence and absence, and why it ends in a
transumptive interplay of earliness and lateness. You can
be too early or too late, but it makes no sense to say that
you are finally too early or finally too late, unless you are
talking about death. Meaning in poems, as Vico first saw
or at least said, is always a matter of survival, and so we
might say that poems no more can discourse truly of the
poet's own death than anyone ever quite dies in his own
dreams.

We can map the *Triumph* therefore as the complete
poem it is, while remembering that a phrase like "complete poem" is oxymoronic. Here, utilizing my own shorthand, is the mapping:

Lines 1–20, the induction: *clinamen.* Dialectical opposition of sun and stars, as presence/absence of nature/
poetry; rhetorical irony of saying "dawn" and meaning
"twilight"; reaction-formation on Shelley's part against
Wordsworthian natural piety; deeper irony implied (as
figure-of-thought) of presence of natural sun and absence

of stars (poets) preparing for overwhelming presence of chariot of Life, a presence blanker than any absence.

Lines 21–40, the induction completed: *tessera*. Imagery of recurrence, of vision as part of whole that is repetition of vision; synecdoche of poet's vision for all of reality; psychically a reversal into the opposite as Shelley moves from imaginative activity into passive reception of a vision not his own, and so at least purgatorial of the self.

Lines 41–175, the pageant: *kenosis*. Imagery of emptying-out of captives of Life; metonymy of fiction of the leaves; Life the Conqueror as metonymy of death; Chariot of Life as undoing of Merkabah; dance of victims as undoing of Eros; metonymy of foam for sexual passion; metonymy of shade for death-in-life; psychic defense of undoing Shelley's own vision of love, as in St. Ignatius: "My Eros is crucified."

Lines 176–300, epiphany of Rousseau as surrogate for Wordsworth: *daemonization*. The Sublime collapsed into the Grotesque; litotes as reversed hyperbole; infernal imagery of the depths of degradation; powerful repression of Shelley's own desire to carry through the Rousseau-Wordsworth dream of natural redemption; imagery of the great, those on intellectual heights, thrown down.

Lines 300–411, Rousseau's account of his imaginative genesis, culminating in his yielding to the "Shape all light": *askesis*. Imagery of inside subjectivity and outward nature; sublimation of greater vision to lesser as Rousseau drinks of Shape's cup of Nepenthe; radical metaphor of the poem, the tripartite metaphor of three lights: the original one, the Shape's, Life's.

Lines 412–end, Rousseau's vision after his sublimation, Shelley's own reaction, transumption of *Intimations* Ode: the *apophrades*. Return of Wordsworth, but somewhat in Shelley's own colors; imagery of belatedness; deliberate refusal to bring about metaleptic reversal; death of earliness and joy; introjection of past, and so of Wordsworthian defeat; projection of poetic future, and so abandonment of what has become merely a life-in-death.

Those are the contours of misprision in *The Triumph of Life*; I shall not try to demonstrate them exhaustively in a commentary, but shall move instead to the image of the chariot in the poem, to see how Shelley, on the threshold of his proper greatness, handled the difficult process of troping further upon what we already have seen to be the prime image of transumption in Western tradition. Here is the Shelleyan parody of a transumptive mode, far in spirit but perhaps not far in technique from Nietzschean parody:

And as I gazed methought that in the way
  The throng grew wilder, as the woods of June
    When the South wind shakes the extinguished day.—

And a cold glare, intenser than the noon
    But icy cold, obscured with   light
The Sun as he the stars. Like the young moon

    When on the sunlit limits of the night
Her white shell trembles amid crimson air
    And whilst the sleeping tempest gathers might

Doth, as a herald of its coming, bear
    The ghost of her dead Mother, whose dim form
Bends in dark ether from her infant's chair,

    So came a chariot on the silent storm
Of its own rushing splendour, and a Shape
    So sate within as one whom years deform

Beneath a dusky hood & double cape
    Crouching within the shadow of a tomb,
And o'er what seemed the head, a cloud like crape,

    Was bent a dun & faint aetherial gloom
Tempering the light; upon the chariot's beam
    A Janus-visaged Shadow did assume

The guidance of that wonder-wingèd team.
    The Shapes which drew it in thick lightnings
Were lost: I heard alone on the air's soft stream

The music of their ever moving wings.
All the four faces of that charioteer
    Had their eyes banded . . . little profit brings

Speed in the van & blindness in the rear,
    Nor then avail the beams that quench the Sun
Or that his banded eyes could pierce the sphere

Of all that is, has been, or will be done.—

                                        [74–104]

Dante and Milton both relate their chariot-visions to
the Sun; Shelley parodies both when the cold light of his
chariot emits beams that quench the sun, but that still do
not avail as a light to guide the chariot properly. The
larger parody involved is profound, and has been unex-
amined in the canonical commentaries of *The Triumph of
Life*. What does it mean to substitute the equivocal
figure, Life, for the Enthroned Man of Ezekiel, and
Beatrice in Dante, and Milton's warlike Christ? What kind
of transumptive parody is this, when Death-in-Life becomes the conqueror? Shelley has another precursor
here, Spenser, whose Lucifera rides in a triumph that is
also a demonic parody of the Ezekiel-tradition, but Shelley's Life is not an allegorical opposition to the enthroned
beings of tradition, as Lucifera is. Life is not a light-
bearer, a son or daughter of the morning fallen into
darkness. Life is merely Life, our Life, everybody's life,
natural existence, the repetition we all dubiously enjoy
and endure. What is Shelley doing to tradition here?
    A. C. Charity, commenting on Dante's quest, compares
it to Kierkegaard's program of *becoming a Christian,* which
is the positive meaning of "repetition," according to Kierkegaard. Shelley, as always, is not interested in becoming
a Christian, but rather in the perpetual struggle of *becoming a poet,* and then remaining a poet, by continually
becoming a poet again. It is surprising how much of
Shelley's poetry, on close analysis, is obsessed with the

careers of Wordsworth and Coleridge, who had ceased to be strong poets at just about the time when Shelley became one. Lamenting Keats, in *Adonais,* it is still clearly Wordsworth and Coleridge that Shelley has in mind when he writes of Keats that:

> From the contagion of the world's slow stain
> He is secure, and now can never mourn
> A heart grown cold, a head grown gray in vain;
> Nor, when the spirit's self has ceased to burn,
> With sparkless ashes load an unlamented urn.

So much echoes here; Shelley's own cry, at the close of the *Ode to the West Wind:*

> Scatter, as from an unextinguished hearth
> Ashes and sparks, my words among mankind!

Two stanzas before, in *Adonais,* Shelley had chided, as I would interpret it, Wordsworth and Coleridge, by crying out "Thou canst not soar where he is sitting now—" and then contrasting Keats's perpetual glowing in the burning fountain of the Eternal, to the sitters who are told: "thy cold embers choke the sordid hearth of shame." The line, "Thou canst not soar where he is sitting now," echoes Milton's Satan, in Book IV, lines 828–29, declaring himself in Eden to the two angelical sentries, Ithuriel and Zephon, in a passage that Keats had echoed in the *Ode to Psyche.* Satan says:

> Know ye not mee? ye knew me once no mate
> For you, there sitting where ye durst not soar.

So Wordsworth and Coleridge are unkindly but not too inaccurately (in 1821) being viewed as an Ithuriel and Zephon pair, knowing not Keats (or Shelley), but living on with an extinguished poetic hearth and writing sparkless verses. But this had been an obsession of Shelley's poetry ever since its real beginnings in 1815, when he had addressed lyrics to Wordsworth and to Coleridge lamenting them as sell-outs, and when he had anticipated (seven years prematurely) his own death, in *Alastor*, where "those who remain behind" are the two Romantic precursor poets, there dubbed not Ithuriel and Zephon, "But pale despair and cold tranquillity," the former being Coleridge and the latter Wordsworth.

As a transumptive parody, Shelley's vision in *The Triumph of Life* addresses itself more even to Wordsworth and Coleridge than it does to Milton and Dante. Shelley shrewdly implies that the Ezekiel-Revelation chariot contains the contrasting epigraph-emblems of both the *Dejection* Ode and the *Intimations* Ode, the pale despair of the portent of an oncoming storm, and the image of the rainbow, sign that the storm is over, with cold tranquillity ensuing. That is why, in *The Triumph of Life*, the onrushing chariot is heralded by the old moon in the new moon's arms, as in the fragment of *Sir Patrick Spens* that begins Coleridge's Ode, and that begins Ione's vision in *Prometheus Unbound*. And that is why, in *The Triumph of Life*, Rousseau encounters Iris or the rainbow just before confronting Wordsworthian Nature as the "Shape all light," as in the fragment of his own "My heart leaps up" that Wordsworth uses to begin the *Intimations* Ode.

I am suggesting then that there is no mystery about Life in *The Triumph of Life*. Life is precisely what has triumphed over Wordsworth and Coleridge, that is, over their imaginative integrity and autonomy as strong poets. Life is the conqueror of poets, the death-in-life that they sought to fend off by divination. Most certainly, Life in this particular sense is what Shelley had always feared, and clearly it is what he rejects in his sublimely suicidal last poem. Rousseau might just as well be named Wordsworth or Coleridge in the poem, except that Shelley was too tactful and urbane to thus utilize those who were still, technically speaking, alive.

But why then the chariot, as the poem's central trope, since it is hardly a dominant image in Wordsworth or in

Coleridge? We return to the paradox of poetic origins; poetry is not an art passed on by *imitation,* but by *instruction.* There is no instruction without a Scene of Instruction, a primal fixation upon a precursor (however composite, however idealized) and such a fixation is also a primal repression, in which what is repressed is the acute demand for divination, the ephebe's sense that his own powers are preternatural and autonomous. Before the winter of 1814–15, Shelley wrote badly; he was a very weak poet. After he read deeply in Wordsworth and Coleridge, particularly Wordsworth, he was able to write *Alastor* and the powerful 1816 poems, including *Mont Blanc.* Becoming a poet had meant accepting a primal fixation upon a quasi-divine precursor. For Shelley, as for so many other poets, the problem of continuity or discontinuity with precursors became merged with the problem of continuity in and with one's own poetic self.

Like other poets, Shelley first tried to achieve a perspectivizing stance in relation to precursors through the limiting trope of metaphor. Fire is the prime perspectivizing metaphor of Romanticism, and to burn through context, the context of precursors and of nature, is the revisionary aim of that metaphor. Fire becomes the "inside" or "subjectivity" while nature becomes the context or the "outside" in this unconvincing but prevalent Promethean trope. That is why Shelley begins *Alastor* by addressing earth, air, and water as though he were one with their brother-element of fire. Behind this, ultimately, is the image of fire that went from Heraclitus to the Stoics and from them to the Gnostic system of Valentinus, which Shelley so strongly and so oddly resembles. For the Stoics, fire was rational; they spoke of "the fiery mind of the universe." But, to the Valentinians, the fire was the dark affection or passion they called "ignorance," which contained within itself the three lesser dark passions that had brought about the Fall into nature: "grief, fear and bewilderment." We can see in Shelley a fearful passage of the image of fire, from *Prometheus Unbound,* where it is essentially rational, to *Adonais,* where it is still Stoic and rational but where an element of Gnostic dark affection or "ignorance" has been admitted into the metaphor. In *The Triumph of Life,* the fire of Eros and the cold, glaring light are no longer rational at all, but are given over wholly to the dark passion of Gnostic "ignorance."

Shelley had learned, for himself, what Milton had illustrated by the career of Satan; the metaphor of fire (which is the Prometheus-phase of poetic quest) must "fail," in that its perspectivism is necessarily self-defeating, for all of its "insides" and "outsides" are endlessly equivocal and reversible. Yet post-Enlightenment poetry, as Shelley understood, was in one phase at least a questing for fire, and the defensive meaning of that fire was discontinuity. "The fire for which all thirst" or burning fountain of *Adonais* may have an ultimate source in Plotinus, but its immediate continuity was with the "something that doth live" in our embers that still gave Wordsworth joy, in the final stanzas of the *Intimations* Ode. Those "embers" of Wordsworth, still smoldering in the *Ode to the West Wind,* flare up for a last time in *Adonais,* and then find their continuity, after Shelley, in what Yeats called the Condition of Fire, which has its flamings in Browning and Pater while en route to Yeats.

When the fire metaphor had failed Shelley, he turned in the *Triumph* back to the transumptive image of the chariot, which we have seen him attempt before in his poetry. The chariot, as a trope, succeeds in breaking continuity, in the sense that continuity equals nature or the *res extensa* of Descartes. The fire is a limitation; the chariot substitutes for it as a representation. The fire is a sublimation; the chariot is an introjection of futurity, and a projection of lost or past time. Shelley was a strong poet and a central poet, and he knew instinctively what Vico knew overtly, that poetic meaning is always concerned with the struggle for poetic survival. To avoid the poetic fate of Wordsworth, he had turned to the image of fire. It had failed him. He turned back therefore from Wordsworth to the image of the chariot that the anti-mythological Wordsworth would not handle. Wallace Stevens is Wordsworthianizing when he says: "The solar chariot is junk." Shelley says, in effect, the solar chariot and all the other chariots are obsolete, all right, as Wordsworth had said, but nevertheless Life came riding along in such a chariot, and triumphed over Wordsworth.

But whether Shelley, in terms of poetic meaning, accomplishes a successful transumption of the fundamental Wordsworthian metonymy of gleam for imagination, is quite another matter. The cold light of the chariot overcomes the light of the Wordsworthian Shape, even as the light of nature overcomes the earlier light of Rousseau, or of the young Wordsworth. Yet in what I have called the *apophrades* or final part of Shelley's poem, from the "new Vision" of line 411, until the end, the meaning that returns is wholly a Wordsworthian kind of meaning, and the colors of the return flicker a little uncertainly, so that we cannot tell at times if they are Shelley's transformations, or if they are survivals still very much Wordsworth's own. Let us try a somewhat closer reading of the last two parts of the poem, beginning with Rousseau's account of his origins from line 300 on.

Rousseau's vision describes a Wordsworthian process of imaginative rebirth or restoration, but a process that ends in a catastrophe. He awakens first into the earlier world of "there was a time," by way of a parody of the *Intimations* Ode. In this awakening, he still beholds the visible trace of a greater imaginative anteriority, "a gentle trace / Of light diviner than the common Sun." In the synaesthetic splendor of a "confusing sense" he sees and hears "A shape all light," whom we may describe as a sublimating metaphor for everything that Wordsworth called "nature." In response to her seductive summons, he yields up to her the metaphoric fire of his poethood, in Shelley's cruellest parody of the Wordsworthian "O joy! that in our embers / Is something that doth live." Seven years of brooding on the imaginative failure of Coleridge and of Wordsworth, that is, of their failure to carry their youthful imagination intact into middle age, culminates in this frightening vision:

> 'And still her feet, no less than the sweet tune
> To which they moved, seemed as they moved, to blot
>   The thoughts of him who gazed on them, & soon
>
> 'All that was seemed as if it had been not,
> As if the gazer's mind was strewn beneath
>   Her feet like embers, & she, thought by thought,
>
> 'Trampled its fires into the dust of death . . .'

This is the end, in Shelley, of the fire of sublimation, the hope that poetic discontinuity or autonomy could be achieved by a radical or Nietzschean perspectivism. With the bursting on sight of the new vision, are we any less in the world of Wordsworth's poetry?

> 'So knew I in that light's severe excess
> The presence of that shape which on the stream
>   Moved, as I moved along the wilderness,
>
> 'More dimly than a day appearing dream,
>   The ghost of a forgotten form of sleep,
> A light from Heaven whose half extinguished beam
>
> 'Through the sick day in which we wake to weep
> Glimmers, forever sought, forever lost.—
>   So did that shape its obscure tenour keep
>
> 'Beside my path, as silent as a ghost,
>   But the new Vision, and its cold bright car,
> With savage music, stunning music, crost
>
> 'The forest . . .'

[424–35]

How much, besides the chariot itself, had Shelley added to Wordsworth here? The Wordsworthian equivalent is the poignant (if less sublime):

> At length the Man perceives it die away,
> And fade into the light of common day.

Only the chariot, transformed from its glorious riders to Life's destructive vehicle, was Shelley's own, as Shelley clearly knew. After seven years of struggle with Wordsworth's poetry, Shelley's work still battled to keep itself from being flooded out by the precursor's. He had learned, finally and superbly, the Miltonic lesson of transumptive allusion, yet he could not bring himself to apply it to Wordsworth as he had applied it to the Bible, Dante, and Milton. Why? Because the primal fixation upon Wordsworth, and consequent repression of self, was simply too great, would be my answer, an answer that I would illustrate by citing the most famous single passage of Shelley's prose, the last paragraph of *A Defence of Poetry:*

... For the literature of England, an energetic development of which has ever preceded or accompanied a great and free development of the national will, has arisen as it were from a new birth. In spite of the low-thoughted envy which would undervalue contemporary merit, our own will be a memorable age in intellectual achievements, and we live among such philosophers and poets as surpass beyond comparison any who have appeared since the last national struggle for civil and religious liberty. The most unfailing herald, companion, and follower of the awakening of a great people to work a beneficial change in opinion or institution, is poetry. At such periods there is an accumulation of the power of communicating and receiving intense and impassioned conceptions respecting man and nature. The persons in whom this power resides, may often as far as regards many portions of their nature, have little apparent correspondence with that spirit of good of which they are the ministers. But even whilst they deny and abjure, they are yet compelled to serve, the power which is seated upon the throne of their own soul. It is impossible to read the compositions of the most celebrated writers of the present day without being startled with the electric life which burns within their words. They measure the circumference and sound the depths of human nature with a comprehensive and all-penetrating spirit, and they are themselves perhaps the most sincerely astonished at its manifestations; for it is less their spirit than the spirit of the age. Poets are the hierophants of an unapprehended inspiration; the mirrors of the gigantic shadows which futurity casts upon the present; the words which express what they understand not; the trumpets which sing to battle, and feel not what they inspire; the influence which is moved not, but moves. Poets are the unacknowledged legislators of the world.

Unquestionably, the poets of whom Shelley is speaking here are not himself, Byron, and Keats, but primarily Wordsworth and secondarily Coleridge. It does not matter, Shelley says, that as men Wordsworth and Coleridge have become Tories in politics, pillars of the established Church in religion, and mere time-servers in literature. "Even whilst they deny and abjure" the imagination, Wordsworth and Coleridge serve its power. Wordsworth is a hierophant or expounder of the mysterious, even though he himself cannot apprehend what he expounds. Wordsworth is a transumptive mirror of futurity, and sings Shelley on to the battle of poetry long after Wordsworth himself is uninspired. And then comes the beautifully summarizing formula: Wordsworth is the unmoved mover, as an *influence*. The famous, much misinterpreted last sentence, "Poets are the unacknowledged legislators of the world," clearly needs to be interpreted in the context of the paradox that Shelley himself calls poetic "influence." The late W. H. Auden had a passionate dislike of Shelley, and once went so far as to interpret the last sentence of the *Defence of Poetry* as meaning that Shelley thought that poets were in league with the secret

police. An unacknowledged legislator is simply an unacknowledged influence, and since Shelley equates
Wordsworth with the *Zeitgeist,* it is hardly an overestimate
to say that Wordsworth's influence created a series of laws
for a world of feeling and thinking that went beyond the
domain of poetry. Very strong poet that he was, Shelley
nevertheless had the wisdom and the sadness of knowing
overtly what other poets since have evaded knowing, except in the involuntary patterns of their work.
Wordsworth will legislate and go on legislating for your
poem, no matter how you resist or evade or even unconsciously ignore him.

I do not want to end on such a tone of realistic sorrow
and wisdom, even though the superbly intelligent Shelley
is not ill-represented by such a tone. He knew that he
could not escape the shadow of Wordsworth, and of and
in that knowing he made his own poetry. I end by apply-
ing to him the last stanza of his own *Hymn of Apollo.* He
would not have wanted us to think of him as the speaker
of these lines, but he came as close, I think, as any poet
since Wordsworth, down to our present day, to justifying
our going beyond his intentions, and hearing the poet
himself in this great declaration:

> I am the eye with which the Universe
>   Beholds itself and knows itself divine;
> All harmony of instrument or verse,
>   All prophecy, all medicine is mine,
> All light of art or nature;—to my song
> Victory and praise in its own right belong.

5

Keats: Romance Revised

Paul de Man engagingly remarks that "it is one of Keats's most engaging traits that he resists all temptation to see himself as the hero of a tragic adventure." De Man says also of Keats that "he lived almost always oriented toward the future," the pattern of his work being thus "prospective rather than retrospective." These are moving observations, and I honor them. They surmise a Keats whose vision "consists of hopeful preparations, anticipations of future power rather than meditative reflections on past moments of insight or harmony." As does Angus Fletcher, de Man sees Keats as one of the *liminal* visionaries, akin surely to Coleridge, to Hart Crane, perhaps to an aspect of Stevens. De Man points to all those phrases in Keats's poems and letters "that suggest he has reached a threshold, penetrated to the borderline of a new region which he is not yet ready to explore but toward which all his future efforts will be directed." If de Man were wholly right, then Keats ought to be happily free of the Shadow of Milton and of Wordsworth, the composite precursor that both inspired and inhibited him. There can be no more extreme posture of the spirit, for a strong poet, than to take up, perpetually, a prospective stance. I regret taking up a more suspicious or demystifying stance than de Man does, but Keats can charm even the subtlest and most scrupulous of deconstructors. No strong poet, of necessity, is wholly liminal in his vision, and Keats was a very strong poet, greatly gifted in the revisionary arts of misprision. I begin therefore by suggesting that de Man's observation accurately describes one of Keats's prime composite tropes, but also declines (on de Manian principle, of course) to examine the psychic defenses that inform Keats's liminal trope.

Keats no more resembles Nietzsche's Zarathustra than Nietzsche himself did. I myself, perhaps wrongly, tend to read Zarathustra as a highly deliberate Nietzschean parody of the prospective stance that frequently distinguishes the High Romantic poet. Nietzsche had read and brooded upon Shelley, and also upon that indeliberate parodist, Poe. The contrary to prospective vision, in Blakean rather than Nietzschean terms, is the cycle of the being Blake called Orc, who would like to tear loose from Nature's wheel, but cannot. Nietzsche dreamed an antithetical vision, the Eternal Return of the Same, which is transumptive in stance. But these dialectical resources, whether Blakean or Nietzschean, were not congenial to Keats's genius. He was an experiential or retrospective poet at least as much as he was visionary or prospective, and as a poet who lived fully the life of poetry, and very little life of any other kind, he was compelled to one of the fiercest and most problematic struggles with the Covering Cherub of poetic influence that the language affords us.

My primary text in this discourse will be the second and greater of Keats's *Hyperion* fragments or heroic torsos, *The Fall of Hyperion*. I must remark, before commencing a reading of the poem, that here I cannot agree with de Man at all, for in *The Fall of Hyperion* Keats does yield to the temptation to see himself as the hero of a romance that is in the process of turning into tragedy. By the point at which the fragmentary *The Fall of Hyperion* breaks off, Keats (perhaps despite himself) has become the quest-hero of a tragic adventure.

Certainly he had resisted such a temptation for nearly the whole of his writing-life, consciously opposing himself in this to Byron and to Shelley, and emulating the pre-

cursor he shared with them, Wordsworth, who had made
an aesthetic and moral choice against tragedy, and who
had refused to identify himself with his own isolate selfhood, the Solitary of *The Excursion*. But in *The Fall of
Hyperion*, and perhaps only there, Keats did write at least
the sketch of a tragic romance, a prophetic sketch in that
the poem has vital descendants both direct and indirect.
A dance-play like Yeats's savage *A Full Moon in March* is a
direct descendant, while Hart Crane's *The Bridge* is an
indirect but remarkably close descendant, and so, I begin
to suspect, is Stevens's *Esthétique du Mal*.

In reading Keats as having been a revisionist of Romance, I need to commence by revising the way I have
read him in the past, for he too has suffered, and from
other critics as well as myself, by the kinds of misreading
that canon-formation enforces. In the past, I would have
given an account of Keats's development somewhat as
follows: after the subjectivizing disorders that rhetorically
disfigured *Endymion*, Keats returned to the austere program of his own *Sleep and Poetry*, by attempting to write in
what he himself disarmingly called "the more naked and
Grecian manner" of the first *Hyperion*. But he discovered
that his supposedly more objective epic could not be
freed of the not-so-naked and no-so-Grecian manner of
Paradise Lost, and so he broke off, on the polemical plea
that, as he put it: "English must be kept up." His rallying
cry became the rather transparent self-deception of:
"Back to Chatterton!" which of course turned out to
mean: "Back to Wordsworth!" Turning to the not un-
Wordsworthian Cary translation of the *Purgatorio*, Keats
then attempted his own purgatorial vision in *The Fall of
Hyperion*, and did not so much break that off as discover,
quite suddenly, that he had finished the poem as much as
it could be finished. This canonical or Bloomian misreading traced a kind of cycle, in which Keats went from
Romantic subjectivism to a kind of "Modernist" reaction
against Wordsworthian internalization, only to discover at

last that the Wordsworthian mode was the authentic and inescapable one for the would-be strong poet. Though I would still have found a critique of Wordsworthianism in *The Fall of Hyperion,* I would have centered any reading of the poem in the movement of a return to Wordsworth, under whatever cover and with whatever saving difference.

So once I would have thought, but now no more. I don't know if I have submitted to a new control, but I do think my sense of how poems make us read them has undergone a distress in which the reader's soul too is humanized, and made more aware of the necessity of error. Keats could not read Milton or Wordsworth without troping what he read, and we do the same to Keats.

Like Shelley, Keats is a poet of the transumptive mode, which is necessarily both retrospective and prospective, as I have been trying to show. In my last chapter, on Shelley, I emphasized Shelley's radical development of the prime Western poetic image of transumption, the Merkabah. In tracing the conflict between fire as the prime image of perspectivizing and the chariot as the image of overcoming belatedness, I concluded that Shelley's yielding to the chariot is equivocal, and unwilling. His heart remained in and with the Condition of Fire; the Fire, he insisted, for which all thirst. Keats, as I surmise we will see, gives himself more graciously to the chariot, to the great image of human and poetic continuity. Here is Keats's own early version of the chariot, from *Sleep and Poetry,* the programmatic poem he wrote at the hopeful age of twenty-one. After a passage of cheerfully erotic wish-fulfillments, involving at least three "white-handed nymphs in shady places," Keats addresses himself to higher things:

> And can I ever bid these joys farewell?
> Yes, I must pass them for a nobler life,
> Where I may find the agonies, the strife
> Of human hearts: for lo! I see afar,

> O'er sailing the blue cragginess, a car
> And steeds with streamy manes—the charioteer
> Looks out upon the winds with glorious fear.

The chariot is the throne-world in motion, but here the throne-world is that of Apollo, or rather of the Apollo of Collins, the Apollo of Sensibility, and not the High Romantic Apollo of Nietzsche. Keats's oxymoron of "glorious fear" suggests Collins's use of fear as a psychic defense and rhetorical trope, of "fear" as the repression of the daemonic force of a belated creativity that needs to forget that it knows itself as a belatedness. "Glorious fear," in Keats or Collins, therefore means a creative repression, as here in Collins's *Ode to Fear:*

> Dark power, with shuddering meek submitted thought,
> Be mine to read the visions old,
> Which thy awakening bards have told . . .

We associate Shelley with rhetorical speed and glancing movement, while Keats, like Collins, is deliberately slow-paced, at times approaching a stasis. The chariot or throne-in-motion is therefore less congenial to Keats than a stationary throne-world, and so his prime transumptive image returns us to the source of Ezekiel's Merkabah in the throne-vision of Isaiah. Keats's version of the Hekhaloth or heavenly halls has been too little admired, or studied. Here are Book I, lines 176–200, of the first *Hyperion:*

> His palace bright
> Bastioned with pyramids of glowing gold,
> And touched with shade of bronzèd obelisks,
> Glared a blood-red through all its thousand courts,
> Arches, and domes, and fiery galleries;
> And all its curtains of Aurorian clouds
> Flushed angerly: while sometimes eagle's wings,
> Unseen before by Gods or wondering men,
> Darkened the place; and neighing steeds were heard,

Not heard before by Gods or wondering men.
Also, when he would taste the spicy wreaths
Of incense, breathed aloft from sacred hills,
Instead of sweets, his ample palate took
Savour of poisonous brass and metal sick:
And so, when harboured in the sleepy west,
After the full completion of fair day,—
For rest divine upon exalted couch
And slumber in the arms of melody,
He paced away the pleasant hours of ease
With stride colossal, on from hall to hall;
While far within each aisle and deep recess,
His wingèd minions in close clusters stood,
Amazed and full of fear; like anxious men
Who on wide plains gather in panting troops,
When earthquakes jar their battlements and towers.

Partly, Keats is writing in the mode of Walter Savage
Landor here, a mode of marmoreal reverie, but partly he
evokes (consciously, I think) the omen-ridden world of
Shakespeare's Roman tragedies, particularly *Julius Caesar.*
But these surface similarities or allusions induce no anxieties in Keats, and so do little to determine the tropes
and images of the first *Hyperion.* The true precursor-text
is the vision of Heaven in *Paradise Lost,* a Heaven in which
the impending Fall of Satan and his Host is scarcely a
major disturbance, in which the actual War between the
faithful and the rebels is at most a minor annoyance for
God, the smashing of a few Divine breakfast dishes. The
passage that I have just quoted from *Hyperion* is a misprision of the Miltonic Heaven, but it is not itself a Miltonic
kind of misprision, in that it is not transumptive; that is, it
does not project the Miltonic Heaven into belatedness,
while establishing instead its own earliness. It fails to do
to Milton's Heaven what Milton did to the Olympus of
Homer, and this failure is at the heart or one might say
nerve of its powerful uneasiness, an uneasiness that has a

thematic function, certainly, but that transcends even thematic necessity. The tropes of this passage (lines 176–200) are all tropes of representation, and yet they over-represent.

Let me return to, and now adumbrate, a distinction I ventured in *A Map of Misreading*, between ratios (tropes, defenses, images) of limitation and ratios of representation. I said there that "limitations turn away from a lost or mourned object towards either the substitute or the mourning subject, while representations turn back towards restoring the powers that desired and possessed the object. Representation points to a lack, just as limitation does, but in a way that *re-finds* what could fill the lack. Or, more simply: tropes of limitation also represent, of course, but they tend to limit the demands placed upon language by pointing to a lack both in language and the self, so that limitation really means recognition in this context. Tropes of representation also acknowledge a limit, point to a lack, but they tend to strengthen both language and the self."

I quote this gnomic passage because I am now ready to unpack it, to illustrate it by the passage of *Hyperion* under consideration and, I hope, to illuminate Keats's lines by the application of my distinction. But I want to return my distinction to its Kabbalistic source, in order to be reminded that "limitation" and "representation" are highly dialectical terms in the context of poetic interpretation. The Lurianic *zimzum* is not so much a contraction or a withdrawal as it is a concentration upon a point, a kind of intensification of God as he takes a step inside himself. A poetic image of limitation tends to cluster in three areas: presence and absence, fullness and emptiness, insideness and outsideness. In the dialectic of rhetorical irony or of defensive reaction-formation, absence tends to dominate over presence, yet this is more a pointing to an absence or a lack, in language or the self, than it is itself a state of absence. Similarly, in the metonymic reductiveness from images of fullness to those of emptiness, these defensive undoings, regressions, and isolations indicate more a *recognition* of emptiness, whether of the empty word or the empty self, than they actually mean an emptiness itself. Most crucially, in the sublimating perspectivism of metaphorical images, though the emphasis in poems tends most often to be upon the outsideness of objects, sharply distinguished from the inwardness of subjective consciousness, the ratio or trope does not so much limit meaning to the aching sense of a loss of inwardness, but rather concentrates attention upon the process of perspectivizing itself. The Lurianic *zimzum,* as a master, composite ratio or trope of limitation, betrays in its most problematic kinds of meaning its usefulness as a paradigm for all tropes of limitation. *Zimzum* is the ultimate *askesis* because it is God's own *askesis,* His self-truncation, but paradoxically it strengthens rather than weakens God, by concentrating Him, and by making Creation possible. The great Renaissance commonplace, most beautifully phrased by Tasso and by Sidney, that only the poet truly merited the term of Creator, as God did, took on a special force in the context of Lurianic Kabbalah, which is I think why figures like Bruno and Pico were so enraptured by Kabbalah.

But this digression has gone out and away, apparently, from the passage of Keats's *Hyperion* in question, for there I said we meet only tropes of representation, even of overrepresentation, which I think is largely true of the first *Hyperion* as a poem, and is another indication of why the earlier *Hyperion* is so much less moving and magnificent than its replacement in *The Fall of Hyperion.* Though tropes of representation also acknowledge limits, and point to lacks, primarily they tend to strengthen both language and the self. Can we not say of the first *Hyperion*, and not just of its single passage under discussion, that the poem's language tries to be stronger than the poem's language can sustain being, and also that Keats's

own poetic self is being put under too strong a burden
throughout, both as the impersonal narrator and as the
Apollo of the fragmentary third book? Too much is being
refound, and nearly all at once, throughout the first
Hyperion, and the poem as a whole, at least as it stands,
implies and even exemplifies too sharp a turning-back
towards restoring our mutilated human powers, powers
for not only desiring a totality, but even for hoping to
possess the object of such desire. The function of images
or tropes of limitation is to turn us away from the lost or
mourned object, and so to bring us back to either a
sublimated substitute for the object or, more crucially, a
reconsideration of ourselves as mourning subjects. In the
first *Hyperion*, Keats took up too directly the burden of
Miltonic representation, with a mass of universalizing
synecdoches, Sublime hyperboles, and—as we will see—
transumptive or metaleptic reversals of tradition. To recognize himself again, Keats had to write *The Fall of Hyperion* and his five great odes, and both the *Fall* and the
Odes do follow the structure or pattern of ratios that
Wordsworth and most strong post-Wordsworthian poets
have followed.

I return, at last, to lines 176–200 of Book I of *Hyperion*,
to demonstrate some of these conclusions, after which I
will proceed to the main business of this discourse, which
is to give a full antithetical reading of *The Fall of Hyperion*,
and by it come back full circle to the starting point of my
dissent from de Man, which was my insistence that Keats
was as much a retrospective as a prospective poet, and
also that in his last major work he was compelled, despite
himself, to see himself as a hero of quest-romance on the
very threshold of becoming a tragic hero. It was a
threshold that he did not cross, in poetry or in life, and I
hope to surmise before I end this chapter why he would
(or could) not cross it in the poem.

When we first confront Hyperion in the earlier poem,
he is remarkably balanced between Sublime and Gro-

tesque representation, a balance that, I hasten to add, belongs to Keats's art alone, and not to Hyperion himself, for Hyperion is suffering what we tend to call a failure of nerve, or even a nervous breakdown. At this point Hyperion as Sun God reminds us too well that Freud's formulation of the defense of repression centers it in the psychic area of hysteria. We see and hear a Sublime being, but we are aware, all too uneasily, that this hyperbolical sublimity is founded upon a really fierce repression:

> Blazing Hyperion on his orbèd fire
> Still sat, still snuffed the incense, teeming up
> From man to the sun's God; yet unsecure:
> For as among us mortals omens drear
> Fright and perplex, so also shuddered he—
> Not at dog's howl, or gloom-bird's hated screech,
> Or the familiar visiting of one
> Upon the first toll of his passing-bell,
> Or prophesyings of the midnight lamp;
> But horrors, portioned to a giant nerve,
> Oft made Hyperion ache.

[166–76]

A God who shudders at divinations is in the process of ceasing to be a God, and too nervous a God is a grotesque God. The meaning of Hyperion's repression here rises from its interplay with the grand repressive God of Book III of *Paradise Lost*. From the first moment we see him, Milton's God, unlike Milton's Satan, has no relation whatsoever to the stance and condition of being a poet. From our first encounter with him, Keats's Hyperion is a touch closer to Milton's Satan than Keats would care for him to have been, since like Satan Hyperion is not so much a God in dread of losing his kingdom as he is a poet in dread of losing his poetic powers or mortal godhead. An obsession with divination, a fear of futurity, is the mark of Hyperion, of Satan, and of Blake's Urizen, and its human meaning is the peculiar poetic property not so

Poetry and Repression

much of Milton as of Wordsworth, a truth that Keats
knew perhaps better than we can know it.

I come now to the particular passage of the first *Hyperion* that I have been circling in upon, the Hekhaloth or
heavenly halls of the nervous Hyperion, in the Sublime
pathos that will be almost the last of his glory. Here I will
want to start with a formula that sums up the revisionary
element in lines 176–200: Keats gives us *an earliness that
works as a lateness,* almost the reverse of the Miltonic
scheme of transumptive allusion. Milton knowingly sac-
rifices the living present, the moment of his empirical
being as he writes, in order to achieve an ontological
earliness that triumphs over almost the entire tradition
that produced him, and makes us see that tradition as
being belated in contrast to him. I do not think that
Keats, any more than Milton or Wordsworth, ever sought
that all-but-impossible union between the ontological and
empirical self, *in a poem,* that became the peculiarly
American tradition of Romantic poetry, from Emerson
and Whitman on to Hart Crane and A. R. Ammons. But,
in the first *Hyperion*, Keats is not yet the master of transumptive allusion that, following Milton, he was to become. We can date the transition to Keats's maturity as a
poet very precisely, since it was by April 1819 that he
gave up the first *Hyperion* for good, and it was during the
month from April 20 to May 20, that he fully found
himself in the writing of the *Ode to Psyche.*

Let us examine Hyperion's palace. Its characteristic imagery is of height and depth, but we may be reminded by it
of Blake's comment upon Dante: "In equivocal worlds up &
down is equivocal." Hyperion is still sitting exalted, but he
acts like ourselves, beings *beneath* the sun. His Shakespearean palace, at once Roman and exotically Eastern, is both
"glowing" and "touched with shade," the light also showing
an equivocal height and depth. The images of what ought to
be earliness crowd upon us: a rising sun; clouds accompany-
ing Aurora, goddess of the dawn; eagles never seen before,

and horses never heard before, whether by Gods or men. But all these have to be taken on the lateness of "the sleepy west," of incense turned to "savour of poisonous brass." The Sun God, moving through his domain, is imaged lastly by his angelic attendants or minor Titans, who are waiting for the final lateness of an apocalyptic earthquake. Keats has achieved a surprising immediacy here, but at a triple cost: the only future is a final fall, or utter projection; there is no past surviving into the present, except for a grotesque parody of the Sublime; and the present is introjected as a pure anxiety. I suggest that a full-scale reading of the first *Hyperion* would show that this passage is a part standing for the whole of the fragment. There are essentially only two ratios in the first *Hyperion,* and they are a *kenosis* and a *daemonization,* in uneasy alternation. The fragment vacillates between a defensive isolation of Sublime tradition, through metonymic reduction, and a powerful repression of the Sublime that fails to make the passage from hyperbole to a metaleptic reversal, that is to say from a perpetually mounting force of still greater repression to a stance finally the poet's own.

In contrast, I turn at last to *The Fall of Hyperion,* which is at once Keats's revision of romance and also his acceptance of the necessity of internalizing romance. This supposed fragment is an entire poem, showing the total structure of misprision, the complete patterning of images that Romantic or belated poetry demands. It is not accidental that, of all the Great Odes, the *Ode to Psyche* most resembles *The Fall of Hyperion,* for it was the *Ode to Psyche* that Keats, with high good humor, came to terms with his own belatedness. As I have sketched an antithetical reading of the *Ode to Psyche* in *A Map of Misreading,* I will leap over that poem here and take its pattern of misprision as a prelude to the richer working-out of the same pattern in *The Fall of Hyperion.*

The fundamental principle of an antithetical or Kabbalistic criticism is that, in poetic texts, tropes are best understood as psychic defenses, because they *act as de-fenses*, against the tropes of anteriority, against the poems of the precursors. Similarly, in poetic texts, the poet's (or his surrogate's) psychic defenses are best understood as tropes, for they trope or turn against anterior defenses, against previous or outworn postures of the spirit. I shall illustrate this principle by contrasting the opening lines of *The Fall of Hyperion* to part of the opening passage of Wordsworth's *The Excursion*, Book I, lines 77 ff., that describes the Wanderer:

> Oh! many are the Poets that are sown
> By Nature: men endowed with highest gifts,
> The vision and the faculty divine;
> Yet wanting the accomplishment of verse
> . . . .
> Nor having e'er, as life advanced, been led
> By circumstances to take unto the height
> The measure of themselves, these favoured Beings,
> All but a scattered few, live out their time,
> Husbanding that which they possess within,
> And go to the grave, unthought of . . .

The first verse-paragraph of *The Fall of Hyperion* may be thought of as a *clinamen* away from this passage of Wordsworth, among others, one of which might be *The Excursion*, Book IV, lines 1275 ff., yet another panegyric in praise of (let it be admitted) that egregious bore, the Wanderer or the censorious Wordsworthian superego:

> Here closed the Sage that eloquent harangue,
> Poured forth with fervour in continuous stream,
> Such as, remote, 'mid savage wilderness,
> An Indian Chief discharges from his breast
> Into the hearing of assembled tribes,
> In open circle seated round, and hushed
> As the unbreathing air, when not a leaf
> Stirs in the mighty woods. —So did he speak:

> The words he uttered shall not pass away
> Dispersed like music that the wind takes up
> By snatches, and lets fall, to be forgotten ...

Behind both Wordsworthian passages is an anxiety of Wordsworth's, that the part of his mind represented by the Wanderer may be inimical to poetry, as opposed to the more dangerous part represented by the Solitary, who in Shelley and in the Keats of *Endymion* becomes a figure nearly identical with poetry itself. I think we have underestimated Keats's savagery in *The Fall of Hyperion,* and that he begins the poem with a very bitter rhetorical irony that is his psyche's reaction-formation to this Wordsworthian anxiety:

> Fanatics have their dreams, wherewith they weave
> A paradise for a sect; the savage too
> From forth the loftiest fashion of his sleep
> Guesses at Heaven; pity these have not
> Traced upon vellum or wild Indian leaf
> The shadows of melodious utterance.
> But bare of laurel they live, dream, and die;
> For Poesy alone can tell her dreams,
> With the fine spell of words alone can save
> Imagination from the sable charm
> And dumb enchantment. Who alive can say,
> Thou art no Poet—mayst not tell thy dreams?
> Since every man whose soul is not a clod
> Hath visions, and would speak, if he had loved,
> And been well nurtured in his mother tongue.
> Whether the dream now purposed to rehearse
> Be poet's or fanatic's will be known
> When this warm scribe my hand is in the grave.

[1–18]

What is present, and what is absent in these lines, and why does Keats commence his poem with them? "Fanatics" here mean believing Christians, and so "dreams" here mean religious conceptualizations of a heavenly paradise, or else yet more "primitive" mythologies of paradise. Keats's distinction is between dreams and the telling of dreams, which he defines as poetry. Keats's irony, the *clinamen* directed against Wordsworth, is that fanatic and savage alike are present only as dreamers, but absent as poets, and by Keats's allusive implication Wordsworth's Wanderer, who is all but one with the poet writing most of *The Excursion,* is at once fanatic and savage, a complex dreamer but not a poet. But there is a deeper irony here, though it is still a figuration, still a saying of one thing while meaning another. Keats's concern is purgatorial and self-directed; is *he* present only as dreamer, and absent as poet? He is to rehearse a dream for us, but is he poet or fanatic? Can he tell his dream, which must mean something beyond a rehearsal, or will *The Fall of Hyperion* fail even as *Hyperion* failed? As he says himself, the answer came after he was in the grave, and never more greatly than from this poem. But I need to digress here, as few poems open more profoundly than this does, or confront a reader with so problematic a distinction.

The problem of the status and significance of poetry must be resolved at last in the area where our understanding of the following will meet: dreaming, and the telling of dreams in poetry, and the analogy: sex, and the telling of sex in love. The dialectic of Romantic love, which involves dream and identity, is the core problem. In *The Fall of Hyperion,* Keats moves himself and Moneta from one state of Identity to another state, still of Identity, but involving a self less insistent and more given to the sympathetic imagination. The first state is that of the dream, the second that of the dream's telling.

Geza Roheim, the most interesting speculative mind to arise on the Freudian Left, thought that there was only one basic dream, and that all we needed to understand, finally, was our motive for telling it. Wittgenstein in effect sàys that the dream and the motive alike cannot be spoken of; for him there is only the telling of dreams. To Freud, it does not matter whether the telling is "accurate" or not, just as it does not matter that the therapeutic image is intruded into the patient's consciousness by the analyst. But it matters to a poet that he get his "dream" right, and matters even more that he draw inevitable images *out of* the consciousness of his proper readers, whether in his own time or afterwards. It is because *pleasure* is legitimately one of his criteria, that the poet has his advantage. Perhaps the Stevensian criteria for poetry as the Supreme Fiction can be modified, to be more active: it must abstract, or withdraw perception from belatedness to earliness; it must *cause* change; it must *create* pleasure; it must humanize; all of these appropriate criteria also, surely, for the other Supreme Fiction—Romantic Love.

Is there an analogy between the strong poet's desire for priority and the motives or necessity for *telling*, whether of dreams in poetry or sexuality in love? We border on the realm of solipsism again; priority perhaps means not being first, but being alone, and is the demonic form of the apocalyptic impulse to be integrated again. "I sure should see / Other men here," Keats says to Moneta, and then adds: "But I am here alone." Yet he has not come to tell her his dreams, but to listen to hers, or rather to hear her study the nostalgias. I will return to this stance of faithful listening to the Muse when it comes to dominate the poem, but for now I return to the poem's opening, this time to map it through to the end.

Let us call the opening verse-paragraph, with its reverberations directed against Wordsworth's Wanderer, Keats's poetic reaction-formation against the anxiety of Wordsworthian presence, a conscious *illusio* that knows at once that Keats is an elected poet, but also that in this poem of trial he will not be free to tell his deepest dreams. The answering restitution or representation is in the noble synecdoche of the next, long verse-paragraph, lines 19–80, where Keats antithetically completes both Book V of *Paradise Lost* and his own *Ode to Psyche*. Notice that there is no entrance into this movement of the poem except for the abrupt "Methought I stood," and it is this unmerited and unexplained re-entry into the earthly paradise which is the only dream that Keats will tell in this poem. The recall of lines 60–63 of the *Ode to Psyche* establishes the new poem's largest difference from earlier Keats; the "wreathed trellis of a working brain," there, has been externalized, here, just as the Miltonic dream of Angels and humans feasting together is seen here as belonging to a naturalistic and recent past. Keats stands in a microcosm of the poet's paradise, drinks the honey of Eden, and enters what would be a dream-within-a-dream if it were not so insistently and persuasively a vision of Instruction. When he wakes from his swoon, he is in a poet's purgatory, a ruined sanctuary of every dead faith, and defensively he is turned dangerously against himself, without as yet overtly knowing it.

To stand before the purgatorial stairs is to stand in the realm of displacements, where the center of a dream lances off into indirect byways, into reductions and emptyings-out of things into aspects of things. Rhetorically this is the realm of metonymy, an object-world where there are no resemblances but only contiguities. In lines 81–181 of *The Fall of Hyperion* Keats confronts his Muse in a state of heightened awareness, but also in a state of reified vulnerability. The Keatsian *kenosis* is neither a Wordsworthian regression nor a Shelleyan undoing, but rather resembles Stevens, Keats's descendant, in being a radical isolation. The passage begins just after a repetition of the *Ode to Psyche*'s reduction of dead religion to a metonymic catalog, and continues in a curious tone of the cataloger of contiguities, who cannot summon haste or urgency even to ward off his own destruction until the last possible moment. I will concentrate in this movement upon one moment only, where Keats nearly undoes himself. Moneta has just spoken, with the bitter eloquence that marks her, not so much warning the poet as harshly proclaiming the quick death she confidently expects for him. The purgatorial steps, she says, are immortal, but Keats is only so much dust and sand, a mass of displacements. The poet who had preached disinterestedness is at first so disinterested that he almost fails to move in time. Characteristically, he is roused only by hearing his own involuntary shriek, a rousing or being stung that sets him moving:

> I heard, I looked: two senses both at once,
> So fine, so subtle, felt the tyranny
> Of that fierce threat and the hard task proposed.
> Prodigious seemed the toil; the leaves were yet
> Burning—when suddenly a palsied chill
> Struck from the pavèd level up my limbs,
> And was ascending quick to put cold grasp
> Upon those streams that pulse beside the throat:
> I shrieked, and the sharp anguish of my shriek
> Stung my own ears—I strove hard to escape
> The numbness; strove to gain the lowest step.
> Slow, heavy, deadly was my pace: the cold
> Grew stifling, suffocating, at the heart;
> And when I clasped my hands I felt them not.
> One minute before death, my iced foot touched
> The lowest stair; and as it touched, life seemed
> To pour in at the toes ...

This is, at the least, a strong revision of a romance commonplace; the quester's ordeal of recognition, which is not so much a crisis of self-recognition as it is the agony of being brought to what Yeats called "the place of the Daemon." Keats describes in himself a suffering that is at the threshold of strength, even a pragmatic weakness that becomes a poetic power. This is a quester so detached that he broods first on the fineness and subtlety of his

own hearing and seeing, before he bothers to consider
the danger he confronts. It is as though various reductions of himself—hearing, sight, chilled limbs, tubercular
symptoms—were contiguous with the emblems of
danger—the harsh voice of the seeress, the burning
leaves, the stairs—but so displaced from a universe of
resemblances that the contiguity assumed a solitary emphasis as a characteristic. But why does Keats, as a poet,
so empty himself out here? Why does he station himself
so deliberately, as though he were one more falsely reified entity in a world of such entities, so that the
prophetess Moneta becomes yet another such, and so a
kind of false prophetess? Freud tells us that the dream-
world necessarily involves displacement, which rhetorically becomes the mode of metonymy, of so troping or
turning from the literal that every complex thing is replaced by a simple, salient aspect of that thing. Keats
enters his own poem in the self-proclaimed role as poet,
indeed as *the* poet of his own time. Why should he have to
undergo such an emptying-out of the poetic self in what
is, after all, his annunciation as a strong poet?

I suggest that Keats, a startlingly clear intellect, had a
proleptic understanding that there is no breakthrough to
poetic strength without a double distortion, a distortion
of the precursors and so of tradition, and a self-distortion
in compensation. There is no growth into poetic strength
without a radical act of interpretation that is always a
distortion or misprision and, more subtly, without the
necessity of so stationing the poet's ontological self that it
too is held up to an interpretation that necessarily will
also be distortion or misprision. Keats differs only in
degree from previous strong poets by his *acceptance* of
these necessities. The prime function of Moneta in the
poem is to *misinterpret* Keats, but by so misinterpreting she
canonizes him, in a dialectical reversal of her attitude that
I now would say does not leave her at the end misunderstanding him any less radically than she misun-

derstands him when first he stands before her purgatorial stairs. As the Muse, Moneta presides over the canon of poetry and mythology and dead religion, but the canon is a grand ruin, as the poem makes clear. The great sanctuary of Saturn is a wreck, and to be accepted by Moneta as the properly qualified quester is to join an enterprise of disaster. By courteously troping or turning the harsh Muse into accepting him, Keats wins a dubious blessing, as he well knows. It is as though romance is poised already on the verge of what it will become in Tennyson's *The Holy Grail,* where Percivale's quest will destroy everything it touches, or in Browning's *Childe Roland to the Dark Tower Came,* where just the quester's glance will be enough to deform and break all things it views.

We have reached that point in *The Fall of Hyperion* where Keats, mounting up into the shrine of Moneta, mounts up into the Sublime, through the characteristic, paradoxical defense of repression, and by the trope of hyperbole, a trope of excess, of the violent overthrow. A theoretical digression opens before me, in which I hope to clarify not only the poem, but my own antithetical theory of poetry, or rather of the antithetical element in post-Enlightenment poetry.

Richard Wollheim, in his book *On Art and the Mind,* reminds us that Freud knew his favorite models differed in their own purposes from the purposes of art. Freud's models were the dream, the neurotic symptom, the tendentious joke, and all of these have a directness and an immediacy that art fortunately does not have and does not seek. A poem, as Freud well knew, was not a dream, nor a joke, nor a symptom. But Freud, as a humanistic scientist, and Wollheim, as an analytical philosopher, do not know that a poem *is* a kind of error, a beautiful mistake or open lie, that does have the function of, somehow, *telling a dream.* Wollheim, following and expounding Freud, says that a poem does not avail itself of a drop in

consciousness or attention in order to become the sudden
vehicle of buried desires. But here I think Wollheim is not
close enough to what poems actually do, perhaps because
he is more interested in the visual arts and less in poetry.
Poems, I would insist, indeed do just the reverse of what
Wollheim says they don't do, but as this is a dialectical
reversal it too is frequently reversed, and so poems do
refute Wollheim, not in theory but in the ways they behave. It is by the mode of sublimity that poems suddenly
do become the vehicle of buried desires, by violent
heightenings of consciousness or attention. But these
heightenings can drop away just as suddenly, and abandon us to the consequences of repression, a process
rhetorically manifested through the substitution of the
trope of litotes for that of hyperbole, by a turning to an
underthrow of language that plunges us from the Sublime down into its dialectical brother, the Grotesque.

I would say then that Wollheim, following Freud, is
only partly right, because Freud was only partly right,
about poetry. Poetic meaning, or the absence of it, exists
in the psychic and linguistic gap that separates repression
from sublimation. It is true that art, for Freud, does not
link up directly with wish and impulse expressing themselves in neurosis, but it does link up, for Freud, and I
think in actuality, with defense, and psychic defense need
not be or become neurotic, though sorrowfully it usually
is or does. Wollheim wisely says that when you abandon
the false and non-Freudian equation, neurosis = art, you
lose all justification for thinking of art as showing a single
or unitary motivation, since except for the relative in-
flexibility of a neurosis there is no single, unchanging,
constant form that our characters or temperaments assume, but rather endless vicissitudes of impulse and feeling, constant formings and re-formings of fantasy, and
while there *are* patterns in these, they are as flexible as
those of art. I accept Wollheim's formulation of this principle, but with a vital, antithetical proviso—these pat-

terns in feeling and fantasy are frequently defensive without being neurotic, and there are patterns in poetic imagery, rhetoric, and stance that are also defensive, without being neurotic. Wollheim says that art for Freud was constructive as well as expressive, and I would add that what poetry constructs can be a healthy defense against the real dangers of both the inner and the outer life.

Wollheim usefully adds that there is a gap in Freud's account of art, a gap that I think a more antithetical criticism of poetry can help to fill. Freud's vision or poem of the mind developed (as Wollheim indicates) through three stages: first, one in which the unconscious was identified with repression; second, one in which the unconscious was seen as the primary process of mental functioning; third, in which the unconscious attained a function that went beyond defense, and beyond the ongoing functions of the mind. In this third and final stage, Freud's vision is surprisingly close to Blake's, for the unconscious plays its part as what Blake called the Devourer, binding energy and so building up the ego, the role Blake assigned to Urizen, so that in Freud's final stage the unconscious has turned potentially reasonable. The defenses of projection and introjection are seen by Freud as capable of being transformed beyond defense into a healthful, constructive, ongoing process of *identification*, a Freudian vision in which he again followed the poets, as I have been trying to show, with my emphasis upon schemes of transumption as the characteristic post-Miltonic poetic mode for successfully concluding poems. Wollheim remarks: "In a number of celebrated passages Freud equated art with recovery or reparation on the path back to reality. But nowhere did he indicate the mechanism by which this came about. By the time he found himself theoretically in a position to do so, the necessary resources of leisure and energy were, we must believe, no longer available to him."

It is in the absence of this third-stage Freudian model
that I have proposed a Kabbalistic model or paradigm for
the image-patterning, for the movement of tropes and
defenses towards the strengthening of the poetic ego, that
I think is characteristic of the major poets of the last
several centuries. But Keats in particular, and in *The Fall
of Hyperion* more than anywhere else, gives us yet another
critical reason for following Gnostic or Kabbalistic
paradigms of belatedness rather than hypothesizing what
a mature Freudian psychoesthetics might have become.
Most students of Freud would agree that for him the
dream and/or the unconscious are at once three things—a
representation, a staged scene, and a distortion. But a
poem is all three at once also, and we can distinguish
between a poem and a dream or unconscious process,
simply by remarking that the dream or unconscious process is overdetermined in its *meanings,* since we are discovering, if I am right, that belated poems suffer an
increasing overdetermination in *language,* but an increasing *under-determination in meaning.* The dream or the
symptom has a redundancy of meaning, but the
Wordsworthian or modern poem has an apparent dearth
of meaning, which paradoxically is its peculiar strength,
and its demand upon, and challenge to, the interpretative
powers of the reader.

I return to Keats confronting Moneta. Poetic images
are not just condensations or displacements of signs,
which would make all poetic images either metaphors or
metonymies, and hence all *images-of-limitation.* Poetic images, whether as synecdoches, hyperboles, or transump-
tions, also transform signs, whether by antithetical completion, by heightening, or by the final illusion of making
the sign appear to be earlier than it actually is. But whatever the images of a dream may try to be, they *do* tend to
be only images of limitation, and so the dream-tropes are
irony, metonymy, metaphor, or in Freudian language:
distortion, displacement, condensation. To understand a

dream, the dreamer must tell it as a text, which means that he must translate or interpret it into either the language of Freudian reduction, or into the restituting language of poetry, as Keats does. In the scene we have now reached, with Keats facing Moneta after ascending the purgatorial stairs, the language joins the issue for us, between the Freudian, reductive view of repression, and the poetic or Sublime translation or interpretation of repression.

According to Freud, repression is a *failure in translation,* and since I would insist that a strong poem is a triumph of repression, and *not* of sublimation, then I would acknowledge that there must be *some* failure in translation or interpretation in order for a dream to become a poem, which is another way of stating the necessity of *misreading,* if strong poems are to be written or indeed if they are to be read. Just as no dream has a meaning except in relation to other dreams, so that in some clear sense the meaning of a dream can be only another dream, so also poems behave in relation to other poems, as my theory hypothesizes. I want now to break back into Keats's text, at line 134, by venturing this new antithetical formula: *Within a poem the Sublime can only result when translation fails, and so when misprision is heightened, through hyperbole, to a daemonic climax.* The great climax of *The Fall of Hyperion* will be seen to be a revision of the Wordsworthian version of romance, a revision dependent upon an even greater repression than Wordsworth had to accomplish.

The dialogue between Keats and Moneta concerns the problematic of poetic identity, which is an extreme form of the idea of an autonomous ego. Keats, in his speculation upon identity, is part of a very complex nineteenth-century questioning of the notion of a single, separate self, a questioning that culminated in the analytics of Nietzsche, Marx, and Freud, but which may be stronger in the poets even than it was in the great speculators. Is the poetic identity or autonomous ego only a reification? Emerson, who identified the power of poetry with what he called unfixing and clapping wings to solid nature, certainly rejects any notion of a fixed poetic identity or of a single, confined human ego. Nietzsche, on more language-centered grounds, did the same in denying what he called the unnecessary hypothesis of the human subject. There are insights in Keats that may be more subtle than all but a few in nineteenth-century traditions, and these insights tend to cluster around the image of the sole self or poetic identity as a negation of the human. In *Endymion*, Keats had celebrated love and friendship for their work in destroying the autonomy of the self, and had called "crude and sore / The journey homeward to habitual self." But Keats, I think, protested too much his zeal to overcome self-concern, and I think also that Keats has deceived his critics into literalizing his figuration of destroying the self. I am very startled when a critic as demystifying and demystified as Paul de Man says of Keats: "He almost succeeds in eliminating himself from his poetry altogether," or again that "the only threat that Keats seems to experience subjectively is that of self-confrontation." I would venture the paradox that Shelley, who so overtly dramatizes himself in his poetry, is nevertheless far more authentically selfless than Keats in poetry, as he was in life. Keats's speculations on selfhood and identity are not so much deceptive or even self-deceiving as they are evidences of a remarkable repression of anxiety, and also of a will-to-poetic power, and simply cannot be read and accepted at anything near face-value.

Shall we not call Moneta the Muse of repression? Criticism has not explained, nor even attempted to explain, her initial hostility to Keats. It is more than haste that Keats represses as he approaches her altar; it is the highest kind of poetic ambition, which is the dream of an active divination, of the poet becoming a god. All through Keats's poetry, critics rightly have seen different aspects of the same situation recur: a mortal, human male quester-poet confronts an immortal, divine, female Muse-principle, and almost always in a context in which the quester-poet is threatened by death, a death marked by privation, particularly by the cold. But Moneta paradoxically is at once the most ultimately benign and the most immediately hostile of these Muses. Keats asks her the wholly modest question, "What am I that should so be saved from death?" And she snaps that all he has done is "dated on" his doom. When Keats says that he is "encouraged by the sooth voice of the shade," he does *not* mean "consoling" but "truthful," for while he is as courteous as she is abrupt, the truth is that he is now as harsh as she is, because it is harsh to confront truth so directly, or at least what one takes to be truth. What could be harsher, or more apparently un-Keatsian, than the shocking hyperbole that Keats allows himself here?

>   Then shouted I
> Spite of myself, and with a Pythia's spleen,
> "Apollo! faded! O far flown Apollo!
> Where is thy misty pestilence to creep
> Into the dwellings, through the door crannies
> Of all mock lyrists, large self worshippers
> And careless Hectorers in proud bad verse.
> Though I breathe death with them it will be life
> To see them sprawl before me into graves.
>   [202–10]

    These are not the accents of a poet who has eliminated himself from his own poetry, or for whom self-confrontation is the only subjective threat. What is audible here is spleen all right, and I am afraid that this rancor, from our perspective, is precisely the "good will" on Keats's part that Moneta praises and reciprocates. Keats has done something audacious and only dubiously successful; he purports to speak for Apollo, and to have Moneta speak for all the dead gods of poetry. It is from *that* undemonstrable perspective that Keats so cruelly

condemns Shelley, Wordsworth, and Byron, and so it is
by being as cruel as Moneta, but towards *other poets,* that
Keats has found acceptance by her.

There is no reason to condemn the prevalent critical
idolatry of Keats, which as I have remarked elsewhere is a
rather benign literary malady. But I do think that such
idolatry has blinded us from seeing just what is happening in *The Fall of Hyperion,* and perhaps also in *Lamia.* We
have overcanonized Keats, and so we do not read him as
he is, with all his literary anxieties and all his high and
deep repression plain upon him. From the hyperbolical
Sublime of Pythian spleen that he shares with Moneta,
Keats attempts the great description of Moneta's face in
lines 256–81, which may be the most remarkable extended metaphor in his poetry. I will not analyze it here,
except to observe that it fails grandly just as all High
Romantic inside/outside metaphors fail, because in attempting to overcome a subject-object dualism it instead
extends such dualism. Yet the passage is terribly moving
because it persuades us that Keats at last has fulfilled his
quest, and has seen what he always wanted to see. He has
revised romance, even his own kind of romance, by recon-
ciling and almost integrating the quester and the object of
quest. He is no knight-at-arms pining for a Belle Dame,
not even the quester after the Melancholy whose "soul
shall taste the sadness of her might, / And be among her
cloudy trophies hung." Yet his Muse suffers "an immortal
sickness which kills not," and is so oxymoronically described that we are bewildered by the shifts-in-perspective
that Keats himself cannot control. "Death is the mother of
beauty" in Keats's disciple, Stevens, because nothing can
be beautiful that does not change, and the final form of
change is death. But Keats defies this obvious wisdom,
since the "immortal sickness" works a constant change
that does not end with death, however unhappy. Earlier
in the poem, Keats has referred to his own oxymoronic
sickness as being "not ignoble," and we can surmise there-

fore that Moneta's "immortal sickness" is the fearful repression that results in the poetry of the Sublime, which is
Keats's own, overt "illness."

What remains in *The Fall of Hyperion* are traces of a
scheme of transumption that Keats sketches without fully
working it through. It emerges in two passages of belatedness reversed into earliness:

> ... whereon there grew
> A power within me of enormous ken
> To see as a god sees, and take the depth
> Of things as nimbly as the outward eye
> Can size and shape pervade ...

> —Now in clear light I stood,
> Relieved from the dusk vale. Mnemosyne
> Was sitting on a square-edged polished stone,
> That in its lucid depth reflected pure
> Her priestess-garments.—My quick eyes ran on ...

The second of these passages seems to allude to an
image in Cary's translation of the *Purgatorio* 9:85-87:
"The lowest stair was marble white, so smooth / And
polish'd, that therein my mirror'd form / Distinct I saw."
As we would expect in the trope of metalepsis, Keats
tropes upon his own earlier trope (and Dante's) of the
purgatorial stairs. What earlier menaced Keats, the cold
stairs that nearly killed him, is now a further means to
vision as Keats projects the past, introjects the future, and
stands knowingly in a moment that is no moment, a
negation of present time. But a transumptive stance,
whether in Milton or in Keats, is not simply a prospective
one. Its emphasis is not upon a time-to-be, but on the
loss-of-being that takes place in present experience.

What then would an antithetical as opposed to a canonical reading of *The Fall of Hyperion* be? All canonical
readings (my own earlier one included) have *naturalized*
the poem; an antithetical reading would abstract the

poem from the irrelevant context of nature, in every sense of "nature." Poems are not "things" and have little to do with a world of "things," but I am not endorsing either the Stevensian notion that "poetry is the subject of the poem." There is no subject *of* the poem or *in* the poem, nor can we make the poem into its own subject. There is a dearth of meaning in a strong poem, a dearth so great that, as Emerson says, the strong poem forces us to invent if we are to read well, or as I would say, if we are to make our misreading stronger and more necessary than other misreadings. *The Fall of Hyperion* is a very strong poem because it impels every reader to return upon his or her own enterprise as a reader. That is the challenge Keats gives us: his stance in relation to Moneta, which means to tradition, which means in turn to the composite precursor, becomes the inevitable paradigm for our stance as readers in relation to his text.

Let me return to the question of a dearth-in-meaning, and elaborate upon it. Only a strong poet can make a dearth-in-meaning, a *zimzum* or limitation that compels subsequent substitution and the *tikkun* or restitution of poetic representation. Any poetaster or academic impostor can write a poem for us that oozes a plenitude of "meaning," an endless amplitude of significances. This late in tradition, we all come to one another smothered in and by meaning; we die daily, facing one another, of our endlessly mutual interpretations and self-interpretations. We deceive ourselves, or are deceived, into thinking that if only we could be interpreted rightly, or interpret others rightly, then all would yet be well. But by now—after Nietzsche, Marx, Freud, and all their followers and revisionists—surely we secretly—all of us—know better. We know that we must be misinterpreted in order to bear living, just as we know we must misinterpret others if they are to stay alive, in more than the merely minimal sense. The necessity of misreading one another is the other daily necessity that accompanies sleep and food, or that is as pervasive as light and air. There is no paradox in what I am saying; I but remind myself of an obvious truth, of *Ananke,* or what Emerson called the Beautiful Necessity.

Keats, revising his lifelong obsession with romance, confronts Moneta as the final form of romance, and sees in her more-than-tragic face the Beautiful Necessity. Of what? Of a mode of repetition in self-destroyings, I think, and a repetition also in the redefinition of romance. I conclude then by asking two questions, both of them in the antithetical context of *The Fall of Hyperion:* what is romance? and what is the repetition of romance?

Freud once described repression as being only a middle stage between a mere, reflex-like defense and what he called an *Urteilsverwerfung* or moral judgment of condemnation. There may be a connection between this description, as Anthony Wilden suggests in his *System and Structure,* and Freud's very difficult essay on "negation," with its much-disputed key sentence: "Through the mediation of the symbol of negation, thought frees itself from the consequences of repression and enriches itself with a content necessary for its accomplishment." Thus freed by negation from the reign of the pleasure-principle, thought (according to Freud) is able to attain the more fixed or devouring forms of the reality-principle or, as Freud says elsewhere, thought at last is enabled to free itself from its sexual past. I would transpose Freud's formula of negation into the realm of poetry, and specifically into the context of *The Fall of Hyperion,* by suggesting that, in Keats's poem, Moneta, as what Freud calls the symbol of negation, mediates for Keats not so as to free his thought from the consequences of repression but so as to show him that his thought cannot be so liberated, if it is to remain *poetic* thought. When she has shown Keats this, then it is his heroism that permits him to accept such dark wisdom. Romance, as Keats teaches us to understand it, cannot break out of the domain of the pleasure-principle even though that means, as Keats knows, that romance must accept the vision of an endless entropy as its fate.

If this is Keatsian or revised romance, then what is the repetition of romance, which is the actual mode of *The Fall of Hyperion* from its first until its final vision of Hyperion: "On he flared"? Though Kierkegaard joked that the dialectic of repetition is easy, he employed his customary rhetorical irony in so joking. At the center of his idea of repetition is the problem of continuity for the individual, a problem that he believed could be solved only by first arriving at a decision, and then by continually renewing it. The best analogue he could find for his vision was the Christian idea of marriage, which he exalted, but pathetically recoiled from personally. Only Christian marriage could give the daily bread that could undergo the severities of repetition, and so finally repetition became meaningless without the perpetual and difficult possibility of *becoming* a Christian.

In Keats, the repetition of romance becomes the perpetual and difficult possibility of *becoming* a strong poet. When Keats persuaded himself that he had mastered such repetition, *as a principle,* then *The Fall of Hyperion* broke off, being as finished a poem as a strong poem can be. Keats had reached the outer threshold of romance, and declined to cross over it into the realm of tragedy. Poised there, on the threshold, his stance is more retrospective than he could have wanted it to be, but there he remains still, in a stance uniquely heroic, in despite of itself.

6

Tennyson: In the Shadow of Keats

Freud, in his essay on "Repression" (1915), says that psychoanalysis shows us:

> . . . that the instinct-presentation develops in a more unchecked and luxuriant fashion if it is withdrawn by repression from conscious influence. It ramifies like a fungus, so to speak, in the dark and takes on extreme forms of expression, which when translated and revealed to the neurotic are bound not merely to seem alien to him, but to terrify him by the way in which they reflect an extraordinary and dangerous strength of instinct. This illusory strength of instinct is the result of an uninhibited development of it in phantasy and of the damming-up consequent on lack of real satisfaction.

Freud emphasized that repression manifested itself particularly in hysteria, but added that it could be observed in "normal" psychology also. Any definition of Freud's notion of "repression" should make clear that what is repressed is not an instinctual drive or desire, but rather the representation of it *in an image*. The repressed image is not wholly confined to the unconscious. However, some aspect of it is, an aspect which distorts, expands, intensifies the aspect still apparent in consciousness. Freud began by using "repression" and "defense" as though they were synonyms, but defense was necessarily always the wider term. Yet, of all the defenses, repression is most sharply differentiated from the others, and again it is the most elaborate of the defenses, being a three-phased process:

1. Primal Repression, directed against representations, but not against the instinct that remains fixated to the representations.

2. Repression proper, which Freud calls "after-pressure."

3. The Return of the Repressed, as dream, or symptom, or lapse in speech or behavior.

Since only representations or images can be repressed, but not desire or drive, we can wonder what motives Freud could ascribe to repression? There can be no repression unless the image threatens unpleasure, Freud insists. We approach therefore, particularly in the context of poetry, a fundamental question, which is doubtless fundamental for psychoanalysis also, but that is not *our* concern. Why must the ego be defended from the representations of its *own* desires? Whatever the answer is in a psychoanalytic context (and Freud is evasive in this area), I am certain that in the context of poetry the answer has to do with the anxiety of influence. The representations that rise up from the id are not wholly the ego's own, and this menaces the poetic ego. For the precursor poem has been absorbed as impulse rather than as event, and the internalized precursor thus rises, or seems to rise, against the ego from what appear to be the alienated representations of the id. It is in this strange area of identity-and-opposition that unpleasure in one's own images becomes a burden for the poetic ego, a burden that provokes defense, which in poetry means misprision, or the trope as a misreading of anteriority.

This essay is to be a discourse on Tennyson and not on Freud, however analogically, and yet I want to keep us in the gray area where poetry and psychoanalysis compete, for a while longer. My concern will be with Tennyson's revisionist genius for internalizing Keats, a process we might have thought impossible but for Tennyson's incredible rhetorical skill. That particular act of revisionary genius, on Tennyson's part, changed poetic history, for it was Tennyson's transformation of Keats that was the largest single factor in British and American poetry from about 1830 until about 1915. I am thinking not only of such various literary phenomena as the Pre-Raphaelites, Pater, aspects of Yeats, and of Wilfred Owen and other Georgians, and Trumbull Stickney and the early Stevens in America, but of hidden, crucial influences such as that of Tennyson on Whitman, and then of Tennyson and Whitman together upon Eliot. But first, I return us to the terrible poetic double-bind relationship of identity-and-opposition, between the formative poetic ego and its internalized precursor.

For the post-Enlightenment poet, identity and opposition are the poles set up by the ephebe's self-defining act in which he creates the hypostasis of the precursor as an Imaginary Other. We can agree with Nietzsche that distinction and difference are humanly preferable to identity and opposition as categories of relationship, but unfortunately strong poets are not free to choose the Nietzschean categories in what has been, increasingly, the most competitive and overcrowded of arts. I am tempted to adopt here the notion of what Jacques Lacan calls the Imaginary Order, which has to do with a world of what Blake called the Crystal Cabinet, a Beulah-world of doubles, illusive images, mirrors and specular identification, except that Lacan says there is no Other in the Imaginary but only others, and for the ephebe there is always the imaginary Other. But I do find useful in poetic, rather than general human terms, Lacan's remark that the ego, the *moi,* is essentially paranoid. The poetic ego is a kind of paranoid construct founded upon the ambivalency of opposition and identity between the ephebe and the precursor. Lacan says also that, in analysis, a passage is made from the "empty word" or Imaginary discourse to the "full word" or Symbolic discourse. Let us adopt our constant subversive principle, which is that many nineteenth- and twentieth-century speculators secretly are talking about poems when they assert that they are talking about people. Translating Lacan, we substitute the word "poet" for the "patient" and the word "poem" for the "analysis," and we arrive at the following: "The poet begins the poem by talking about himself without talking to you, or by talking to you without talking about himself. When he can talk to you about himself, the poem will be over." To this formula, I would add that the blocking agent that gradually gives way here is the imaginary form of the precursor.

The Marxist reply to my way of talking about influence necessarily would have to be that scorn of repetition as overdetermined force which Marx manifests in his powerful *The 18th Brumaire of Louis Napoleon.* Contemporary Marxist theorists, like Althusser or Marcuse or the systems-theorist Wilden, tend to see art as a domain where a return of the repressed can be completed. Thus, Wilden speaks of "transcending the individualistic identities and oppositions of the Imaginary by entering the *collective differences* of the Symbolic." I would say against this Marxist idealizing that the study of poetic misprision demonstrates the necessity of fresher and greater repressions if strong poetry is to survive. The Marxist critics say, in effect: Do not make the mistake of trying to destroy the precursor by taking his place, but rather let the dead bury the dead, and so make the precursor irrelevant. My sad reply must be: No newly strong poet can reduce the significance of the precursor's mastery, because it is not possible for the new or belated poet to transcend the oppositional relationship that is ultimately a negative or dialectical identification with the precursor. That relationship can be transcended only by refusing the perpetual burden and conflict of *becoming a strong poet.* There are no dialectics of liberation that will work in the world of the antithetical, and the dialectics of poetry are never those of nature or of society or of history. I do not know whether psychoanalysis will prove to be the final form or perhaps dubious last achievement of capitalism, but I suspect that really strong modern poetry may prove to be that form, a suspicion in which I follow again the prophet- ic lead of Emerson, or of Wallace Stevens in his Em- ersonian aphorism: "Money is a form of poetry."

I am aware of how incongruous all this seems as an introduction to the poetry of Alfred, Lord Tennyson, but Tennyson was surely one of the most sublimely repressed poets in the language. It is no accident that Tennyson, like his precursor Keats, and like their common ancestor, Spenser, is one of the three most authentically erotic poets in the language. I commence with a marvelous poem of enormous erotic repression, *Mariana*, where I will ask: What does this erotic repression itself repress? Let us recall Freud's profound theory of desire, which speculates that desire always tries to bring about an iden- tity between a present state of nonsatisfaction, and a past state that is recalled as satisfaction, whether truly it was that or not. I am afraid that Freud implies that what desire desires is desire, which means that desire never can be satisfied. On Freud's view, the unconscious component in desire dooms all erotic quests to the worst kind of repetition. Tennyson was the peculiar master of this in- sight, and I suggest now that Tennyson's mastery in this regard came out of a beautiful misprision of Keats. With all this as prologue, I come at last to the superb *Mariana*, a genuine perfection of strong poetry, and a work as genuinely alarming in its deepest implications as are even the darkest speculations of Freud.

The "sources," in a conventional sense, of *Mariana* are traditionally and rightly held to include Keats, particu- larly his rather dreary poem, *Isabella*, which the young Tennyson loved rather more than anyone else has since. Here are stanzas XXX through XXXIV of *Isabella*:

> She weeps alone for pleasures not to be;
> Sorely she wept until the night came on,
> And then, instead of love, O misery!
> She brooded o'er the luxury alone:

His image in the dusk she seem'd to see,
    And to the silence made a gentle moan,
Spreading her perfect arms upon the air,
And on her couch low murmuring, "Where? O where?"

But Selfishness, Love's cousin, held not long
    Its fiery vigil in her single breast;
She fretted for the golden hour, and hung
    Upon the time with feverish unrest—
Not long—for soon into her heart a throng
    Of higher occupants, a richer zest,
Came tragic; passion not to be subdued,
And sorrow for her love in travels rude.

In the mid days of autumn, on their eves
    The breath of Winter comes from far away,
And the sick west continually bereaves
    Of some gold tinge, and plays a roundelay
Of death among the bushes and the leaves,
    To make all bare before he dares to stray
From his north cavern. So sweet Isabel
By gradual decay from beauty fell,

Because Lorenzo came not. Oftentimes
    She ask'd her brothers, with an eye all pale,
Striving to be itself, what dungeon climes
    Could keep him off so long? They spake a tale
Time after time, to quiet her. Their crimes
    Came on them, like a smoke from Hinnom's vale;
And every night in dreams they groan'd aloud,
To see their sister in her snowy shroud.

And she had died in drowsy ignorance,
    But for a thing more deadly dark than all;
It came like a fierce potion, drunk by chance,
    Which saves a sick man from the feather'd pall
For some few gasping moments; like a lance,
    Waking an Indian from his cloudy hall
With cruel pierce, and bringing him again
Sense of the gnawing fire at heart and brain.

Keats's distressed lady is waiting for a murdered man; Shakespeare's Mariana is waiting for a deceiver, who has no intention of arriving. All that Tennyson really wants from *Measure for Measure* is that moated grange; we *know*, all through the poem, *Mariana,* that her lover *could* not arrive, even if he willed to, and that what reverberates in Tennyson's ear are a few lines from *Isabella:* "She weeps alone for pleasures not to be; / Sorely she wept until the night came on ... / And so she pined, and so she died forlorn." Besides Keats, Virgil is the presence almost always haunting Tennyson, and somewhere in the background we see Dido resolving to die, and hear the ominous line: "She is weary of glancing at the curve of heaven" (*Aeneid* IV, 451). But these "sources" have little to do with the truly deep or repressed literary anxieties of the poem *Mariana,* just as the tags from Keats scattered through are essentially ornamental allusions ("athwart the glooming flats," line 20, goes back to "athwart the gloom" of *Sleep and Poetry,* line 146, while "Upon the middle of the night," suggests "Upon the honeyed middle of the night" in *The Eve of St. Agnes,* line 49). Such echoes, as I keep saying, are not matters of poetic influence, nor is style much the issue either. A profound ambivalence towards Keats's influence is the true subject of Tennyson's poem, and the rich repression that fascinates the reader throughout is part of the defensive pattern of misprision clearly at work in the poem. To get at that pattern, we need ask only: why does this poem fascinate so much, what makes it as strong and memorable as it is, why is it so important a poem? Important it certainly is; as much as any poem, it can be said to have invented that whole mode of poetry which in the next generation was called, so very oddly, Pre-Raphaelitism. What is the new, uncanny element that we hear in Tennyson's first stanza?

> With blackest moss the flower-plots
>> Were thickly crusted, one and all:
> The rusted nails fell from the knots
>> That held the pear to the gable-wall.

> The broken sheds looked sad and strange:
>   Unlifted was the clinking latch;
>   Weeded and worn the ancient thatch
> Upon the lonely moated grange.
>   She only said, 'My life is dreary,
>   He cometh not,' she said;
>   She said, 'I am aweary, aweary,
>   I would that I were dead!'

There are the naturalistic particularities of Keats, as globed and tactile as they are in the ode *To Autumn*, yet we are troubled by the impression that what we confront is not nature, but phantasmagoria, imagery of absence despite the apparent imagery of presence. The troublesomeness comes from a sense of excess, from a kind of imagery of limitation that seems to withdraw meaning even as it thickly encrusts meaning. The rusted nails appear no more nor less a morbid growth than the moss does, and the overwhelming impression of absence seems irreversible. We are drawn into an internalization that has brought phantasmagoria very close, yet the language gives such pleasure, such a frustrate ripeness, that we are anything but sorry to be so drawn. We have here, I think, a kind of catachresis imposed upon a rhetorical irony, or psychically Tennyson's reaction-formation to the fascination that Keats had for him.

Catachresis is not so much a trope in itself as it is an abuse of the other tropes. It is a kind of tautology to speak of a "false figure," since all figures are necessarily false, but a catachresis, skillfully used, is a subtly imperfect trope, or a peculiarly extended trope, or a forced one. Derrida seems to suggest that all philosophical tropes are catachreses; Tennyson is not a philosophical poet, but he is peculiarly conscious of his own poetic belatedness from the start, and his rhetorical resources were enormous. In one sense, the whole poem of *Mariana* is an exquisite catachresis of Keats's own modification of the Wordsworthian crisis-poem, but we will come to that sense later. First, let us break from the sequence of *Mariana*, so as to consider its seventh and last stanza:

> The sparrow's chirrup on the roof,
>   The slow clock ticking, and the sound
> Which to the wooing wind aloof
>   The poplar made, did all confound
> Her sense; but most she loathed the hour
>   When the thick-moted sunbeam lay
>   Athwart the chambers, and the day
> Was sloping toward his western bower.
>   Then, said she, 'I am very dreary,
>   He will not come,' she said;
>   She wept, 'I am aweary, aweary,
>   Oh God, that I were dead!'

This stanza is manifestly obsessed with time, and indeed with belatedness. But what kind of belatedness is this, erotic or poetic? If there is any validity at all to my theory of misprision, then sexual anguish, in a belated poetic text, would be, frequently, a mask for influence-anxiety, if only because an erotic blocking-agent, if it is to be handled by a poem, must be treated as though it also was a Covering Cherub or precursor-text doing the work of double-binding. Let me again beat upon the obvious; I am *not* taking away from the poem *Mariana* the fine anguish of Mariana's erotic frustration. But I recur to a point I made about the poem in an earlier essay ("Tennyson, Hallam and Romantic Tradition" in *The Ringers in the Tower*): this Mariana is herself a poetess, her true affliction is the Romantic self-consciousness of Keats and Shelley as solitary questers made yet one generation more belated, and no bridegroom, if he ever arrived, would be able to assuage her malaise. Without pulling the poem into our contemporary areas of the war between men and women, we can still note that what Mariana is longing for is not her belated swain but a priority in poetic invention that would free her from her really deadly obsession that nevertheless is giving her an intense quasi-sexual pleasure, a kind of sublime perversion that no sexual satisfaction could begin to hope to match. Mariana is much more than half in love with easeful death, and in the poem's closing lines she all but identifies death with her own primal narcissism.

I urge us, however, in the final stanza, to concentrate on the astonishingly strong but psychically costly transumption or metaleptic reversal of the most characteristic of Keatsian metonymies, which is the substitution of a near-stasis or slow-pacedness for the language of the sense, for the sounds and sights of passing time. To Mariana, the sparrow's chirrup, the clock's ticking, the poplar's erotic cry in response to the wind's cry, all "confound her sense," which recalls Shelley's transumption of Wordsworth, in *The Triumph of Life,* when he has Rousseau speak of "many sounds woven into one / Oblivious melody, confusing sense." So Mariana also achieves a synaesthetic vision, yet more in Rousseau's victimized way than in Wordsworth's mode of tranquil restoration. What she hates, the poem ends by telling us, is that final near-stasis of light, when the sunbeam holds on, as thick-moted as the harsh luxuriance that opened the poem. Reversing Keats's heroic and proleptic naturalism, she projects and so casts out all past time, which means all erotic otherness, and introjects death, her own death, in despair of present as of the past. The poem is more deliciously unhealthy than all its Pre-Raphaelite and Decadent progeny were to be, and remains the finest example in the language of a embowered consciousness representing itself as being too happy in its unhappiness to want anything more.

Whatever canonical interpretation has said to the contrary, what he does so superbly in *Mariana* is Tennyson's peculiar greatness as a poet. I want in this discourse to trace that greatness now in a sequence of poems: *The Hesperides, Ulysses* (though very briefly, since I have mapped *Ulysses* in *A Map of Misreading*), and then most elaborately in *Tithonus,* with an after-glance at *Tears, Idle Tears,* after which I will conclude with a reading of Tennyson's repressive masterpiece, "Percivale's Quest," as I have called it, excerpting it from *The Holy Grail* in the *Idylls of the King.* But I will begin this sequence with a final glance at *Mariana,* so as to attempt some conclusion about the nature of Tennysonian repression in that poem. Let us look at that celebrated poplar tree, which Leslie Brisman notes as itself deriving from *Sleep and Poetry,* lines 277–78. It enters in the fourth stanza, dominates the fifth, vanishes in the sixth, and acquires an erotic voice in the seventh. Let us dismiss the grotesque notion that it is a phallic emblem; it is a very lone tree, and it represents the Sublime, so that we can call it, grimly and accurately, itself an emblem of repression, of purposeful forgetting or after-pressure, which always leaves a residue or some slight element of return. Far from being a representation of the lover who will not arrive, the poplar represents the Sublime or repressed element in Mariana herself, her own uncanny solipsistic glory. Its shadow falls not only "upon her bed" but significantly "across her brow" as well. As the solitary height above the level waste, the poplar is the precise equivalent of Childe Roland's dark tower, the internalized negative sublime that the quester will not see until it comes upon him or her. In the final stanza, what is the poplar but the High Romantic aeolian harp, or Mariana's song gathered together in its condensed glory?

What then is Mariana repressing? Why, that she doesn't want or need the other who cometh not. What would she do with him, what mental space has she left for him? And what is Tennyson the poet repressing? Only that the most dangerous and powerful and authentic part of his own poetic mind would like to be as perfectly embowered as Mariana's consciousness is, but of course it can't. And yet, Tennyson *has* surpassed Keats in his misprision of Keats's mode, for even Keats is not, could not be, the sustained artist that Tennyson is. To get beyond *Mariana*, as a poem, you must go the way of Dante Gabriel Rossetti, but that is another story, a story of still greater repression.

Before going on to an even more gorgeous triumph of repression, *The Hesperides*, let us worry the notion of repression just a bit longer, by returning to Freud's central essay on the subject:

The process of repression is not to be regarded as something which takes place once for all, the results of which are permanent, as when some living thing has been killed and from that time onward is dead; on the contrary, repression demands a constant expenditure of energy, and if this were discontinued the success of the repression would be jeopardized so that a fresh act of repression would be necessary.

The emphasis here is on energy expended, again and again, and that is how we have got to think of repression, particularly in the context of strong poetry. Repression is, as Derrida surely remarks somewhere, a difference in contending forces, and so necessarily is a strong poem such a difference. It is the constant renewal of repression that is, I am convinced, the clue to the magnificence of Tennyson's style. No poet in English, not even Milton, is so consistently Sublime. Tennyson's most characteristic trope is not even the hyperbole, but is a catachresis or extended abuse of that trope of overthrow or over-emphasis. Tennyson never stops exaggerating, yet never stops giving pleasure by his leaps beyond limits. Take the Miltonic closing trope of *Mariana*: "and the day / Was sloping towards his western bower." It is an elegant allusion to line 31 of *Lycidas,* where the evening star "Toward heaven's descent had sloped his westering wheel," but Tennyson's or rather Mariana's sun is linger-ing belatedly, so that the sloper, when he gets there, will be in much the same closed-in condition as the em-bowered Mariana, so that we are compelled to see that solipsistic damozel as being rather a sloper herself. Keats, in a pungent and somewhat ungracious letter to Shelley, had urged his swifter colleague to be an artist and so serve Spenser's Mammon: load every rift with ore. Tennyson betters Keats's instruction and, as Keats's ephebe, word-paints himself into the most densely inlaid art in the language.

Mariana, as I suggested earlier, can be regarded as a catachresis of the Romantic crisis-ode, as a hyperbolic version of Coleridge's *Dejection* or Keats's *Nightingale.* The catachresis here is the hothouse-forcing of the crisis-situation, since it would be difficult to image a more extreme state of self-consciousness than the one that Mariana so dialectically enjoys. But note Tennyson's curious staging of the poem; he narrates, and she speaks, and yet we find it difficult to keep the narrative and the embowered voices separate from one another. A descendant, odd as it must seem, is Stevens's *Sunday Morning,* where again the narrator and the occasionally speaking woman tend to merge in heightened passages. Let us think of Mariana as Tennyson's Stevensian Interior Paramour or Shelleyan epipsyche, and be prepared to find her hovering elsewhere in his poetry.

It·is at the catachresis of internalized quest or Keatsian revised romance that Tennyson is most gifted, a wonderful instance being *The Hesperides,* a poem that the poet always insisted upon suppressing. Why? I suppose because here the repression is not strong enough, so that there is a dangerous and, evidently to Tennyson, disconcerting partial or apparent return-of-the-repressed. Here is the incantation of the repressive daughters of Hesperus at its properly apocalyptic climax:

Holy and bright, round and full, bright and blest,
Mellowed in a land of rest;
Watch it warily day and night;
All good things are in the west.

Till midnoon the cool east light
Is shut out by the round of the tall hillbrow;
But when the fullfaced sunset yellowly
Stays on the flowering arch of the bough,
The luscious fruitage clustereth mellowly,
Goldenkernelled, goldencored,
Sunset-ripened above on the tree.
The world is wasted with fire and sword,
But the apple of gold hangs over the sea.
Five links, a golden chain, are we,
Hesper, the dragon, and sisters three,
Daughters three,
Bound about
All round about
The gnarlèd bole of the charmèd tree.
The golden apple, the golden apple, the hallowed fruit,
Guard it well, guard it warily,
Watch it warily,
Singing airily,
Standing about the charmèd root.

Though this lovely song intentionally induces a lan-
guorousness in its readers, it requires of its singers a
continual expenditure of repressive energy. As these
ladies had sung previously, trying no doubt to keep their
drowsy dragon awake:

If ye sing not, if ye make false measure,
We shall lose eternal pleasure,
Worth eternal want of rest.

The pleasure they value so highly must be their pride as
poets and as performers, as weavers of an enchantment
so sinuous as to block all questers from fulfillment in an
earthly paradise. Their closing stanza is a celebration of
belatedness, of being perpetually "after the event" by
virtue of always being poised in front of it. As a transumption, this is a catachresis of the Keatsian trope that

unheard melodies are sweeter, and the Hesperides arrive at a stasis that introjects lateness ("All good things are in the west"). There is an implication, throughout, that poetry and repression are an identity, but there is also a manifest anxiety as to the palpable misprision of Keats that is being enacted. The end of quest is to be not in the quester's merging in the identity of others, or of the poethood, but in the perpetual stasis of an earthly paradise preserved by enchantment from the single gratification it affords, and which would end it.

We pass to mature Tennyson, but before turning to *Tithonus*, where the Keatsian influence is so wonderfully engaged and held to a draw, I want very briefly to re-examine *Ulysses*, which is a companion-poem to *Tithonus*. It would seem odd to speak of repression in regard to a poem like *Ulysses*, whether we mean in the speaker of this dramatic monologue, or in Tennyson himself, for however one wants to interpret the poem, it offers us a vehement and highly expressive selfhood. Whether this Ulysses is a hero, or more likely a hero-villain, or whether he is Tennyson knowing he must go on after Hallam's death, or a more equivocal Tennyson confronting his own ambivalences, in any of these cases he would appear to be a consciousness that has forgotten nothing, even unconsciously. Indeed he seems a total purposefulness, fretting at inaction, and far from burying the representations of any impulse, he seems a man who in the drive to fulfill *all* impulses would welcome all self-representations whatsoever. What can this most sublime of questers not know, or not wish to know, whether about himself or about his relation to others? And, if this is somehow Tennyson himself, why ought we to associate the poem with defensive processes of any kind? Finally, what sort of a poem is this *Ulysses* anyway? Where are we to find its precursors, its brothers, its descendants, in our own quest for those inter-poetic relationships and juxtapositions by which meaning is produced?

Vico, more directly than any other theorist, associated meaning with survival, and rhetoric with defense. Tennyson's Ulysses is not interested in mere survival (thus his heartfelt scorn "as though to breathe were life!") but he cares overwhelmingly about *what he means,* and whether he still means what he used to mean. His rhetoric defends against meaningless or mere repetition, against the reduction of life to the metonymy of breath. In the deep sense, his quest for continued meaningfulness is Vichian, for the meaning he seeks will guarantee his survival as the hero, the perpetually early wanderer, rather than the belated, agèd king he has become when we meet him at the opening of his monologue. Surely, this Ulysses is strikingly like one of those magical formalists that Vico describes the primitive godlike men as being. As their lives were what Vico called "severe poems," so this Ulysses had lived a severe poem, and now cannot bear the life he has come home to, in what has turned out to be a mockery of the fulfilled quest. Can it be that by successfully returning home, this Ulysses has understood himself too well, and thus destroyed his own quest for meaning? In Vichian terms, the poet's quest for divination has been ruined in this quester, which is why he must set out again if he is to survive.

I want to quote part of one of what Vico calls his "Corollaries concerning Poetic Tropes, Monsters, and Metamorphoses," because I believe that Vico is a much better guide than Freud to the curious affinity or even identity between strong poetry and a kind of repression. Vico, in his axiom 405, notes that in language most of the expressions relating to inanimate things are formed by metaphor from the human body, senses, or passions. He then cites his own axiom 120: "Beware of the indefinite nature of the human mind, wherever it is lost in ignorance man makes himself the measure of all things." Even so, Vico says, man through rhetoric "has made of himself an entire world." In what follows, Vico suddenly achieves an astonishing insight:

So that, as rational metaphysics teaches that man becomes all things by understanding them, this imaginative metaphysics shows that man becomes all things by *not* understanding them; and perhaps the latter proposition is truer than the former, for when man understands he extends his mind and takes in the things, but when he does not understand he makes the things out of himself and becomes them by transforming himself into them.

Behind this axiom is the central Vichian principle: you only know what you yourself have made, which means that to know yourself is to have made yourself. Whatever one thinks of the truth of Vico's vision, it certainly applies to Tennyson's Ulysses, who is a severe poet and a Vichian primitive solipsist. When Tennyson's quester says: "I am a part of all that I have met" he means: "I understand only myself, and so everything I have met I have made out of myself, and I have become all things by transforming myself into them." One step further on from Tennyson's Ulysses is Browning's Childe Roland; another step on is Pater's Marius, and the final step is taken by the Hoon of Wallace Stevens who can proclaim triumphantly:

I was the world in which I walked
And what I saw or heard came not but from myself
And there I found myself more truly and more strange.

What Vico saw is that truly poetic metaphysics was founded upon a sacred solipsism, which Vico called "ignorance," or rather that imagination takes its flight when the mind *represses* its own knowing and its own understanding. What Tennyson's Ulysses represses is his own knowledge, of himself and of his relation to others, so that by this repression he can be driven out, away from home, to seek knowledge again. To *know* is to have become belated; not to know, not to understand, is to become early again, however self-deceivingly. What is the relation between this odd catachresis of a transumptive stance, and the celebrated Negative Capability of Keats? Keats spoke of "when man is capable of being in uncertainties, Mysteries, doubts, without any irritable reaching after fact & reason" and added that one must be capable "of remaining content with half knowledge." This is the wisdom of the *aporia,* of knowing we must end in uncertainty, and surely Tennyson's Ulysses is a grand parody of such intellectual heroism. Ulysses asserts he wants full knowledge, and actually wants no knowledge at all, except the Vichian transformation of the self into everything unknown, meaning into everything encountered.

With *Tithonus,* the Vichian repression of understanding achieves an even more intense version of the Sublime, yet one that is also more recognizably in the shadow of Keats. Vico, if I understand him (which in my own terms means if I misread him strongly enough), is saying that poetic repression is a mode of Knowing, or even that rhetoric is a mode of knowing *by negation.* The absolute exquisiteness of the rhetoric of Tennyson's *Tithonus* may mask a profound loss of the self by way of a negation of knowing that becomes a new kind of repressive knowing. Or, more simply, what is Tithonus repressing?

> The woods decay, the woods decay and fall,
> The vapours weep their burthen to the ground.
> Man comes and tills the fields and lies beneath,
> And after many a summer dies the swan.
> Me only cruel immortality
> Consumes: I wither slowly in thine arms.
> Here at the quiet limit of the world,
> A white-haired shadow roaming like a dream
> The ever-silent spaces of the East,
> Far-folded mists, and gleaming halls of morn.

Ostensibly, both *Ulysses* and *Tithonus,* like *Tears, Idle Tears* and the whole of *In Memoriam,* are poems of grief at the loss of Hallam, and of guilt for going on living without Hallam, the guilt of being a survivor, of being humanly as well as poetically belated. We might apply here the insight of Freud, in his "Mourning and Melancholia" essay, that melancholia begins, like mourning, in the loss of the beloved object, but this loss is not the real cause of the melancholia. Instead, the ego splits, with one part attacking the other, and the attacked portion becomes the repressed representation of the lost object (through "identification"). What is thus exposed is the narcissistic element in the love felt for the lost object, so that mourning becomes a process in which self-love is transformed into self-hatred. *Tithonus* shows a pattern not wholly unlike this Freudian insight, but I want to place our emphasis elsewhere, upon Vico again, and therefore upon the repression that makes Tithonus the extraordinary poet he is.

Or, should we say "aesthete" rather than "poet," just as we should say "hero-villain" rather than "hero" when we speak of Ulysses? I want to approach *Tithonus*, including its surpassingly beautiful opening passage, by way of *Tears, Idle Tears*, a closely related poem, and also like *Tithonus* an act of defense against the composite precursor, Keats-and-Wordsworth. Just as any sensitive reader will hear Wordsworth's Simplon Pass (from *The Prelude*) in the opening of *Tithonus*, so he or she will be haunted by *Tintern Abbey* while brooding upon *Tears, Idle Tears:*

> Tears, idle tears, I know not what they mean,
> Tears from the depth of some divine despair
> Rise in the heart, and gather to the eyes,
> In looking on the happy Autumn-fields,
> And thinking of the days that are no more.
>
> Fresh as the first beam glittering on a sail,
> That brings our friends up from the underworld,
> Sad as the last which reddens over one
> That sinks with all we love below the verge;
> So sad, so fresh, the days that are no more.

> Ah, sad and strange as in dark summer dawns
> The earliest pipe of half-awakened birds
> To dying ears, when unto dying eyes
> The casement slowly grows a glimmering square;
> So sad, so strange, the days that are no more.
>
> Dear as remembered kisses after death,
> And sweet as those by hopeless fancy feigned
> On lips that are for others; deep as love,
> Deep as first love, and wild with all regret;
> O Death in Life, the days that are no more.

Cleanth Brooks has devoted some brilliant pages in *The Well-Wrought Urn* to uncovering the motivation of Tennyson's weeper. I myself would say that we cannot uncover the motivation, because of the patterns of repression in the poem. Whatever else we read it as being, *Tears, Idle Tears* is a lament of belatedness, in which part at least of the poet's burden is his inability to achieve any priority in the wording of his own very authentic grief. The dominant imagery of the poem is hyperbolical *depth*, buried passion, and buried in more than one sense, though the poem's largest trope of representation is the Virgilian noble synecdoche, in which weeping for a particular loss is a part of which the tears of universal nature are the whole. In the poem's closing lines, Tennyson tropes upon Wordsworth's double trope in the *Intimations* Ode, of "Heavy as frost, and deep almost as life!" that ends the first movement of the ode, and "Thoughts that do often lie too deep for tears," the ode's final line. The weight that Wordsworth called "custom," a death-in-life, lay deep almost as life, until it was transumed by thoughts of such depth that they transcended tears. But Tennyson beautifully reverses the trope, by metalepsis; the depth greater than "custom" and greater than thoughts of human sympathy, is the repressed depth of lost first love, the true death-in-life that cannot be reversed into an earliness: "the days that are no more."

Though Tennyson defends against Wordsworth's presence, in a poem actually composed at Tintern Abbey again, the tropes of limitation he employs defend rather against Keats, whose ode *To Autumn* is more deeply involved in the lyric repressions of *Tears, Idle Tears.* In *his* ode, Keats looks on the happy autumn fields, and does not weep, does not lament the loss of earliness, the absence of the songs of spring. The bird songs of late-summer/early-autumn intimate to Keats one of his liminal states, a threshold vision poised or held open to the possibility of tragedy, but above all *open,* to whatever may come. This *aporia,* or beautiful uncertainty, is too strong a limitation for Tennyson to accept. But for Tennyson the bird song is not another metonymy for death, like the glittering beam and the sail in the previous stanza, and like the strange metaphoric transformation of Keats's characteristic open casement in "when unto dying eyes / The casement slowly grows a glimmering square." So gorgeous a lyric is *Tears, Idle Tears,* in its dark undoings of Keats's heroism, that we do not pause long enough to suspect a little how perceptive, how aesthetic a vision, is being achieved despite those tears. They are "idle" enough in that they do nothing to blind this weeper.

I think *that* is where the emphasis falls in Tennyson's even more beautiful reverie of a grieved aesthete, his *Tithonus,* where the mourning is necessarily more primal and terrible, being for the monologist's own lost youth and beauty. But, quite evidently, not for lost love, as the grand link between Tithonus and Ulysses is their palpable, solipsistic inability to have loved anyone but their own former selves. As I have said elsewhere, one would not wish to be in a boat with Tennyson's Ulysses, who has the knack of surviving while others drown. Equally, unlike poor Aurora, one wouldn't wish to be in the same bed with Tithonus. But of course it all depends on how one reacts to a really primal narcissism—which will involve another brief digression into how criticism might set about reclaiming the pirated poetic element from yet another of Freud's fundamental insights.

Freud's final insight in regard to narcissism was his realization that it was a defensive movement against the death-drive. His original insight had seen narcissism as the element in the ego that made the ego an image, an imaginary object, rather than an hypostasis of reason. In the subtle lights of Tennyson's *Tithonus*, it is fascinating to note that Freud began to brood upon narcissistic neuroses in order to explain the psychoses of hypochondria and megalomania, as Tithonus has more than a touch of each. We fall in love, according to Freud, as a defense against a narcissistic cathexis or self-investment when our passion-for-ourself threatens to go too far. But in such falling, we continue to love what represents ourself, whether what we were, or what we would like to have been. If Tithonus had fallen in love with Aurora at all, then it was only to the degree that she was a narcissistic representation of himself. But she has remained splendidly herself, he has withered, and now he loves only death.

I repeat Freud's belated insight, that ultimately narcissism is a defense against the death-instincts. If Tithonus genuinely wants to die, as he asserts, then he has ceased to be a poet (if ever he was one) and he has abandoned also the primal megalomania of his own narcissism. His monologue belies both these assertions, and so is either self-deceptive or rhetorically deceptive towards ourselves, or both together, as would be normal in the characteristic Browning monologue. Something is therefore very equivocal about this dramatic monologue, and so I want to return again to its really gorgeous opening lines. Let us regard this first verse-paragraph as the poem's *clinamen*, its swerve away from the naturalistic affirmations of Wordsworth and of Keats. What is absent in these opening ten lines is simply all of nature; what is present is the withered Tithonus. As Tennyson's reaction-formation against his precursors' stance, these lines are a rhetorical irony, denying what they desire, the divination of a poetic survival into strength. Behind these lines are Wordsworth on the Simplon Pass ("The immeasurable height / Of woods decaying, never to be decayed") but more crucially the entire vision of an early cosmos in Keats's *Hyperion*.

I think that the five remaining verse-paragraphs of *Tithonus* will be found to reveal, in sequence, the five expected revisionary ratios, rather too neatly, but I don't think that this is merely my own compulsion or misprision-neurosis working out; rather it is another indication that *Tithonus* truly is a High Romantic crisis-poem, masking as a dramatic monologue, so that its patterning of defenses, tropes, and images closely follows the models of poems like *Tintern Abbey, Intimations of Immortality, Dejection,* the *Ode to Psyche,* and all their companions. Rather than trace the next five verse-paragraphs through my map of misreading, I will leave that operation to my readers' curiosity or skepticism. Let us assume that my apprehension of the patterns of misprision here will be confirmed. What will that tell us about the poem?

In an essay on Christopher Smart's *Rejoice in the Lamb,* Geoffrey Hartman speaks of Freud as our latest doctor of the Sublime, as a diagnostician of "the pathology of ecstasy," the true culminator of the tradition that goes from Boileau on Longinus through Vico and Edmund Burke on to Kant and Schopenhauer. Hartman's laconic point against a view of defense as a primary phenomenon, whether in the psyche or in poems, is made rather aggressively and ironically when he observes: "Defense mechanisms cannot blossom when there is nothing—no fire or flood—to defend against." Against this, I would name, for Tennyson, Keats as the fire and Wordsworth as the flood. *Tithonus,* as a poem, is at once a narcissistic apotheosis and a powerful repressive reaction against the greatest poets ever to have attempted a humanized Sub-

lime, an attempt made by way of a humanization of the
ancient poetic lust for divination. When Tithonus defensively turns against himself, he turns against the whole
heroic enterprise that would single out the poet as a
candidate for survival:

>   . . . Let me go: take back thy gift:
> Why should a man desire in any way
> To vary from the kindly race of men,
> Or pass beyond the goal of ordinance
> Where all should pause, as is most meet for all?

This is a dark synecdoche, reminding us that the burden of a trope is pathos, and that the ancient war between
rhetoric and a more rational dialectic can never end. But
though he yields to masochism as a vicissitude of instinct,
we would do wrong to take *Tithonus* literally when he says
"take back thy gift," since the gift of immortality in this
poem is also the gift of divination, without which no one
becomes, or remains, a poet. Against this momentary
yielding to an instinctual vicissitude with its strong representation set against the self, Tithonus recoils with an
obsessive force in a psychic defense of limitation, which in
his case is a compulsive return to origins, a regression
conveyed primarily by the metonymy of the Wordsworthian glimmer or gleam, but with a direct eroticism that
derives from Keats:

>   A soft air fans the cloud apart; there comes
> A glimpse of that dark world where I was born.
> Once more the old mysterious glimmer steals
> From thy pure brows, and from thy shoulders pure,
> And bosom beating with a heart renewed.
> Thy cheek begins to redden through the gloom,
> Thy sweet eyes brighten slowly close to mine,
> Ere yet they blind the stars, and the wild team
> Which love thee, yearning for thy yoke arise,
> And shake the darkness from their loosened manes,
> And beat the twilight into flakes of fire.

What is palpable in this lovely passage is that the sexual warmth not only is but always *was* Aurora's, and also that the monologist, a solipsistic aesthete, now and always was no part of "the wild team / Which love thee." Even Ulysses is not so sublimely incapable as is Tithonus of apprehending anyone's emotions except his own. Thus, Aurora's tears are read by Tithonus as his own hysterical fear that his now noxious immortality cannot be withdrawn (which, on the level of Tennyson's own repressions, I would tend to interpret as his own evaded realization that he is doomed to go on seeking to be a strong poet, even though Hallam is dead). Again, in the fifth verse-paragraph, there is the extraordinary passivity of Tithonus as a lover, with its overwhelming emphasis not upon sexual pleasure or fulfillment, but upon the monologist's heightened powers of aesthetic perceptiveness while being embraced.

When, in the final verse-paragraph, we move into the area of East and West, or early and late, the *aprophrades* or introjection of the past has about it the peculiar and unnerving accents of paranoia—not that of Tennyson, I hasten to say, but of the monomaniacal Tithonus. What is most striking to me, about these lines, is their cruelty as the masochistic Tithonus manifests a repressed sadism towards the bereaved and loving Aurora:

> Yet hold me not for ever in thine East:
> How can my nature longer mix with thine?
> Coldly thy rosy shadows bathe me, cold
> Are all thy lights, and cold my wrinkled feet
> Upon thy glimmering thresholds, when the steam
> Floats up from those dim fields about the homes
> Of happy men that have the power to die,
> And grassy barrows of the happier dead.
> Release me, and restore me to the ground;
> Thou seest all things, thou wilt see my grave:
> Thou wilt renew thy beauty morn by morn;
> I earth in earth forget these empty courts,
> And thee returning on thy silver wheels.

Let us grant that the monologist's situation is extreme,
but his presumably unconscious cruelty transcends even
that extremity. Is it really necessary for him to assure her:
"Thou seest all things, thou wilt see my grave"? Need he
finally assure her that, when he is "earth in earth," he will
forget her? I do not believe Tennyson was aware of this
cruelty, and I am suggesting that even in these glorious
closing lines, a profound repression is at work. To grow
endlessly more agèd while remaining immortal is an
oxymoronic or belated version of the divination that is
crucial to strong poetry. The hidden concern of the poem
Tithonus, as of the poem *Ulysses,* is Tennyson's own belatedness as a poet, his arrival on the scene *after the event,*
after the triumph of poetry of "reflection" in Coleridge
and Wordsworth, and of poetry of "sensation" in Shelley
and Keats, to use a critical distinction invented by Hallam.
Hallam's enormous contribution to Tennyson was to overcome the poet's diffidence, and to persuade him that he
could become a third, with Shelley and Keats. Hallam
dead, Tennyson knew not only the guilt of a survivor but
also the obsessive poetic fear of belatedness, the fear that
torments his own Sir Percivale, that every repressed voice
crying from within will proclaim: "This Quest is not for
thee."

With Percivale's Quest from *The Holy Grail,* I come to
my final text from Tennyson, and begin by dismissing as
a palpable evasion his own weak misreading of his own
text, in which Percivale and all the other knights, except
Galahad, represent a flawed Christianity, flawed in Percivale's case by an ascetic, otherworldly mysticism, a sort
of St. John of the Cross Catholic temperament. But the
Percivale we meet in the poem is hardly a mystical ascetic,
but rather a highly familiar compound ghost, the High
Romantic antithetical quester, whose every movement is
contra naturam, even in spite of himself. We are back in
that central current that goes from Spenser, in the
Prothalamion, and from Spenser's Colin Clout to the *Penseroso* of Milton and the equivocal heroism of Satan quest-

ing onwards through Chaos to reach Eden, the New World. These are Percivale's ultimate ancestors, but much closer are the Solitary of Wordsworth, and the Solitary's younger brothers in Childe Harold, Endymion, and, above all others, the doomed, driven Poet of *Alastor*. Contemporary with Percivale is Browning's Roland as well as Tennyson's Ulysses, while looming up are the Oisin and Forgael of Yeats, and the Nietzschean parody of all these in Stevens's Crispin, or the antithetical quester reduced to the state of *The Comedian as the Letter C*.

I am suggesting that, in Percivale, the repressed element in Tennyson's poethood emerges fully, in a fury of questing that deforms and breaks all it encounters more devastatingly than even Childe Roland's vision wrecks upon his world. Hypnotic and incantatory as Tennyson is almost always capable of being, I know nothing in him as phantasmagoric, as Sublime, as much charged with a greatly controlled hysteria of repression as Percivale's destructive quest:

> 'And I was lifted up in heart, and thought
> Of all my late-shown prowess in the lists,
> How my strong lance had beaten down the knights,
> So many and famous names; and never yet
> Had heaven appeared so blue, nor earth so green,
> For all my blood danced in me, and I knew
> That I should light upon the Holy Grail.

> 'Thereafter, the dark warning of our King
> That most of us would follow wandering fires,
> Came like a driving gloom across my mind.
> Then every evil word I had spoken once,
> And every evil thought I had thought of old,
> And every evil deed I ever did,
> Awoke and cried, "This Quest is not for thee."
> And lifting up mine eyes, I found myself
> Alone, and in a land of sand and thorns,
> And I was thirsty even unto death;
> And I, too, cried, "This Quest is not for thee."

'And on I rode, and when I thought my thirst
Would slay me, saw deep lawns, and then a brook,
With one sharp rapid, where the crisping white
Played ever back upon the sloping wave,
And took both ear and eye; and o'er the brook
Were apple-trees, and apples by the brook
Fallen, and on the lawns. "I will rest here,"
I said, "I am not worthy of the Quest;"
But even while I drank the brook, and ate
The goodly apples, all these things at once
Fell into dust, and I was left alone,
And thirsting, in a land of sand and thorns.

'And then behold a woman at a door
Spinning; and fair the house whereby she sat,
And kind the woman's eyes and innocent,
And all her bearing gracious; and she rose
Opening her arms to meet me, as who should say,
"Rest here;" but when I touched her, lo! she, too,
Fell into dust and nothing, and the house
Became no better than a broken shed,
And in it a dead babe; and also this
Fell into dust, and I was left alone.

'And on I rode, and greater was my thirst.
Then flashed a yellow gleam across the world,
And where it smote the plowshare in the field,
The plowman left his plowing, and fell down
Before it; where it glittered on her pail,
The milkmaid left her milking, and fell down
Before it, and I know not why, but thought
"The sun is rising," though the sun had risen.
Then was I ware of one that on me moved
In golden armour with a crown of gold
About a casque all jewels; and his horse
In golden armour jewelled everywhere:
And on the splendour came, flashing me blind;
And seemed to me the Lord of all the world,

Being so huge. But when I thought he meant
To crush me, moving on me, lo! he, too,
Fell into dust, and I was left alone
And wearying in a land of sand and thorns.

'And I rode on and found a mighty hill,
And on the top, a city walled; the spires
Pricked with incredible pinnacles into heaven.
And by the gateway stirred a crowd; and these
Cried to me climbing, "Welcome, Percivale!
Thou mightiest and thou purest among men!"
And glad was I and clomb, but found at top
No man, nor any voice. And thence I past
Far through a ruinous city, and I saw
That man had once dwelt there; but there I found
Only one man of an exceeding age.
"Where is that goodly company," said I,
"That so cried out upon me?" and he had
Scarce any voice to answer, and yet gasped,
"Whence and what art thou?" and even as he spoke
Fell into dust, and disappeared, and I
Was left alone once more, and cried in grief,
"Lo, if I find the Holy Grail itself
And touch it, it will crumble into dust."

I have quoted all of this sequence, so as not to lose any
of its cumulative force. But what is this force? I think we
recognize in it, all of us, one of our own nightmares, the
nightmare that is centered upon our own self-
destructiveness, and so upon our own murderousness
also, our aggressive instinct whose aim is the destruction
of the object. As the greatest of modern moralists—true
successor of Pascal, Montaigne, Schopenhauer, Emerson,
Nietzsche—Freud is the inevitable authority to cite in any
account of the aggressive instinct or drive-towards-death,
though the poetic variant, in Tennyson, will hardly be an
exact equivalent of the Freudian insights. Rather, Tennyson's vision of Percivale's Quest, and Freud's vision of the

death instinct (particularly in *Beyond the Pleasure Principle*)
will be found to have a troublesome resemblance suggesting that both are complex misprisions of a common precursor, of a larger mental form to which Vico remains the
surest guide I have been able to discover.

Though Percivale's Quest might seem to sustain the
analysis of the ascetic ideal as given by Nietzsche in *Towards the Genealogy of Morals,* this apparent similarity has
more to do with Tennyson's overt intention than with his
actual representation of Percivale, in the poem. What we
encounter in Percivale, as in the wandering Poet of Shelley's *Alastor,* is a repressed aggressive instinct, or what
Freud calls the death instinct directed outwards. But
clearly, Percivale's deathliness intends to be directed
against his own self. What does it mean that Tennyson is
compelled to make of Percivale a consuming force that
devastates everything it encounters?

Freud's very problematic final theory of the instincts
posits a group of drives that work towards reducing all
tensions to a zero-point, so as to carry everything living
back to an inorganic state. Freud's formulation is difficult,
because it suggests that a self-destructive drive back towards origins is a universal phenomenon. As a theory,
Freud's notion here is frankly daemonic, and related to
his dark insight that all repetition phenomena may mask
a regressive element in every human instinct. To account
for life's ambivalence towards itself, Freud resorted to a
more radical dualism than he had entertained earlier.
The id became the center for representing every instinctual demand, with none assigned to the ego, which
means that ultimately every desire, whether for power or
for sexual fulfillment, is in some sense linked to the desire
for death. Without pretending to be summarizing the full
complexity of Freud's speculations, I will leave the notion
of the death instincts there, except to note that Freud was
compelled to adopt a new formulation in this area, the
Nirvana Principle, which he took from Schopenhauer by

way of a suggestion of the English psychoanalyst Barbara Low.

The Nirvana Principle, introduced in *Beyond the Pleasure Principle* (1920), is the psyche's drive to reduce all excitation within itself, whether the origin of the excitation be internal or external, to the zero-level, or as close to zero as possible. I have invoked all of this Freudian speculation in order to get us to the Nirvana Principle, for that is the actuality of Percivale's Quest, despite Percivale's apparent intention and Tennyson's stated and overt intention. Percivale believes he is questing for the Holy Grail, but in reality he quests for Schopenhauer's quasi-Buddhistic Nirvana, where desire shall vanish, the individual self fade away, and quietude replace the strong poet's search for a stance and word of his own. Percivale, I am suggesting, is as close as Tennyson can come, not to a return of the repressed, but to an absolute or total freshening of self-repression. And though *The Holy Grail* is ostensibly a critique of Percivale and an exaltation of Galahad, and even of the humane and sweet Ambrosius, what any reader is going to remember is that sublime and terrific destructive march to the zero-point that is the litany of Percivale's quest. Reflect even upon the exchange between Ambrosius and Percivale that ends the account of Percivale's ruinous march. Ambrosius cries out, in the name of common humanity:

> 'O brother, saving this Sir Galahad,
> Came ye on none but phantoms in your quest,
> No man, no woman?'

> Then Sir Percivale:
> 'All men, to one so bound by such a vow,
> And women were as phantoms . . .'

How shall we read "such a vow"? Only I think, despite Tennyson's intentions, as the vow to be a strong poet, whatever the human cost. Percivale, in the deep sense, is

Tennyson the poet, unable to get out of or beyond the shadow of Galahad, the quester who beholds and becomes one with a strength that resists the Nirvana Principle. I am not proposing any simple equation of Galahad = Keats, but a more complex formula in which Galahad does represent the High Romantic quest, and Percivale the belated quest of Victorian Romanticism. Tennyson was too sublimely repressed a poet to develop very overtly his ambivalence towards his prime precursors, and the death of Hallam, who was the great champion of Keats, augmented the repression. But Tennyson too was a preternaturally strong poet, and we have seen something of his strength at misprision. The shadow of Keats never did abandon him wholly, and so the stance of belatedness became a kind of second nature for him. But what he may have lacked in priority of stance, he greatly compensated for in priority of style. He prophesies his true ephebe, the late T. S. Eliot, and time, I am persuaded, will show us how much stronger a poet Tennyson was. than Eliot.

7

Browning: Good Moments and Ruined Quests

One of the principles of interpretation that will arise out
of the future study of the intricacies of poetic revisionism,
and of the kinds of misreading that canon-formation en-
genders, is the realization that later poets and their critical followers tend to misread strong precursors by a fairly
consistent mistaking of literal for figurative, and of
figurative for literal. Browning misread the High Romantics, and particularly his prime precursor, Shelley, in this
pattern, and through time's revenges most modern poets
and critics have done and are doing the same to Browning. I am going to explore Browning, in this chapter, as
the master of misprision he was, by attempting to show
our tendency to read his epiphanies or "good moments"
as ruinations or vastations of quest, and our parallel tendency to read his darkest visions-of-failure as if they were
celebrations.

I will concentrate on a small group of Browning's
poems including *Cleon, Master Hugues of Saxe Gotha, A
Toccata of Galuppi's, Abt Vogler,* and *Andrea del Sarto,* but I
cannot evade for long my own obsession with *Childe Roland to the Dark Tower Came,* and so it and its contrary
chant, *Thamuris Marching,* will enter late into this discourse. Indeed, I want to end with a kind of critical
self-analysis, and ask myself the question: why am I obsessed by the *Childe Roland* poem, or rather, what does it
mean to be obsessed by that poem? How is it that I cannot
conceive of an antithetical practical criticism of poetry

without constantly being compelled to use *Childe Roland*
as a test case, as though it were the modern poem proper,
more even than say, *Tintern Abbey* or *Byzantium* or *The Idea
of Order at Key West?* Is there a way to make these questions center upon critical analysis rather than upon psychic self-analysis?

In Browning's prose *Essay on Shelley,* there is an
eloquent passage that idealizes poetic influence:

There is a time when the general eye has, so to speak, absorbed
its fill of the phenomena around it, whether spiritual or material, and desires rather to learn the exacter significance of what
it possesses, than to receive any augmentation of what is possessed. Then is the opportunity for the poet of loftier vision, to
lift his fellows. . . . The influence of such an achievement will
not soon die out. A tribe of successors (Homerides) working more
or less in the same spirit, dwell on his discoveries and reinforce
his doctrine; till, at unawares, the world is found to be subsist-
ing wholly on the shadow of a reality, on sentiments diluted
from passions, on the tradition of a fact, the convention of a
moral, the straw of last year's harvest.

Browning goes on to posit a mighty ladder of authentic
poets, in an objective and subjective alternation, who will
replace one another almost endlessly in succession, concerning which, "the world dares no longer doubt that its
gradations ascend." Translated, this means: "Wordsworth
to Shelley to Browning," in which Browning represents a
triumph of what he calls the objective principle. Against
Browning's prose idealization, I will set his attack upon
the disciples of Keats in his poem *Popularity:*

> And there's the extract, flasked and fine,
>   And priced and saleable at last!
> And Hobbs, Nobbs, Stokes and Nokes combine
>   To paint the future from the past,
> Put blue into their line.

For "Hobbs, Nobbs, Stokes and Nokes" we might read
Tennyson, Arnold, Rossetti, and whatever other con-

temporary Keatsian, whether voluntary or involuntary, that Browning wished to scorn. But the next stanza, the poem's last, would surely have cut against Browning himself if for "John Keats" we substituted "Percy Shelley":

> Hobbs hints blue,—straight he turtle eats:
>> Nobbs prints blue,—claret crowns his cup:
> Nokes outdares Stokes in azure feats,—
>> Both gorge. Who fished the murex up?
> What porridge had John Keats?

The vegetarian Shelley, according to his friend Byron, tended to dine on air and water, not fit fare for the strenuously hearty Browning, who in his later years was to become London's leading diner-out. But though Browning seems not to have had the slightest *personal* consciousness of an anxiety of influence, he wrote the most powerful poem ever to be explicitly concerned with the problem. This is the dramatic monologue *Cleon,* in which the imaginary jack-of-all-arts, Cleon, is in my judgment a kind of version of Matthew Arnold, whose *Empedocles on Etna* Browning had been reading. Arnold's Empedocles keeps lamenting his own and the world's belatedness, a lament that becomes a curious kind of inauthentic overconfidence in Cleon's self-defense:

> I have not chanted verse like Homer, no—
> Nor swept string like Terpander, no—nor carved
> And painted men like Phidias and his friend:
> I am not great as they are, point by point.
> But I have entered into sympathy
> With these four, running these into one soul,
> Who, separate, ignored each other's art.
> Say, is it nothing that I know them all?

Browning could enjoy the belatedness of Arnold or Rossetti, because no poet ever felt less belated than this exuberant daemon. We remember the malicious epithet applied to him by Hopkins: "Bouncing Browning." I think we can surmise that poetic belatedness as an affliction, whether conscious or unconscious, always rises in close alliance with ambivalence towards the prime precursor. Browning felt no ambivalence towards Shelley, such as Yeats had towards Shelley, or Shelley towards Wordsworth, or Wordsworth towards Milton. Browning loved Shelley unbrokenly and almost unreservedly from the age of fourteen, when he first read him, until his own death at the age of seventy-seven. But ambivalence is not the only matrix from which the anxiety of influence rises. There is perhaps a darker source in the guilt or shame of identifying the precursor with the ego-ideal, and then living on in the sense of having betrayed that identification by one's own failure to have become oneself, by a realization that the ephebe has betrayed his own integrity, and betrayed also the covenant that first bound him to the precursor. That guilt unmistakably was Browning's, as Betty Miller and others have shown, and so the burden of belatedness was replaced in Browning by a burden of dissimulation, a lying-against-the-self, rather than a lying-against-time.

But is not that kind of shame only another mask for the guilt-of-indebtedness, the only guilt that ever troubles a poet-as-poet? Certainly, Shelley for Browning was precisely the "numinous shadow" or ancestor-god whose baleful influence is stressed by Nietzsche. Rather than demonstrate this too obviously, whether by recourse to Browning's poem *Pauline* or by an examination of the unhappy episode in which the young Browning yielded to his stern mother's Evangelical will, I think it more interesting to seek out what is most difficult in Browning, which is the total contrast between his optimism, a quality both temperamental and theoretical, and the self-destructive peculiarities of his men and women. I want to start by puzzling over the grotesque and unique poem, *Master Hugues of Saxe-Gotha,* with its curious and central contrast between the charming organist who speaks the monologue and the heavy pseudo-Bachian composer, also invented by Browning, whose name is the poem's title. The relationship between performer and composer *is* the poem. This relationship is *not* a displaced form of the ambivalence between ephebe and precursor, because the performer's reading/misreading of the composer is very different from the later poet's interpretation of an earlier one, or anyone's reading/misreading of any poet. It is true that a performance is an interpretation, but a performance lacks the vital element of revisionism that makes for fresh creation. The charm of the poem *Master Hugues of Saxe-Gotha,* like the chill of the somewhat similar but greater poem, *A Toccata of Galuppi's,* is precisely that we are free of the burden of misprision and that the performer in each poem is more like a reciter of a text than he is like a critic of a text. Yet it remains true that you cannot recite any poem without giving some interpretation of it, though I would hazard the speculation that even the strongest recital, acting, or performance is at best a weak reading/misreading, in the technical antithetical senses of "weak" and "strong," for again there is no strength, poetic or critical, without the dialectics of revisionism coming into play.

The organist earnestly wants to understand Hugues without revising him, but evidently the world is right and the poor organist wrong, in that less is meant than meets the ear in Hugues' mountainous fugues. Hugues is a kind of involuntary musical nihilist, who in effect would rather have the void as purpose than be void of purpose. The organist is not only old-fashioned in his devotion to Hugues but, as we might say now, old-fashioned in his devotion to meaning. Yet skepticism, a suspicion concerning both meaning-in-Hugues and meaning-in-life, has begun to gain strength in the organist, despite himself. His quasi-desperate test-performance of Hugues, thematically racing the sacristan's putting-out of the light, moves from one sadly negative conclusion to a larger negation, from "But where's music, the dickens?" to:

Is it your moral of Life?
    Such a web, simple and subtle,
Weave we on earth here in impotent strife,
    Backward and forward each throwing his shuttle,
Death ending all with a knife?

The very reluctance of the organist's interpretation
convinces us of its relevance to Hugues. Hugues will not
"say the word," despite the organist's plea, and the organist lacks the strength to break out on his revisionary
own and do what he wants to do, which is "unstop the
full-organ, / Blare out the *mode Palestrina*," akin to the
gentle simplicity of his own nature. Yet we must not take
the organist too literally; after all, there is nothing whatsoever to prevent him from playing Palestrina to his own
satisfaction in the moments of light that remain to him.
But it is the problematical, cumbersome, absurdly intricate Hugues who obsesses him, whose secret or lack of
a secret he is driven to solve. Despite himself, the organist
is on an antithetical quest, like absolutely every other
monologist in Browning. The luminous last line of the
poem is to be answered, emphatically: "Yes!"

While in the roof, if I'm right there,
    . . . Lo you, the wick in the socket!
Hallo, you sacristan, show us a light there!
    Down it dips, gone like a rocket.
What, you want, do you, to come unawares,
Sweeping the church up for first morning-prayers,
And find a poor devil has ended his cares
At the foot of your rotten-runged rat-riddled stairs?
    Do I carry the moon in my pocket?

If the organist is right, then the gold in the gilt roof is a
better emblem of a final reality than the spider web
woven by Hugues. But fortunately the darkening of the
light breaks in upon an uneasy affirmation, and leaves us

instead with the realization that the organist is subject as well as object of his own quest for meaning. Hugues goes on weaving his intricate vacuities; the organist carries the moon in his pocket. Has the poem ended, however humorously, as a ruined quest or as a good moment? Does Browning make it possible for us to know the difference between the two? Or is it the particular achievement of his art that the difference cannot be known? Does the organist end by knowing he has been deceived, or does he end in the beautiful earliness of carrying imagination in his own pocket, in a transumptive allusion to the Second Spirit in one of Browning's favorite poems, Shelley's *The Two Spirits: An Allegory*? There the Second Spirit, overtly allegorizing desire, affirms that the "lamp of love," carried within, gives him the perpetual power to "make night day." Browning is more dialectical, and the final representation in his poem is deeply ambiguous. But that is a depth of repression that I want to stay with, and worry, for a space, if only because it bothers me that *Master Hugues of Saxe-Gotha,* like so many of Browning's poems, ends in an *aporia,* in the reader's uncertainty as to whether he is to read literally or figuratively. Browning personally, unlike Shelley, was anything but an intellectual skeptic, and that he should create figures that abide in our uncertainty is at once his most salient and his most challenging characteristic.

A Toccata of Galuppi's can be read as a reversal of this poem, since it appears to end in the performer's conscious admission of belatedness and defeat. But Browning was quite as multiform a maker as poetic tradition affords, and the *Toccata* is as subtle a poem as ever he wrote. It invokes for us a grand Nietzschean question, from the Third Essay of *On the Genealogy of Morals:* "What does it mean when an artist leaps over into his opposite?" Nietzsche was thinking of Wagner, but Browning in the *Toccata* may be another instance. Nietzsche's ultimate answer to his own question prophesied late Freud, if we take the answer to be: "All great things bring about their own destruction through an act of self-overcoming." I think we can say rather safely that no one was less interested in *Selbstaufhebung* than Robert Browning; he was perfectly delighted to be at once subject and object of his own quest. Like Emerson, whom he resembles only in this single respect, he rejoiced always that there were so many of him, so many separate selves happily picnicking together in a single psyche. From a Nietzschean point of view, he must seem only an epitome of some of the most outrageous qualities of the British empirical and Evangelical minds, but he is actually more sublimely outrageous even than that. There are no dialectics that can subsume him, because he is not so much evasive as he is preternatural, wholly daemonic, with an astonishing alliance perpetual in him between an impish cunning and endless linguistic energy. I think we can surmise why he was so fascinated by poets like Christopher Smart and Thomas Lovell Beddoes, poets who represented the tradition of Dissenting Enthusiasm carried over into actual madness. With energies like Browning's, and self-confidence like Browning's, it took a mind as powerful as Browning's to avoid being carried by Enthusiasm into alienation, but perhaps the oddest of all Browning's endless oddities is that he was incurably sane, even as he imagined his gallery of pathological enthusiasts, monomaniacs, and marvelous charlatans.

There are at least four voices coldly leaping along in *A Toccata of Galuppi's,* and only one of them is more or less Browning's, and we cannot be certain even of that. Let us break in for the poem's conclusion, as the monologist first addresses the composer whose "touch-piece" he is playing, and next the composer answers back, *but only through the monologist's performance,* and finally the speaker-performer acknowledges his defeat by the heartlessly brilliant Galuppi:

XI

But when I sit down to reason, think to take my stand nor
    swerve,
While I triumph o'er a secret wrung from nature's close re-
    serve,
In you come with your cold music till I creep through every
    nerve.

XII

Yes, you, like a ghostly cricket, creaking where a house was
    burned:
'Dust and ashes, dead and done with, Venice spent what Venice
    earned.
The soul, doubtless, is immortal—where a soul can be dis-
    cerned.

XIII

'Yours, for instance: you know physics, something of geology,
Mathematics are your pastime; souls shall rise in their degree;
Butterflies may dread extinction,—you'll not die, it cannot be!

XIV

'As for Venice and her people, merely born to bloom and drop,
Here on earth they bore their fruitage, mirth and folly were
    the crop:
What of soul was left, I wonder, when the kissing had to stop?

XV

'Dust and ashes!' So you creak it, and I want the heart to scold.
Dear dead women, with such hair, too—what's become of all
    the gold
Used to hang and brush their bosoms? I feel chilly and grown
    old.

The "swerve" *is* the Lucretian *clinamen*, and we might
say that Galuppi, like Lucretius, assaults the monologist-
performer with the full strength of the Epicurean argument. One possible interpretation is that Browning, as a

fierce Transcendentalist of his own sect, a sect of one, is
hammering at the Victorian spiritual compromise, which
his cultivated speaker exemplifies. That interpretation
would confirm the poem's seriocomic opening:

I

Oh Galuppi, Baldassaro, this is very sad to find!
I can hardly misconceive you; it would prove me deaf and
    blind;
But although I take your meaning, 'tis with such a heavy mind!

Galuppi's triumph, on this reading, would be the
dramatic one of shaking up this cultivated monologist,
who first half-scoffs at Galuppi's nihilism, but who ends
genuinely frightened by the lesson Galuppi has taught,
which is a lesson of mortality and consequent mean-
inglessness. But I think that is to underestimate the
monologist, who is a more considerable temperament
even than the organist who plays Hugues and can bear
neither to give Hugues up nor accept Hugues' emptiness.
Galuppi is no Hugues, but a powerfully sophisticated
artist who gives what was wanted of him, but with a
Dance-of-Death aspect playing against his audience's desires. And the speaker, who knows physics, some geology,
a little mathematics, and will not quite abandon his Christian immortality, is at least as enigmatic as the organist,
and for a parallel reason. Why cannot he let Galuppi
alone? What does he quest for in seeing how well he can
perform that spirited and elegant art? Far more even
than Galuppi, or Galuppi's audience, or than Browning,
the speaker is obsessed with mortality:

X

Then they left you for their pleasure: till in due time, one by
    one,
Some with lives that came to nothing, some with deeds as well
    undone,
Death stepped tacitly and took them where they never see the
    sun.

One of the most moving elements in the poem is its erotic nostalgia, undoubtedly the single sphere of identity between the monologist and Browning himself. Eros crowds the poem, with an intensity and poignance almost Shakespearean in its strength:

V

Was a lady such a lady, cheeks so round and lips so red,—
On her neck the small face buoyant, like a bell-flower on its
bed,
O'er the breast's superb abundance where a man might base his
head?

VI

Well, and it was graceful of them—they'd break talk off and
afford
—She, to bite her mask's black velvet—he, to finger on his
sword,
While you sat and played Toccatas, stately at the clavichord?

VII

What? Those lesser thirds so plaintive, sixths diminished, sigh
on sigh,
Told them something? Those suspensions, those solutions—
'Must we die?'
Those commiserating sevenths—'Life might last! we can but
try!'

VIII

'Were you happy?'—'Yes.'—'And are you still as happy?'—'Yes.
And you?'
—'Then, more kisses!'—'Did *I* stop them, when a million
seemed so few?'
Hark, the dominant's persistence till it must be answered to!

IX

So, an octave struck the answer. Oh, they praised you, I dare
say!
'Brave Galuppi! that was music! good alike at grave and gay!
I can always leave off talking when I hear a master play!'

Nothing in the poem is at once so moving and so shocking as the monologist's final "Dear dead women, with such hair, too—," for this spiritual trimmer is very much a sensual man, like his robust creator. It is the cold Galuppi who is more the dualist, more the artist fulfilling the Nietzschean insight that the ascetic ideal is a defensive evasion by which art preserves itself against the truth. But where, as readers, does that leave us, since this time Browning elegantly has cleared himself away? His overt intention is pretty clear, and I think pretty irrelevant also. He wants us—unlike the monologist, unlike Galuppi, unlike Galuppi's hard-living men and women—to resort to his ferocious version of an antithetical Protestantism, which is I think ultimately his misprision of Shelley's antithetical humanism. Yet Browning's art has freed us of Browning, though paradoxically not of Shelley, or at least of the strong Lucretian element in Shelley. Has the monologist quested after Galuppi's truth, only to end up in a vastation of his own comforting evasions of the truth? That would be the canonical reading, but it would over-literalize a metaleptic figuration that knowingly has chosen not to attempt a reversal of time. When the speaker ends by feeling "chilly and grown old," then he has introjected Galuppi's world and Galuppi's music, and projected his own compromise formulations. But this is an *illusio*, a metaleptic figuration that is on the verge of becoming an opening irony or reaction-formation again, that is, rejoining the tone of jocular evasion that began the poem. Nothing has happened because nothing has changed, and the final grimness of Browning's eerie poem is that its speaker is caught in a repetition. He will pause awhile, and then play a toccata of Galuppi's again.

Let us try a third music-poem or improvisation, the still more formidable *Abt Vogler*, where the daemonic performer is also the momentary composer, inventing fitfully upon an instrument of his own invention, grandly solitary because there is nothing for him to interpret except his own interpretation of his own creation. The canonical readings available here are too weak to be interesting, since they actually represent the poem as being pious. The historical Vogler was regarded by some as a pious fraud, but Browning's Vogler is too complex to be regarded either as an impostor or as sincerely devout. What matters most is that he is primarily an extemporizer, rather than necessarily an artist, whether as performer or composer. The poem leaves open (whatever Browning's intentions) the problem of whether Vogler is a skilled illusionist, or something more than that. At the least, Vogler is self-deceived, but even the self-deception is most complex. It is worth knowing what I must assume that Browning knew; Vogler's self-invented instruments sounded splendid only when played by Vogler. Though the great temptation in reading this poem is to interpret it as a good moment precariously attained, and then lost, I think the stronger or antithetical reading here will show that this is very nearly as much a poem of ruined quest as *Childe Roland* or *Andrea del Sarto* is.

Abt Vogler is one of those poems that explain Yeats's remark to the effect that he feared Browning as a potentially dangerous influence upon him. If we could read *Abt Vogler* without interpretative suspicion (and I believe we cannot), then the poem would seem to be a way-station between the closing third of *Adonais* and Yeats's Byzantium poems. It establishes itself in a state of being that seems either to be beyond the antithesis of life and death, or else that seems to be the state of art itself. Yet, in the poem *Abt Vogler,* I think we have neither, but something more puzzling, a willed phantasmagoria that is partly Browning's and partly an oddity, a purely visionary dramatic monologue.

Vogler, we ought to realize immediately, does not seek the purposes of art, which after all is hard work. Vogler is daydreaming, and is seeking a magical power over nature or supernature, as in the debased Kabbalist myth of Solomon's seal. Vogler is not so much playing his organ as enslaving it to his magical purposes, purposes that do not distinguish between angel and demon, heaven and hell. Vogler is no Blakean visionary; he seeks not to marry heaven and hell, but merely to achieve every power that he can. And yet he has a moving purpose, akin to Shelley's in *Prometheus Unbound,* which is to aid earth's mounting into heaven. But, is his vision proper something we can grant the prestige of vision, or is there not a dubious element in it?

v

All through my keys that gave their sounds to a wish of my soul,
  All through my soul that praised as its wish flowed visibly forth,
All through music and me! For think, had I painted the whole,
  Why, there it had stood, to see, nor the process so wonder-worth:
Had I written the same, made verse—still, effect proceeds from cause,
  Ye know why the forms are fair, ye hear how the tale is told;
It is all triumphant art, but art in obedience to laws,
  Painter and poet are proud in the artist-list enrolled:—.

Being made perfect, when the subject is someone like Vogler, is a somewhat chancy phenomenon. Unlike the sublimely crazy Johannes Agricola, in one of Browning's earliest and most frightening dramatic monologues, Vogler is not a genuine Enthusiast, certain of his own Election. Stanza VI has a touch of *Cleon* about it, and stanza VII is clearly *unheimlich,* despite the miraculous line: "That out of three sounds he frame, not a fourth sound, but a star." But with Stanzas VIII and IX, which are this poem's *askesis* or sublimation, it is not so easy to distinguish Vogler from Browning, or one of the beings always bouncing around in Browning, anyway:

VIII

Well, it is gone at last, the palace of music I reared;
 Gone! and the good tears start, the praises that come too
  slow;
For one is assured at first, one scarce can say that he feared,
 That he even gave it a thought, the gone thing was to go.
Never to be again! But many more of the kind
 As good, nay, better perchance: is this your comfort to me?
To me, who must be saved because I cling with my mind
 To the same, same self, same love, same God: ay, what was,
  shall be.

IX

Therefore to whom turn I but to thee, the ineffable Name?
 Builder and maker, thou, of houses not made with hands!
What, have fear of change from thee who art ever the same?
 Doubt that thy power can fill the heart that thy power
  expands?
There shall never be one lost good! What was, shall live as
 before;
 The evil is null, is nought, is silence implying sound;
What was good shall be good, with, for evil, so much good
 more;
 On the earth the broken arcs; in the heaven, a perfect
 round.

The poem, from here to the end, in the three final stanzas, is suddenly as much Browning's Magnificat as the *Song to David,* which is deliberately echoed in the penultimate line, is Smart's. But what does that mean, whether in this poem, or whether about Browning himself? Surely he would not acknowledge, openly, that his is the art of the extemporizer, the illusionist improvising? Probably not, but the poem may be acknowledging an anxiety that he possesses, to much that effect. Whether this is so or not, to any degree, how are we to read the final stanza?

XII

Well, it is earth with me; silence resumes her reign:
    I will be patient and proud, and soberly acquiesce.
Give me the keys. I feel for the common chord again,
    Sliding by semitones, till I sink to the minor,—yes,
And I blunt it into a ninth, and I stand on alien ground,
    Surveying awhile the heights I rolled from into the deep;
Which, hark, I have dared and done, for my resting-place is
      found,
    The C Major of this life: so now I will try to sleep.

This descent to C Major separates Vogler totally from Browning again, since of the many keys in which the genuinely musical Browning composes, his resting place is hardly a key without sharps or flats. Browning has his direct imitation of Smart's *Song to David* in his own overtly religious poem, *Saul,* and so we can be reasonably certain that Vogler does not speak for Browning when the improviser belatedly stands on alien ground, surveying the Sublime he had attained, and echoes Smart's final lines:

> Thou at stupendous truth believ'd;—
> And now the matchless deed's atchiev'd,
>   DETERMINED, DARED, and DONE.

What Vogler has dared and done is no more than to have dreamed a belated dream; where Browning is, in regard to that Promethean or Shelleyan a dream, is an enigma, at least in this poem. What *Abt Vogler,* as a text, appears to proclaim *is* the impossibility of our reading it, insofar as reading means being able to govern the interplay of literal and figurative meanings in a text. Canonically, in terms of all received readings, this poem is almost an apocalyptic version of a Browningesque "Good Moment," a time of privilege or an epiphany, a sudden manifestation of highest vision. Yet the patterns of revisionary misprision are clearly marked upon the poem, and they tend to indicate that the poem demands to be read figuratively against its own letter, as another parable of ruined quest, or confession of imaginative failure, or the shame of knowing such failure.

I turn to *Andrea del Sarto,* which with *Childe Roland to the Dark Tower Came,* and the meditation entitled *The Pope* in *The Ring and the Book,* seems to me to represent Browning at his greatest. Here there would appear to be no question about the main issue of interpretation, for the canonical readings seem fairly close to the poem in its proclamation that this artist's quest is ruined, that Andrea stands self-condemned by his own monologue. Betty Miller has juxtaposed the poem, brilliantly, with this troubled and troublesome passage in Browning's *Essay on Shelley*:

Although of such depths of failure there can be no question here we must in every case betake ourselves to the review of a poet's life ere we determine some of the nicer questions concerning his poetry,—more especially if the performance we seek to estimate aright, has been obstructed and cut short of completion by circumstances,—a disastrous youth or a premature death. We may learn from the biography whether his spirit invariably saw and spoke from the last height to which it had attained. An absolute vision is not for this world, but we are permitted a continual approximation to it, every degree of which in the individual, provided it exceed the attainment of the masses, must procure him a clear advantage. Did the poet ever attain to a higher platform than where he rested and exhibited a result? Did he know more than he spoke of?

On this juxtaposition, Andrea and Browning alike rested on a level lower than the more absolute vision they could have attained. Certainly Andrea tells us, perhaps even shows us, that he knows more than he paints. But Browning? If he was no Shelley, he was also no Andrea, which in part is the burden of the poem. But only in part, and whether there is some level of *apologia* in this monologue, in its patterning, rather than its overt content, is presumably a question that a more antithetical practical criticism ought to be capable of exploring.

Does Andrea overrate his own potential? If he does, *then there is no poem,* for unless his dubious gain-in-life has paid for a genuine loss-in-art, then he is too self-deceived to be interesting, even to himself. Browning has complicated this matter, as he complicates everything. The poem's subtitle reminds us that Andrea was called "The Faultless Painter," and Vasari, Browning's source, credits Andrea with everything in execution but then faults him for lacking ambition, for not attempting the Sublime. Andrea, in the poem, persuades us of a wasted greatness not so much by his boasting ("At any rate 'tis easy, all of it! / No sketches first, no studies, that's long past: / I do what many dream of, all their lives . . ."), but by his frightening skill in sketching his own twilight-piece, by his showing us how "A common greyness silvers everything—." Clearly, this speaker knows loss, and clearly he is the antithesis of his uncanny creator, whose poetry never suffers from a lack of ambition, who is always Sublime where he is most Grotesque, and always Grotesque when he storms the Sublime. Andrea does not represent anything in Browning directly, not even the betrayed relationship to the heroic precursor, yet he does represent one of Browning's anxieties, an anxiety related to but not identical with the anxiety of influence. It is an anxiety of representation, or a fear of forbidden meanings, or in Freudian language precisely a fear of the return-of-the-repressed, even though such a return would cancel out a poem-as-poem, or is it *because* such a return would end poetry as such?

Recall that Freud's notion of repression speaks of an unconsciously *purposeful* forgetting, and remind yourself also that what Browning could never bear was a sense of *purposelessness.* It is purposelessness that haunts Childe Roland, and we remember again what may be Nietzsche's

most powerful insight, which closes the great Third Essay
of *Towards the Genealogy of Morals.* The ascetic ideal,
Nietzsche said, by which he meant also the aesthetic ideal,
was the only *meaning* yet found for human suffering, and
mankind would rather have the void *for* purpose than be
void *of* purpose. Browning's great fear, purposelessness,
was related to the single quality that had moved and
impressed him most in Shelley: the remorseless purposefulness of the Poet in *Alastor,* of Prometheus, and of
Shelley himself questing for death in *Adonais.* Andrea, as
an artist, is the absolute antithesis of the absolute idealist
Shelley, and so Andrea is a representation of profound
Browningesque anxiety.

But how is this an anxiety of representation? We enter
again the dubious area of *belatedness,* which Browning is
reluctant to represent, but is too strong and authentic a
poet to avoid. Though Andrea uses another vocabulary, a
defensively evasive one, to express his relationship to
Michelangelo, Raphael, and Leonardo, he suffers the
burden of the latecomer. His Lucrezia is the emblem of
his belatedness, his planned excuse for his failure in
strength, which he accurately diagnoses as a failure in
will. And he ends in deliberate belatedness, and in his
perverse need to be cuckolded:

> What would one have?
> In heaven, perhaps, new chances, one more chance—
> Four great walls in the New Jerusalem,
> Meted on each side by the angel's reed,
> For Leonard, Rafael, Agnolo and me
> To cover—the three first without a wife,
> While I have mine! So—still they overcome
> Because there's still Lucrezia,—as I choose.
>
> Again the Cousin's whistle! Go, my Love.

Can we say that Andrea represents what Shelley
dreaded to become, the extinguished hearth, an ash

without embers? We know that Shelley need not have feared, yet the obsessive, hidden fear remains impressive. Browning at seventy-seven was as little burned out as Hardy at eighty-eight, Yeats at seventy-four, or Stevens at seventy-five, and his *Asolando,* his last book, fiercely prefigures Hardy's *Winter Words,* Yeats's *Last Poems,* and Stevens's *The Rock,* four astonishing last bursts of vitalism in four of the strongest modern poets. What allies the four volumes (*The Rock* is actually the last section of Stevens's *Collected Poems,* but he had planned it as a separate volume under the title *Autumn Umber*) is their overcoming of each poet's abiding anxiety of representation. "Representation," in poetry, ultimately means self-advocacy; as Hartman says: "You justify either the self or that which stands greatly against it: perhaps both at once." We could cite Nietzsche here on the poet's Will-to-Power, but the more orthodox Coleridge suffices, by reminding us that there can be no origination without discontinuity, and that only the Will can interrupt the repetition-compulsion that *is* nature. In the final phases of Browning, Hardy, Yeats, and Stevens, the poet's Will raises itself against Nature, and this antithetical spirit breaks through a final anxiety and dares to represent itself as what Coleridge called self-determining spirit. Whether Freud would have compounded this self-realizing instinct with his "detours towards death" I do not know, but I think it is probable. In this final phase, Browning and his followers (Hardy and Yeats were overtly influenced by Browning, and I would suggest a link between the extemporizing, improvising aspect of Stevens, and Browning) are substituting a transumptive representation for the still-abiding presence of Shelley, their common ancestor.

I want to illustrate this difficult point by reference to Browning's last book, particularly to its *Prologue,* and to the sequence called *Bad Dreams.* My model, ultimately, is again the Lurianic Kabbalah, with its notion of *gilgul,* of lifting up a precursor's spark, provided that he is truly one's precursor, truly of one's own root. *Gilgul* is the ultimate *tikkun,* as far as an act of representation can go. What Browning does is fascinatingly like the pattern of *gilgul,* for at the end he takes up precisely Shelley's dispute with Shelley's prime precursor, Wordsworth. By doing for Shelley what Shelley could not do for himself, overcome Wordsworth, Browning lifts up or redeems Shelley's spark or ember, and renews the power celebrated in the *Ode to the West Wind* and Act IV of *Prometheus Unbound.* I will try to illustrate this complex pattern, after these glances at *Asolando,* by returning for a last time (I hope) to my personal obsession with *Childe Roland to the Dark Tower Came,* and then concluding this discourse by considering Browning's late reversal of *Childe Roland* in the highly Shelleyan celebration, *Thamuris Marching.*

The *Prologue* to *Asolando* is another in that long series of revisions of the *Intimations* Ode that form so large a part of the history of nineteenth- and twentieth-century British and American poetry. But Browning consciously gives a revision of a revision, compounding *Alastor* and the *Hymn to Intellectual Beauty* with the parent poem. What counts in Browning's poem is not the Wordsworthian gleam, called here, in the first stanza, an "alien glow," but the far more vivid Shelleyan fire, that Browning recalls seeing for the first time, some fifty years before:

> How many a year, my Asolo,
>   Since—one step just from sea to land—
> I found you, loved yet feared you so—
>   For natural objects seemed to stand
> Palpably fire-clothed! No—
>
> No mastery of mine o'er these!
>   Terror with beauty, like the Bush
> Burning but unconsumed. Bend knees,
>   Drop eyes to earthward! Language? Tush!
> Silence 'tis awe decrees.

> And now? The lambent flame is—where?
>   Lost from the naked world: earth, sky,
> Hill, vale, tree, flower,—Italia's rare
>   O'er-running beauty crowds the eye—
> But flame? The Bush is bare.

When Shelley abandoned the fire, then it was for the transumptive trumpet of a prophecy, or in *Adonais* for the same wind rising ("The breath whose might I have invoked in song / Descends on me") to carry him beyond voice as beyond sight. Browning, as an Evangelical Protestant, fuses the Shelleyan heritage with the Protestant God in a powerfully incongruous transumption:

> Hill, vale, tree, flower—they stand distinct,
>   Nature to know and name. What then?
> A Voice spoke thence which straight unlinked
>   Fancy from fact: see, all's in ken:
> Has once my eyelid winked?
>
> No, for the purged ear apprehends
>   Earth's import, not the eye late dazed:
> The voice said 'Call my works thy friends!
>   At Nature dost thou shrink amazed?
> God is it who transcends.'

This is an absolute logocentrism, and is almost more than any poem can bear, particularly at a time as late as 1889. Browning gets away with it partly by way of a purged ear, partly because his Protestantism condenses what High Romanticism normally displaces, the double-bind situation of the Protestant believer whose God simultaneously says "Be like Me in My stance towards Nature" and "Do not presume to resemble Me in My stance towards nature." The sheer energy of the Browningesque daemonic Sublime carries the poet past what ought to render him imaginatively schizoid.

But not for long, of course, as a glance at *Bad Dreams*

will indicate, a glance that then will take us back to the
greatest of Browning's nightmares, the demonic romance
of *Childe Roland*. *Bad Dreams III* is a poem in which the
opposition between Nature and Art *has* been turned into
a double-bind, with its contradictory injunctions:

> This was my dream! I saw a Forest
> Old as the earth, no track nor trace
> Of unmade man. Thou, Soul, explorest—
> Though in a trembling rapture—space
> Immeasurable! Shrubs, turned trees,
> Trees that touch heaven, support its frieze
> Studded with sun and moon and star:
> While—oh, the enormous growths that bar
> Mine eye from penetrating past
> Their tangled twine where lurks—nay, lives
> Royally lone, some brute-type cast
> In the rough, time cancels, man forgives.
>
> On, Soul! I saw a lucid City
> Of architectural device
> Every way perfect. Pause for pity,
> Lightning! Nor leave a cicatrice
> On those bright marbles, dome and spire,
> Structures palatial,—streets which mire
> Dares not defile, paved all too fine
> For human footstep's smirch, not thine—
> Proud solitary traverser,
> My Soul, of silent lengths of way—
> With what ecstatic dread, aver,
> Lest life start sanctioned by thy stay!
>
> Ah, but the last sight was the hideous!
> A city, yes,—a Forest, true,—
> But each devouring each. Perfidious
> Snake-plants had strangled what I knew
> Was a pavilion once: each oak
> Held on his horns some spoil he broke

By surreptiously beneath
Upthrusting: pavements, as with teeth,
Griped huge weed widening crack and split
    In squares and circles stone-work erst.
Oh, Nature—good! Oh, Art—no whit
    Less worthy! Both in one—accurst!

In the sequence of *Bad Dreams,* Browning himself, as
interpreter of his own text, identifies Nature with the
husband, Art with the wife, and the marriage of Art and
Nature, man and woman—why, with Hell, and a
sadomasochistic sexual Hell, at that. But the text can
sustain very diverse interpretations, as the defensive intensity of repression here is enormously strong. The City
is of Art, but like Yeats's Byzantium, which it prophesies,
it is also a City of Death-in-Life, and the previous vision
of the forest is one of a Nature that might be called
Life-in-Death. Neither realm can bear the other, in both
senses of "bear"—"bring forth" or "tolerate." Neither is
the other's precursor, and each devours the other, if they
are brought together. This is hardly the vision of the
Prologue to *Asolando,* as there seems no room for either
Browning or God in the world of the final stanza.
Granted that this is nightmare, or severe repression
partly making a return, it carries us back to Browning at
his most problematic and Sublime, to his inverted vision
of the Center, *Childe Roland to the Dark Tower Came.*

As the author of two full-scale commentaries on this
poem (in *The Ringers in the Tower,* 1971, and in *A Map of
Misreading,* 1975) I reapproach the text with considerable
wariness, fairly determined not only that I will not repeat
myself, but also hopefully aiming not merely to uncover
my own obsessional fixation upon so grandly grotesque a
quest-romance. But I recur to the question I asked at the
start of this discourse; is there an attainable *critical* knowledge to be gathered from this critical obsession?

Roland, though a Childe or ephebe on the road to a

demonic version of the Scene of Instruction, is so consciously belated a quester that he seems at least as much
an obsessive interpreter as anything else purposive that
he might desire to become. He out-Nietzsches Nietzsche's
Zarathustra in his compulsive will-to-power over the interpretation of his own text. It is difficult to conceive of a
more belated hero, and I know of no more extreme
literary instance of a quest emptying itself out. Borges
accurately located in Browning one of the precursors of
Kafka, and perhaps only Kafka's *The Castle* rivals *Childe
Roland* as a Gnostic version of what was once romance.
Nearly every figuration in the poem reduces to ruin, yet
the poem, as all of us obscurely sense, appears to end in
something like triumph, in a Good Moment carried
through to a supreme representation:

> There they stood, ranged along the hill-sides, met
>> To view the last of me, a living frame
>> For one more picture! in a sheet of flame
> I saw them and I knew them all. And yet
> Dauntless the slug-horn to my lips I set,
>> And blew. '*Childe Roland to the Dark Tower came.*'

Surely it is outrageous to call this a Supreme or even a
Good Moment? The stanza just before ends with the
sound of loss: "one moment knelled the woe of years."
Wordsworth and Coleridge had viewed the Imagination
as compensatory, as trading off experiential loss for poetic gain, a formula that we can begin to believe was an
unmitigated calamity. Is it the peculiar fascination of
Childe Roland, as a poem, that it undoes every High
Romantic formula, that it exposes the Romantic imagination as being merely an accumulative principle of repression? But such negation is itself simplistic, and evades
what is deepest and most abiding in this poem, which is
the representation of *power.* For here, I think, is the
kernel of our critical quest, that Kabbalistic point which is

at once *ayin*, or nothingness, and *ehyeh*, or the representation of Absolute Being, the rhetorical irony or *illusio* that
always permits a belated poem to begin again in its quest
for renewed strength. Signification has wandered away,
and Roland is questing for lost and forgotten *meaning*,
questing for *representation*, for a seconding or re-advocacy
of his own self. Does he not succeed, far better than
Tennyson's Ulysses and Percivale, and far better even
than the Solitaries of the High Romantics, in this quest
for representation? Let us grant him, and ourselves, that
this is a substitute for his truly impossible original objective, for that was the *antithetical*, Shelleyan dream of re-
begetting oneself, of breaking through the web of nature
and so becoming one's own imaginative father. Substitution, as Roland shows, need not be a sublimation, but can
move from repression *through* sublimation to climax in a
more complex act of defense.

Psychoanalysis has no single name for this act, unless
we were willing (as we are not) to accept the pejorative
one of paranoia for what is, from any point of view that
transcends the analytic, a superbly valuable act of the will.
Roland teaches us that what psychoanalysis calls "introjection" and "projection" are figurations for the spiritual
processes of identification and apocalyptic rejection that
exist at the outer borders of poetry. Roland learns, and
we learn with him, that the representation of power *is*
itself a power, and that this latter power or strength is the
only purposiveness that we shall know. Roland, at the
close, is re-inventing the self, but at the considerable
expense of joining that self to a visionary company of
loss, and loss means loss of *meaning* here. The endless
fascination of his poem, for any critical reader nurtured
upon Romantic tradition, is that the poem, more clearly
than any other, nevertheless does precisely what any
strong Romantic poem does, at once de-idealizes itself far
more thoroughly than we can de-idealize it, yet points
also beyond this self-deconstruction or limitation or reduction to the First Idea, on to a re-imagining, to a

power-making that no other discursive mode affords. For Roland, as persuasively as any fictive being, warns us against the poisonous ravishments of truth itself. He and his reader have moved only through discourse together, and he and his reader are less certain about what they know than they were as the poem began, but both he and his reader have endured unto a representation of more strength than they had at the start, and such a representation indeed turns out to be a kind òf restitution, a *tikkun* for repairing a fresh breaking-of-the-vessels. Meaning has been more curtailed than restored, but strength is revealed as antithetical to meaning.

I conclude with a great poem by Browning that is his conscious revision of *Childe Roland*: the marvelous late chant, *Thamuris Marching,* which is one of the finest unknown, unread poems by a major poet in the language. Twenty-two years after composing *Childe Roland,* Browning, not at the problematic age of thirty-nine, but now sixty-one, knows well that no spring has followed or flowered past meridian. But *Childe Roland* is a belated poem, except in its transumptive close, while all of *Thamuris Marching* accomplishes a metaleptic reversal, for how could a poem be more overwhelmingly early than this? And yet the situation of the quester is objectively terrible from the start of this poem, for Thamuris *knows* he is marching to an unequal contest, a poetic struggle of one heroic ephebe against the greatest of precursors, the Muses themselves. "Thamuris marching," the strong phrase repeated three times in the chant, expresses the *exuberance of purpose,* the Shelleyan remorseless joy in pure, self-destructive poetic quest, that Browning finally is able to grant himself.

Here is Browning's source, *Iliad* II, 594 ff:

>   . . . and Dorion, where the Muses
> encountering Thamyris the Thracian stopped him from singing,
> as he came from Oichalia and Oichalian Eurytos;
> for he boasted that he would surpass, if the very Muses,

daughters of Zeus who holds the aegis, were singing against
    him,
and these in their anger struck him maimed, and the voice of
    wonder
they took away, and made him a singer without memory;
                                        [Lattimore version]

Homer does not say that Thamyris lost the contest, but
rather that the infuriated Muses lost their divine temper,
and unvoiced him by maiming his memory, without
which no one can be a poet. Other sources, presumably
known to Browning, mention a contest decided in the
Muses' favor by Apollo, after which those ungracious
ladies blinded Thamyris, and removed his memory, so as
to punish him for his presumption. Milton, in the invocation to light that opens Book III of *Paradise Lost*, exalted
Thamyris by coupling him with Homer, and then associated his own ambitions with both poets:

> Nightly I visit: nor sometimes forget
> Those other two equall'd with me in Fate,
> So were I equall'd with them in renown,
> Blind Thamyris and blind Maeonides.

Milton presumably had read in Plutarch that Thamyris
was credited with an epic about the war waged by the
Titans against the Gods, the theme that Browning would
associate with Shelley and with Keats. Browning's
Thamuris marches to a Shelleyan *terza rima*, and marches
through a visionary universe distinctly like Shelley's, and
overtly proclaimed as being *early*: "From triumph on to
triumph, mid a ray / Of early morn—" Laughing as he
goes, yet knowing fully his own doom, Thamuris marches
through a landscape of joy that is the deliberate point-
by-point reversal of Childe Roland's self-made phantasmagoria of ordeal-by-landscape:

> Thamuris, marching, laughed 'Each flake of foam'
> (As sparklingly the ripple raced him by)
> 'Mocks slower clouds adrift in the blue dome!'

For Autumn was the season; red the sky
Held morn's conclusive signet of the sun
To break the mists up, bid them blaze and die.

Morn had the mastery as, one by one
All pomps produced themselves along the tract
From earth's far ending to near Heaven begun.

Was there a ravaged tree? it laughed compact
With gold, a leaf-ball crisp, high-brandished now,
Tempting to onset frost which late attacked.

Was there a wizened shrub, a starveling bough,
A fleecy thistle filched from by the wind,
A weed, Pan's trampling hoof would disallow?

Each, with a glory and a rapture twined
About it, joined the rush of air and light
And force: the world was of one joyous mind.

[19–36]

From Roland's reductive interpretations we have
passed to the imagination's heightened expansions. And
though this quest is necessarily for the fearful opposite of
poetic divination, we confront, not ruin, but the Good
Moment exalted and transfigured, as though for once
Browning utterly could fuse literal and figurative:

Say not the birds flew! they forebore their right—
Swam, reveling onward in the roll of things.
Say not the beasts' mirth bounded! that was flight—

How could the creatures leap, no lift of wings?
Such earth's community of purpose, such
The ease of earth's fulfilled imaginings—

So did the near and far appear to touch
In the moment's transport—that an interchange
Of function, far with near, seemed scarce too much;

[37–45]

Roland's band of failures has become the glorious band
of precursors among whom Thamuris predominates. The

Shelleyan west wind of imagination rises, Destroyer and
Creator, as Thamuris, eternally early, stands as the true
ephebe, "Earth's poet," against the Heavenly Muse:

> Therefore the morn-ray that enriched his face,
> If it gave lambent chill, took flame again
> From flush of pride; he saw, he knew the place.
>
> What wind arrived with all the rhythms from plain,
> Hill, dale, and that rough wildwood interspersed?
> Compounding these to one consummate strain,
>
> It reached him, music; but his own outburst
> Of victory concluded the account,
> And that grew song which was mere music erst.
>
> 'Be my Parnassos, thou Pangaian mount!
> And turn thee, river, nameless hitherto!
> Famed shalt thou vie with famed Pieria's fount!
>
> 'Here I await the end of this ado:
> Which wins—Earth's poet or the Heavenly Muse.'

There is the true triumph of Browning's art, for the
ever-early Thamuris is Browning as he wished to have
been, locked in a solitary struggle against the precursor-
principle, but struggling *in* the visionary world of the
precursor. Roland rode through a Gnostic universe in
which the hidden God, Shelley, was repressed, a repression that gave Browning a negative triumph of the Sublime made Grotesque. In *Thamuris Marching,* the joyous
struggle is joined overtly, and the repressed partly returns, to be repressed again into the true Sublime, as
Browning lifts up the sparks of his own root, to invoke
that great mixed metaphor of the Lurianic Kabbalah.
There is a breaking-of-the-vessels, but the sparks are scattered again, and become Shelley's *and* Browning's words,
mixed together, among mankind.

8

Yeats, Gnosticism, and the Sacred Void

The Valentinian Speculation chronicles the Fall of the Muse-principle, the Sophia, who in her leap forward found herself alone in the primal abyss, the Sacred Void, suffering a state that is called "ignorance" by the central Valentinian text, *The Gospel of Truth*:

It was this ignorance concerning the Father which produced Anguish and Terror. Anguish became dense like a fog, so that no one could see. Therefore Error became fortified. It elaborated its own Matter in the Void.

Yeats was slyly fond of the epithet that the Neoplatonist Proclus bestowed upon Christianity; Proclus called it "the barbarian theosophy," and declined to distinguish it from Gnosticism. The classical scholar, E. R. Dodds, rather more detachedly than Proclus or Yeats, concludes that the Gnostic tendency was strong in St. Paul, and agrees that it is impossible to divide sharply between Church and Gnosis.

Yeats is the most canonized poet of the twentieth century, more so even than Eliot, and most criticism of Yeats gives the impression of having been written while the critic was posturing upon his knees. Yeats was a supernaturalist (with much skepticism mixed in) and in some sense a religious poet, but the religion was a syncretic Gnosticism. In itself, of course, this is matter neither for praise nor for blame, but we ought to be clear about it. Canonical misreading provokes anticanonical misreading as a corrective, but since I published a 500-page commentary attempting just that, in 1970, I intend to devote this discourse on Yeats to a rather more sympathetic account of the Gnostic tendency in him. Yeats is safely in the canon, and nobody, myself included, wants him out, or could get him out even if that were desired. Himself a great revisionist, and so an unscrupulous distorter of Romantic tradition, Yeats has suffered and will go on suffering the weak misreadings that canon-formation affords. This hardly matters, and is peculiarly inevitable anyway, because Yeats was deliberately an *antithetical* poet and interpreter. The dominant influences upon him were the antithetical fourfold: Shelley, Blake, Nietzsche, Pater, to whom as an *antithetical* theorist he added himself as a fifth.

My own personal interest in the problems of formulating an *antithetical* practical criticism, founded on a view of poetic influence as misprision and revisionism, started with the difficulties I encountered in trying to write a book upon Yeats's relationship to his precursors, a book that found itself compelled first to center upon Yeats's systematic treatise, *A Vision,* and ultimately upon the far more beautiful and suggestive tractate by Yeats, *Per Amica Silentia Lunae,* now easily available in the collection of Yeats's prose called *Mythologies.* From 1902 on, Yeats was a steady reader of Nietzsche. I suggest that the crucial influences upon a poet must come early in his development, even as Shelley, Blake, and Pater affected Yeats early on. That Nietzsche, whom he read after he turned thirty-seven, influenced Yeats so strongly is due to Nietzsche's reinforcement of the earlier influences. Yeats himself associated Nietzsche with Blake, saying that "Nietzsche completes Blake and has the same roots." He might have said, more accurately, that Nietzsche was allied to Pater, but then the Yeatsian misprision soon compounded Nietzschean elements with aspects of Shelley, Blake, and Pater into one composite *antithetical* precursor anyway.

The term "antithetical" Yeats took from the Third Essay of the *Genealogy of Morals,* where Nietzsche asked for the antagonist of the ascetic ideal to come forward: "Where do we find an antithetical will expressing itself in an antithetical ideal?" In *The Will to Power,* no. 884, Nietzsche speaks of "the *strong* German type" as "existing blithely among antithesis, full of that supple strength that guards against convictions and doctrines by employing one against the other and reserving freedom for itself." Denis Donoghue is accurate in locating Nietzsche as the origin of Yeats's concept of the hero; as Donoghue says: "The hero is an antithetical fiction; his idiom is power, will; his sense of life dynamic, theatrical." In *Per Amica Silentia Lunae,* Yeats first stated his formula of the *antithetical:* "The other self, the anti-self or the antithetical self, as one may choose to name it, comes but to those who are no longer deceived, whose passion is reality."

From Plutarch and the Gnostics and Neoplatonists, Yeats took the notion of the Daimon as the proper figure for the *antithetical.* The evolution of the Daimon in Yeats is curious. In *Per Amica,* it is clearly a father or precursor-figure, "an illustrious dead man," but Yeats insists that "the Daimon comes not as like to like but seeking its own opposite, for man and Daimon feed the hunger in one another's hearts." "The Daimon is our destiny," Yeats says, thinking he cites Heraclitus, but Heraclitus actually said that character or *ethos* was fate or the *daimon,* whereas Yeats's remark is a powerful tautology. The tautology suits Yeatsian solipsism, with its drive towards the ultimate suprarealism that Yeats, following Shelley and Pater, called the Condition of Fire. At the center of *Per Amica* is Yeats's Gnostic version of what I have called the Scene of Instruction, the state of heightened demand that carries a new poet from his origins into his first strong representations. Yeats mediates his Scene of Instruction through the agency of the Daimon, which we can translate here simply as "precursor":

> The Daimon, by using his mediatorial shades, brings man again and again to the place of choice, heightening temptation that the choice may be as final as possible, imposing his own lucidity upon events, leading his victim to whatever among works not impossible is the most difficult.

In *A Vision,* the double cone or vortex or gyre is the dominant image, with the subjective cone "called that of the *antithetical tincture* because it is achieved and *defended* by continual conflict with its opposite." This image in turn is made coherent through a more complex and advanced doctrine of the Daimon, which I have expounded at some length in my commentary upon *A Vision* (see my *Yeats,* pp. 265–78), but briefly the Daimon for Yeats is now both the Muse-principle and the self-destructive principle that expresses itself in passionate heterosexual love. Neither of these meanings is wholly traditional, and Yeats's transformation of the daemonic is therefore worth some explanation. E. R. Dodds observes that for the second and third centuries A.D. the daemonic simply meant what the unconscious means now. By using the daemonic in his special senses, Yeats relates the term to repression, both to the aesthetic repression that gives poetry, and to the mode of repression we call or miscall sexual "love." But the traditional meaning of the daemonic, as Dodds shows, is ultimately the Platonic one: the daemonic interprets the gods to men, and men to the gods, which means that the daemonic is the channel between divine will and mortal wish, or simply constitutes the whole basis of Eros.

Freud's essay in the daemonic is his striking investigation of the *Unheimlich* or "Uncanny" of 1919, which relates the uncanny or daemonic to repetition-compulsion:

Our analysis of instances of the uncanny has led us back to the old animistic conception of the universe, which was characterized by the idea that the world was peopled with the spirits of human beings, and by the narcissistic overestimation of subjective mental processes (such as the belief in the omnipotence of thoughts, the magical practices based upon this belief, the carefully proportioned distribution of magical powers or "mana" among various outside persons and things), as well as by all those other figments of the imagination with which man, in the unrestricted narcissism of that stage of development, strove to withstand the inexorable laws of reality. It would seem as though each one of us has been through a phase of individual development corresponding to that animistic stage in primitive men, that none of us has traversed it without preserving certain traces of it which can be re-activated, and that everything which now strikes us as "uncanny" fulfills the condition of stirring those vestiges of animistic mental activity within us and bringing them to expression.

On this view, the daemonic is the survival of an archaic narcissism, which is defined as our faith that mind can triumph over matter. Let us, as readers of poetry, be very wary about what Freud is saying, for he is destroying the whole enterprise of literary Romanticism, if we give him our entire allegiance, as surely we do not. He is coming to us here as the greatest of reductionists, wiping away moonlight like mud. It is painful to see Sigmund Freud as Mrs. Alfred Uruguay, but it would be more painful still to abandon the mount of vision. The central formula of Coleridgean Romanticism, of which Yeats, Stevens, Hart Crane may have been the last Sublime representatives, is "the power of the mind over the universe of death," in which the mind's power means the Imagination, and the universe of death means all of the object-world. This formula, Freud is telling us, is only a survival, a trace returned from the repression of an archaic narcissism. The daemonic or Sublime is thus merely another evasion of the unacceptable necessity of dying. But Freud is harsher even than this, and his analysis of the uncanny takes us even farther into the problematics of repression:

In the first place, if psychoanalytic theory is correct in maintaining that every emotional affect, whatever its quality, is transformed by repression into morbid anxiety, then among such cases of anxiety there must be a class in which the anxiety can be shown to come from something repressed which *recurs.* This class of morbid anxiety would then be no other than what is uncanny, irrespective of whether it originally aroused dread or some other affect. In the second place, if this is indeed the secret nature of the uncanny, we can understand why the usage of speech has extended *das Heimliche* into its opposite *das Unheimliche*; for this uncanny is in reality nothing new or foreign, but something familiar and old-established in the mind that has been estranged only by the process of repression. This reference to the factor of repression enables us, furthermore, to understand Schelling's definition of the uncanny as something which ought to have been kept concealed but which has nevertheless come to light.

On Freud's view, we cannot distinguish the daemonic, or uncanny, or Sublime, from a particular variant of repetition-compulsion, whose affect is morbid anxiety. Translated into Yeatsian terms, early or late, this means that awareness of the precursor, or of the presence of the Muse, or of sexual love, are all compulsive repetitions of an obsessional anxiety. Here I have no quarrel with Freud, though I wish I did. But Yeats had such a quarrel, as would have had the entire tradition of the daemonic in poetry, from Homer through Goethe. Here is Goethe on the daemonic, as recorded by Eckermann:

I cannot rid myself of the notion that the daemons, who enjoy teasing us and joy at our pain, set up individuals so alluring that everyone aspires towards them, yet so great that no one can reach them. So they set up Raphael . . . Mozart . . . Shakespeare . . .

The daemonic, Goethe added at a later time, was not present in his Mephistopheles, for the daemonic had nothing in it of the spirit that denies, being positive and efficacious, as in Goethe himself. The argument between poetry and Freud, I would judge, reduces to this: can there be, as Goethe thought, a daemonic without morbid anxiety, or is the daemonic only an archaic and narcissistic survival?

I think that this argument, between Freud and the daemonic poets, is an ancient one, and could be traced back through different versions until we reached the quarrel between Plotinus and the Gnostics. Plotinus, unlike his later followers, finally evolved into an Hellenic rationalist, and his great essay against the Gnostics marked the crucial point of this evolution. Let us venture the following formula: the conflict here, whether between Plotinus and the Gnostics, or Descartes and Vico, or Freud and the poets, is between two views of the human condition as flawed or fallen. The more rational dualisms—Plotinian, Cartesian, or Freudian—accept as natural and inevitable the separation between body and consciousness, as well as the continued association of the two entities. So even Plotinus speaks of a descent of the soul into the body as being an instinctual necessity. The less rational dualisms—Gnostic, Vichian, and poetic-daemonic—maintain not only the prestige of monistic origins but assign a particular prestige to the phenomenon of the uncanny, that Freud analyzes as being marked always by evidences of acute anxiety. What Freud sees as archaic narcissism is seen by Gnosticism as the call to salvation, by Vico as Poetic Wisdom, and by Yeats as the *antithetical* imagination.

I do not believe that this argument between Freud and a permanent element in poetic tradition can or should be reconciled or explained away. There is, as I have indicated previously, no fully articulated Freudian view of art, because Freud in his final phase never got round to working one out, but he would have had grave difficulties in persuading himself that the strongest art represented a sublimation of human instinctual drives, whether sexual, or whether aggressively directed towards death. I am not inclined however to blame Freud for what is now called psychoanalytic literary criticism, since none of it that I have read merits being called either psychoanalysis or literary criticism.

Yeats's Gnosticism was in small part a consequence of his reading Gnostic texts, though generally in dubious versions or misleading contexts, but primarily I think that Yeats's Gnosticism was inherent in him, temperamentally and spiritually. Yeats's various occultisms, including his own System, with its often bizarre ventures into philosophy of history, Yeats himself took rather dialectically. He was invariably skeptical of his own credulity but also impatient with his own skepticism. There was also a fair amount of posturing in his stances, particularly in his Nietzscheanism, which was essentially theatrical. But his Gnosticism seems to me his natural religion: sincere, consistent, thoroughgoing, and finally a considerable aid to his poetry, however dubious it may seem in its human or social consequences. I hope to be clear on this; I am *not* saying that Yeats was a Gnostic adept, in the same way that he did become an Hermeticist, a quasi-Kabbalist, a member of the theosophical Order of the Golden Dawn. I *am* saying that the actual religion of Yeats's poetry seems to me closer to the Valentinian Speculation than to any other organized, historical faith of which I have knowledge. Like the Valentinian entity called Error, Yeats elaborated his own matter in the void, and like his masters Pater and Nietzsche he came to regard that void as being in itself partly sacred.

Yeats is hardly unique in his modern Gnosticism. Indeed, it could be argued that a form of Gnosticism is endemic in Romantic tradition without, however, dominating that tradition, or even that Gnosticism is the implicit, inevitable religion that frequently informs aspects of post-Enlightenment poetry, even where that poetry has seemed to be primarily a late phase of Protestantism. I am in no position to condemn Gnosticism anyway, as the kind of criticism I am attempting to develop takes a later Kabbalistic view of textuality and influence as its paradigm, and later Kabbalah relies ultimately upon Gnostic models of catastrophe-creation. Yeats is the representative of more than his own choices, and any reservations I have expressed before or will make now about his Gnostic tendencies have to do with certain consequences he deduced from those tendencies, and not with the tendencies themselves.

Various attempts have been made to account for both ancient and modern Gnosticism, in terms of supposed psychological and social causations, but these have satisfied very few scholars, including those who have formulated them. E. R. Dodds disposes of Erich Fromm on Gnostic and Christian origins by showing that Gnosticism and Gnostic tendencies in early Christianity all came into being in the Antonine period, the last phase of peace and prosperity in the Roman Empire, rather than during the third-century time-of-troubles that Fromm posited as the context in which doctrines of despair arose. Indeed, as Dodds shows, Gnosticism was a prophecy of trouble to come, rather than a reaction to a declining world:

> When Marcus Aurelius came to the throne no bell rang to warn the world that the *pax Romana* was about to be succeeded by an age of barbarian invasions, bloody civil wars, recurrent epidemics, galloping inflation and extreme personal insecurity.

Whatever its historical causations, ancient or modern, Gnosticism is a highly distinctive religion or religious tendency. A brief summary of its salient characteristics may be misleading, but some such summary seems necessary if I am to explore its relevances to Yeats's poetry. Gnosis, as the word itself indicates, means a kind of "knowledge," rather than a mode of thought. This "knowledge" is itself the form that salvation takes, because the "knower" is made Divine in such a "knowing," the "known" being "the alien God." This kind of "knowledge" is anything but what the West has meant by rational "knowledge," from the Greeks until our time, but it is precisely what Yeats means by "knowledge" in his poetry. It is also *not* what normative Judaism and orthodox Christianity have meant by any human "knowledge" of God, for Gnostic "knowledge" transforms man *into* God.

Gnosticism is a doubly radical dualism, a dualism between man and nature, and also between nature and God. Here is a usefully brief summary of the essentials of Gnostic doctrine by Hans Jonas:

> In its theological aspect this doctrine states that the Divine is alien to the world and has neither part nor concern in the physical universe; that the true god, strictly transmundane, is not revealed or even indicated by the world, and is therefore the Unknown, the totally Other, unknowable in terms of any worldly analogies. Correspondingly, in its cosmological aspect it states that the world is the creation not of God but of some inferior principle whose law it executes; and, in its anthropological aspect, that man's inner self, the *pneuma* ("spirit" in contrast to "soul" = psyche) is not part of the world, of nature's creation and domain, but is, within that world, as totally transcendent and as unknown by all worldly categories as is its transmundane counterpart, the unknown God without.

It is what Jonas calls the "anthropological aspect" of Gnosticism that is prominent in Yeats, since Yeats's characteristic poem tends to be a dramatic lyric, frequently turning upon the distinction between what Yeats calls the *antithetical* self and the *primary* soul, which are precisely the *pneuma* and the *psyche,* respectively, of Gnostic formulation. The place of the Gnostic alien or transmundane true God in Yeats is taken, alternately, by death, or by the imagination, which in Yeats is closer to Gnostic transcendence than it is to the Romantic Sublime. What Jonas says of the Gnostic alien God is true also of the Yeatsian imagination; it "does not stand in any positive relation to the sensible world. It is not the essence or the cause of the sensible world, but rather the negation and cancellation" of nature. I think that these similarities of Yeats and the Gnosis account for Yeats's obsession with transmigration, since only Yeats and the Gnosis, so far as I know, make a causal connection between libertinism and reincarnation. The following is the account given of the Cainite Gnostics by Irenaeus (as cited by Jonas), but it could come out of several contexts in Yeats's systematic treatise, *A Vision:*

> The souls in their transmigrations through bodies must pass through every kind of life and every kind of action, unless somebody has in one coming acted everything at once . . . their souls before departing must have made use of every mode of life and must have left no remainder of any sort still to be performed: lest they must again be sent into another body because there is still something lacking to their freedom.

This Gnostic notion of "freedom" as meaning an absolute *completion* of every human impulse, however destructive, is strikingly Yeatsian. But the central Gnostic element in Yeats is the crucial trope of *A Vision* and its "System": the Phases of the Moon, which goes back to the most Yeatsian personage among the Gnostic speculators, the flamboyant Simon Magus, who when he went to Rome took the cognomen of *Faustus,* "the favored one," and so became the ancestor of the Renaissance Faust. Simon, a Samaritan almost uniquely hated by the early Church Fathers, asserted that he was the Messiah. With unrivalled and admirable audacity, Simon picked up a whore in a Tyre brothel, named her Helena, and called her also the fallen Sophia, the "Thought" of God scattered into the broken vessels, whom he now restored and raised up to salvation. Simon also named his Helena *Selene,* the Moon, and gathered twenty-eight disciples, who together with himself and his whore made up the Valentinian *pleroma,*

the thirty Aeons constituting the manifold of unfallen
Divinity. The symbolism of salvation was transferred by
Simon to the great image of the waxing and the waning
of the moon, which in Yeats becomes the central emblem
of the primary and the antithetical cones, or objective and
subjective cycles of history. Rather than continue to ad-
duce Gnostic patterns in Yeats, or link up immediately
Yeats's Gnosticism to his daemonic intensities and both,
whether positively or negatively, to the Freudian defense
of repression, I will proceed now to a consideration of
two of Yeats's most ambitious works in the Sublime mode:
The Second Coming and *Byzantium*, and to very nearly his
last poem, *Cuchulain Comforted*, in order to ask and
perhaps answer the following question: was Yeats's
daemonic Gnosticism his repressive defense against the
anxiety of influence, and in particular against the composite Romantic precursor he had formed out of Shelley,
Blake, and Pater? Is the Yeatsian Sublime a triumph
(however equivocal) of a very belated Romantic questor
over and against the enormous pressures of poetic anteriority? Or, to put the question most plainly: was Yeats's
poetic variety of Gnosticism his own wilful misprision of
Romantic tradition?

The Second Coming is a very powerful piece of rhetoric,
and one of the most universally admired poems of our
century. I attempted a few enlightened reservations about
it in my book on Yeats, and provoked a great deal of
defensive abuse from reviewers and Yeats-idolators, a
reaction that helped instruct me further in the theory of
misprision as defensive troping. I am at least as skeptical
about *The Second Coming* now as I was earlier, but I think
I can elucidate my reservations rather more sharply, by
having recourse to my Kabbalistic map of misprision.

Take the poem's celebrated opening. I would say that
the first six lines require to be read as reaction-formation
or rhetorical irony, while the next two represent a turning against the self that is a despairing or masochistic

synecdoche. In the opening figuration, the center is man, unable as falconer to maintain a control over a "turning and turning" movement that he has trained. But a falconer is also every poet, and the falcon is his trope, and we can translate "turning and turning" as "troping and troping," so that the discipline of falconry represents not only a mastery of nature, but a mastery of language. This representation, either way, is breaking down, or rather falling and shattering outwards, and so the "ceremony of innocence" is indeed an élitist ritual, whether it be the aristocratic sport of falconry, or the poet's art in praise of aristocracy. Yeats, reacting with dismay to the excesses of the Russian Revolution, and with counterrevolutionary fervor and gladness to the excesses of the assault of the German *Freikorps* upon Russia, is saying one thing (falconry) while meaning another (poetry). His reaction-formation is the defense against anteriority (specifically against Shelley, as we will see) that masks his emotional exultation by a deceptive, only apparent emotional revulsion, a rhetorical irony that has been canonically misread as a literal statement. But Yeats is unified in his emotional and intellectual reaction to the Gnostic vision that dominates this poem. He welcomes the second birth of the Egyptian Sphinx both emotionally and intellectually, all canonical misreadings to the contrary.

Yet this opening *illusio* or rhetorical irony indeed limits or withdraws more meaning than it represents, which is why the opening images are so bewildered a dialectical interplay of presence and absence. Meaning has fled or wandered or, more likely, been driven out; the trope will not obey its master, anarchy itself is not significant, coherence is withdrawn, and the image of an élite, of a being chosen, without which poetry is not possible, is engulfed. Out of this flood of limitation, Yeats rescues a single trope of representation, a part/whole image wholly turned against the deepest desires of his own *antithetical* self or Gnostic *pneuma*. A self that worships passionate

intensity finds intensity manifested only by the rabble-
ment, while the best, the aristocrats of Britain, "lack all
conviction." The best gloss on this last phrase can be
found in Yeats's letters of that time, where he bitterly
accuses the British royal family of lacking the conviction
to avenge the murders of their blood-relations, the Czar's
family, recently executed by the Bolsheviks. The second
movement of the poem is lines 9–17, which itself divides
exactly in half with the full colon after "troubles my sight"
in line 13. Here is the poem's *kenosis,* its radical humbling
of its own meaning, by way of a metonymic displacement,
an emptying-out substitution of the Christian Second
Coming for the Gnostic Second Birth, not of the Anti-
christ, but of the mere Demiurge or god of the fallen
world:

> Surely some revelation is at hand;
> Surely the Second Coming is at hand.
> The Second Coming! Hardly are those words out
> When a vast image out of *Spiritus Mundi*
> Troubles my sight:

"Words" is the crucial word here, for Yeats "surely" is
showing us how unsure he is, the repetition of "surely"
betraying his yearning uncertainty. Having used the word
"revelation" he substitutes for it the Christian interpretation. Self-startled into repeating the words "The Second
Coming," he is confronted by a vast image out of a book
he himself has written, for *Spiritus Mundi* is identical with
Anima Mundi, the second part of *Per Amica Silentia Lunae,*
written just two years before. In *Anima Mundi,* following
the lead of the Cambridge Kabbalist and Neoplatonist,
Henry More, Yeats had spoken of images that came before the mind's eye, images out of the Great Memory.
Here, Yeats attains to one of those images through a
defensive act of *isolation,* which on the cognitive level
momentarily burns away the Gnostic context of Yeats's

visionary cosmos. This acute limitation of meaning is restituted as Yeats achieves his daemonic version of the
Sublime, in the truly uncanny passage of his poem:

> somewhere in sands of the desert
> A shape with lion body and the head of a man,
> A gaze blank and pitiless as the sun,
> Is moving its slow thighs, while all about it
> Reel shadows of the indignant desert birds.

I think that if we could answer the question: *what is
being repressed here?*, we would find ourselves better able to
clarify the Yeatsian Sublime. Let us divide our question,
for there are two parts to this repression: literary and
religious-sexual. Yeats is describing a male Sphinx, Egyptian rather than Greek, and in an earlier draft spoke of
"An eye blank and pitiless as the sun," meaning the one-
eyed Egyptian Sphinx associated with the sun-god. The
deepest literary repression here is of Shelley's famous
sonnet *Ozymandias,* which described the "colossal wreck"
of the tomb of Rameses II, a monument that was in the
shape of a male Sphinx. "A gaze blank and pitiless" goes
back to the "shattered visage" of Ozymandias, with its
"sneer of cold command" but particularly to the complex
phrase describing the sculptor's "hand that mocked"
Ozymandias, where "mocked" means both "represented"
and "disdained." Yeats does not mock *his* male Sphinx, in
either sense. His exultant welcome to the Sphinx is both
the sadistic consequence of his relative repression, even in
1919, of a really violent, overexuberant sexuality and,
more intensely, the return of his repressed Gnosticism,
repressed in respect to its real hostility both to nature and
to fallen human history. All of these aspects of repression
will return us to Yeats's notion of the Daimon, once we
have completed our mapping of the poem.

Here is the poem's third and final movement, five
climactic lines of which the first three are a revealingly

limiting metaphor, and the last two a powerful but confused and confusing attempt at a metaleptic reversal or
scheme of transumption:

> The darkness drops again; but now I know
> That twenty centuries of stony sleep
> Were vexed to nightmare by a rocking cradle,
> And what rough beast, its hour come round at last,
> Slouches towards Bethlehem to be born?

The "stony sleep" of the Sphinx associates him with the
"stony sleep" of Blake's Urizen in *The Book of Urizen*.
Those twenty "Christian" centuries can be taken as the
outside term in this metaphor; they represent nature, the
fallen object-world. The "rocking cradle" is the inside
term, standing for the subjective consciousness that is
aware of the Incarnation. Yeats says that his vision is
over, but that he has put on knowledge, if not power,
because he has seen and *known*. He has acquired a "knowing" which tells him that the *antithetical* influx is at hand,
and that the Christian age is over. This "knowing," like
other acts of knowledge in Yeats's poetry, is a sublimation, a condensation of a greater desire or dream, which
would be the Gnostic "knowing" in which Yeats as
"knower" would become one with the vision "known,"
here the antithetical beast. But every poetic sublimation is
an *askesis* or self-curtailment, or another limitation of
meaning. From this limitation Yeats recoils to his poem's
closing representation, which is a rhetorical rather than
an open question. The hour of the rough beast has come
round at last, and yet Yeats stands in no time at the
poem's close, while projecting the twenty Christian centuries and introjecting the *antithetical* age, where the
epiphany at Bethlehem will see the Second Birth of the
Sphinx.

We can read *The Second Coming* as a misprision of Shelley, or perhaps an assimilation of Shelley to Nietzsche,
and then of both to the Gnosis. Echoing throughout the

poem, but particularly in its synecdochal lines 7–8 ("The best lack all conviction, while the worst / Are full of passionate intensity") is the major Shelleyan synecdoche, the lament of the Last Fury in *Prometheus Unbound:*

> The good want power, but to weep barren tears.
> The powerful goodness want: worse need for them.
> The wise want love; and those who love want wisdom;
> And all best things are thus confused to ill.

The final form of this central Shelleyan insight is achieved, as Yeats knew, in *The Triumph of Life:*

> And much I grieved to think how power & will
> In opposition rule our mortal day—
>
> And why God made irreconcilable
> Good & the means of good, and for despair
> I half disdained mine eye's desire to fill
>
> With the spent vision of the times that were
> And scarce have ceased to be . . .

Nietzsche, in *Towards the Genealogy of Morals,* saw art as the *antithetical* opponent of what he had attacked as "the ascetic ideal" since it was art "in which precisely the *lie* is sanctified and the *will to deception* has a good conscience," and so art was much more fundamentally opposed to the ascetic ideal than was science. Yet Nietzsche saw the Romantic artist (Wagner in particular) as being corrupted by the ascetic ideal, and I suspect he would have agreed with Yeats that Shelley was so corrupted, since Shelley *did* try to give human suffering a meaning. What Nietzsche called the "ascetic ideal," Yeats called the *primary,* which he called also the "objective" and the "sentimental," the realm of the soul, and not of the Gnostic *pneuma* or *antithetical* self.

I would summarize this account of *The Second Coming* by saying that what the poem reveals is a successful,

Sublime repression of the Shelleyan influence, by way of a making daemonic or uncanny the characteristic patterning of the post-Wordsworthian crisis-lyric. But that returns me to this discussion's starting point; how can a Gnostic defense be understood from a more rational perspective, whether it be Freud's or belong to some other Western rationalism? If the beast of Yeats's vision in *The Second Coming* is an emanation from his Daimon, as it appears to be, then what is Yeats's relationship to his own vision? Who is making the poem, poet or Daimon?

On Freud's view, Yeats's vision is a partial or distorted Return of the Repressed, manifesting a repetition-compulsion, but that is too partial a view, covering only the poem's *kenosis* or metonymic reduction of itself through isolation, as we have seen. In Yeats the uncanny or repressed spills over into every major trope and into every major psychic defense. And this, I would argue, is the triumph of Yeats's Gnosticism, which is not only beyond Good and Evil (though not quite in the subtler sense that Nietzsche would have desired) but which has broken the bounds also of what Vico meant by Poetic Wisdom or Poetic Divination. Yeats, as a figure or mask *in his own poems,* is much closer to, say, Browning's Childe Roland than he is to Browning, or much closer to Tennyson's Tithonus or Percivale than he is to Tennyson. Following Nietzsche's notion of the Mask as well as Oscar Wilde's, Yeats is the Solitary or *antithetical* quester of his own poetry, and as such he seeks a god who is at once death and the aesthetic state that in *A Vision* is called Phase 15, which is a purely supernatural incarnation. He seeks, like the Error of Valentinus or of Nietzsche, to elaborate his own matter in the Void, but his highly personal swerve away even from Gnosticism allows him to regard the Void itself as being Sacred or daemonic, for does it not contain the splendor of his elaborations?

Let us consider another splendid elaboration in Yeats's

Sublime mode, *Byzantium.* I will begin with another exercise in misprision and its patterns, no doubt mine own as well as Yeats's, by tracing in *Byzantium* the shadows of revisionism. The poem's first stanza divides equally between *clinamen* and *tessera,* four lines of reaction-formation followed by four lines of reversal-into-the-opposite. The *kenosis* of a defensive undoing occupies the first six lines of the second stanza, and is then followed by a sudden mounting into the repressive Sublime of *daemonization,* with "I hail the superhuman," a movement that continues all through the third stanza. The fourth stanza, with its characteristic Romantic metaphor of fire doing the work of sublimation, is this poem's *askesis,* replaced in the fifth and final stanza by the transumptive *apophrades,* with its peculiar balance of introjection and projection defensively represented by the Yeatsian version of the chariot, which is a being borne by dolphins from life to death.

This is the poem's defensive pattern, and it follows the Romantic crisis-poem paradigm more closely even than *The Second Coming* does. I will not pursue this mapping into imagistic detail here, except to note that again it follows the traditional pattern closely, with the imagery of absence at the opening, and the synecdochal representation of "all that man is" reversed into the opposite of the "human form divine," as "the fury and the mire of human veins." The metonymic undoing follows, with the image of unwinding as a kind of emptying out, and the direct metonymies of mouth and breath replacing even the superhuman. The daemonic imagery of high and low is invoked in the third stanza, while the fourth opposes fire and spirits, as inside terms, to storm and dance, as outside ones, with the purgatorial fire refined or sublimated beyond physicality. In the final stanza, "bitter" becomes the equivalent of "late" while "fresh" equals transumptive "early." Our chart of evasions is demonstrated as proleptically accurate in regard to the image patterns of a poem that represses powerfully its very close indebtedness to Shelley and Blake.

I have not attempted a reading/misreading here, whether against the canonical misreadings or my own earlier account of this poem in my book on Yeats. One more misreading, however strong, of *Byzantium,* would be a redundancy; my quarry here is still what Freud called repression or the *unheimlich,* and Yeats the daemonic or the *antithetical,* and what literary tradition has called the Sublime. I want to approach this oxymoronic notion of poetic repression, or hyperbolical representation, through Freud's theory of "Negation," as set forth in his essay of that title, written in 1925, a decade after his essays on "Repression" and on "The Unconcious." I realize now that I employed the Freudian concept of Negation without being aware I was using it in my two books on misprision, particularly in my discussions of the revisionary ratio of *daemonization* or the belated strong poet's Counter-Sublime. In my struggle to understand Yeats's Gnostic Sublime, my repression of Freudian Negation seems to have been startled into a Negation of my own.

Freud defines *Verneinung* as a process in which the ego expresses a repressed thought or desire, but continues the defense of repression by disowning the thought or desire even as it is made overt. "Disowning" here is a kind of "disavowal" rather than a refutation. Negation then, in the Freudian rather than any philosophical sense, means that the repressed rises into cognition, and yet is still to be spoken of as "the repressed":

> Thus the subject-matter of a repressed image of thought can make its way into consciousness on condition that it is *denied* . . . Negation only assists in undoing *one* of the consequences of repression—namely, the fact that the subject-matter of the image in question is unable to enter consciousness. The result is

a kind of intellectual acceptance of what is repressed, though in all essentials the repression persists.

At the end of the essay on "Negation," Freud remarks that since we never discover a "No" in the unconscious, it is fitting that the ego's recognition of the unconscious should be expressed in a negative formula. Certainly we can relate Freud's conceptual insight to the negative element always present in the Romantic Sublime, that self-negation in loss, bewilderment, error, even in an approach to death, that always haunts the *unheimlich* or daemonic aspect of poetic sublimity. A Gnostic Sublime, we must now add, necessarily emphasizes this process of Negation, since both the Gnostic true God and the Gnostic *pneuma* or true, *antithetical* self are utterly alien to all natural or even cosmic imagery. Hence, the powerfully negative aura of the Gnostic Sublime in Yeats's *Byzantium*, where the superhuman is hailed equivocally as "death-in-life" and "life-in-death," respectively Phases 15 and 1 of *A Vision*, both of them phases where human incarnation is negated and so made impossible.

But where then have we taken the interpretation of Yeats's poem? Nowhere much, as yet, for this is still only a clearing of the ground. A poem is a triad, as I have said earlier, following the unlikely combination of Peirce and Proclus. As an idea of thirdness, *Byzantium* involves us in working out the relation of its own text to a composite precursor-text, and of both of these to each of us, who as a reader constitutes a third text. Yet only the overlay effect of our map is preparatory to criticism, for a closer look at the poem's availability to mapping will be a critical act proper. The use of a map is not only to find one's way and to chart the hidden roads that go from poem to poem, but also to train us to see what is truly *there* in the poem, yet might never have been observed if we had not seen it first flatted out upon a necessarily somewhat distorting surface.

The first critical insight that our mapping gives us into *Byzantium* is that this is, intensely, a High Romantic crisis-lyric, a Wordsworthian poem despite all its *antithetical* yearnings; indeed this is a kind of Yeatsian *Intimations Ode*. The biographical facts support such a characterization, since they tell us that Yeats was recovering from a severe illness, at the age of sixty-five, and that by his own account he was attempting to warm himself back into life, through writing this poem. In a clear sense, *Byzantium* is an elegy for the poetic self, and though Yeats was to live for nine more years, he did not know that when he wrote the poem. The poet has a prolepsis of his own death, or rather he achieves a representation of such a prolepsis, by describing a vision of catastrophe-creation, of the Gnostic sort, but confined here to the creation of images, and not of worlds.

The first major representation of the poem is "a starlit or a moonlit dome" that the original publication of the text said "distains / All that man is," not "disdains." In Yeats's Anglo-Irish pronunciation, he would not have distinguished between "distains" and "disdains," but "distains," which means "outshines," appears to have been his original intention, and so "disdains," in his pronunciation, may be taken as meaning both "mocks" and "outshines." "Distains" carries also the memory of Shelley's comparison of life to a dome of many-colored glass, that *stains* the white radiance of eternity. Whereas Shelley's "stains" is a paradox, meaning both "defiles" and "colors," Yeats's "distains" or "disdains" has only negative meaning.

Yeats said repeatedly of the Daimon that it was both the poet's muse and the poet's enemy, an ambivalence that reflects the original meaning of the Daimon in Yeats's work: an "illustrious dead man," the precursor. In *Byzantium*, Yeats-as-Dante, or as the Shelley of *The Triumph of Life*, confronts his Virgil or Rousseau, his guide to the afterlife, as the Daimon: "Shade more than man, more image than a shade." But an image of the precursor, the "numinous shadow" of an ancestor-god, as

Nietzsche called it, can be far more powerful than the precursor himself. Three entities are called "images" in the poem. There are natural images or the *primary*; these, being unpurged, recede as the poem opens. There is the image of the daemonic precursor; its status is ambiguous, and Yeats cannot tell us whether it belongs to Phase 15, complete beauty and "death-in-life," or Phase 1, complete plasticity and "life-in-death." That means Yeats cannot say whether the daemonic image is perfect form, or mere formlessness. That leaves the "bitter furies of complexity," which at the poem's close are broken apart, as in the Gnostic and Kabbalistic breaking-of-the-vessels, and so become images that beget fresh images, catastrophes that are also creations. But here, too, Yeats is equivocal, as he was about previously named "images" in the poem. Syntactically, the last three lines stand alone, even though grammatically all three are governed by the verb "break." This gives a curious rhetorical edge to the three final lines, hinting an autonomy both to "those images" and to "that sea" which the dancing floor actually does not surrender to them.

I suggest that this ambiguity about the status of the "image" in the poem *Byzantium* is a product of what Freud calls "negation," that is, of the daemonic repressed which is revealed and disavowed simultaneously. Yeats, as an authentic strong poet, achieves a belated Sublime at a rather heavy cost. *Byzantium* is a poem about Gnostic salvation or transcendence, which is achieved by an act of *knowing*, but such knowing involves a descent and a loss. We can juxtapose to the close of *Byzantium* a passage from the Valentinian *Gospel of Truth*, which Yeats could not have read, though he had read other Valentinian texts in A. E. Waite's compilation, *The Hermetic Museum*. The advent of salvation or transcendence is necessarily catastrophic in a Gnostic vision:

When the Word appeared, the Word which is in the hearts of those who pronounce It—and It was not only a sound, but It

had taken on a body as well—a great confusion reigned among
the vessels, for some had been emptied, others filled; some
were provided for, others were overthrown; some were sanctified, still others were broken to pieces. All the spaces were
shaken, and confused, for they had no fixity nor stability.
"Error" was agitated, not knowing what it should do. It was
afflicted, and lamented and worried because it knew nothing.
Since the Gnosis, which is the perdition of "Error" and all its
Emanations, approached it, "Error" became empty, there being
nothing more in it.

In an ancient Gnostic text such as this we frequently
miss the Sublime, even when we encounter a doctrine of
transcendence. There are strong passages in the Valentinian *Gospel of Truth*, but this is a weak one, since all
Gnostic texts, out of the ancient world, become rhetorically weaker or more blurred when they speak of salvation, as opposed to when they speak of disaster, of the
Creation-Fall. Yeats was not so much a doctrinal Gnostic,
however eclectic, as he was a naturally Gnostic artist
whose consciously belated situation adapted itself
efficiently to the employment of Gnostic hypostases and
images. His immense advantage, in poems like *The Second
Coming* or *Byzantium*, over ancient Gnostic texts, is not
only the advantage of poetry over the spilled poetry that
is doctrine, however heterodox, but is also the peculiar
strength wrested by him out of his struggle with Romantic tradition. But again, I find myself circling back to the
defensive process of poetic repression, and to Yeats's var-
iations upon the Sublime mode.
   I would choose, as Yeats's finest achievement in the
Sublime, his death-poem, *Cuchulain Comforted*, A Dan-
tesque vision of judgment that is Yeats's condensed equivalent of *The Fall of Hyperion* and *The Triumph of Life*. The
prose draft of this poem identifies the shades as being of
three kinds, all cowards: "Some of us have been put to
death as cowards, but others have hidden, and some even

died without people knowing they were cowards...."
When Yeats versified the poem, he omitted this last
group, thus giving us a hint as to a repressed element in
this last daemonic Sublime of his life.

The poem's beautiful last line is its *apophrades,* echoing
Dante's Brunetto Latini, who is described as being among
the victorious, though justly placed among the damned in
the Inferno. As I have shown in my book on Yeats, the
poem places itself rather precisely, in terms of *A Vision's*
systematic mapping-out of the phases of the life-after-
death. The shades have passed through what Yeats calls
the *Meditation,* and have purged themselves of everything
in their past incarnations except their sense of cowardice.
They are at the very end of the state Yeats names as the
Shiftings, until in the poem's last line they pass out of the
Shiftings and enter into the state of *Beatitude.* Cuchulain,
type of the hero, "a man / Violent and famous," is a stage
behind them, and so needs to be instructed by them, in
an heroic irony on Yeats's part that is much more a
figure-of-thought than a figure-of-speech. Cuchulain, at
the poem's start, is passing out of the *Phantasmagoria,* the
third and last stage of the *Meditation,* and has entered the
Shiftings as soon as he accepts instruction, takes up a
needle, and begins to sew the shroud that marks his
acceptance of passing-over into his antithesis, the world in
which heroism and cowardice blend together as one
communal ecstasy.

I think it palpable that *Cuchulain Comforted* is a much
better poem than *The Second Coming* and *Byzantium,* for it
seems wholly coherent and they do not, but I think also
that its majestic, chastened Sublimity is necessarily the
consequence of a completer repression than the earlier
poems indicate, and moreover a repression in which
there is less disavowal or negation. The mystery of *Cuchulain Comforted* is concealed in the implications of its view
of the afterlife, where what appears to matter is not at all
how you behaved in your last incarnation, but what you

know, as the leader of the shades says, implying strongly
that this knowledge is only attained in the afterlife. Certainly this is Gnosis again, though of a peculiarly original
sort, firmly based upon Yeats's own mythology of death
as worked out in Book III, *The Soul in Judgment,* of *A
Vision.*

Gnostic eschatology, particularly of the Valentinian
sect, is close to Yeatsian eschatology in its larger outlines,
though certainly not in any detail. A good motto to
Cuchulain Comforted would be the best-known Valentinian
formula of salvation, significant for its differences as well
as its similarities to the poem:

> What liberates is the knowledge of who we were, what we
> became; where we were, whereunto we have been thrown;
> whereto we speed, wherefrom we are redeemed; what birth is,
> and what rebirth.

"Equipped with this *gnosis,*" Hans Jonas observes, "the
soul after death travels upwards, leaving behind at each
sphere the psychical 'vestment' contributed by it." As in
Yeats's System, this journey of the *pneuma* has no relation
whatsoever to moral conduct in the fallen world, for
Yeats and the Gnostics share the same antinomianism.
Since Yeats's theoretical human values were always of a
kind that made him abstractly welcome Fascist violence,
whenever it became available for his approval, we need
not be surprised that his self-punishment, in his purgatorial death-poem, involves a leveling equation of what he
believed to be the highest virtue, heroism, with its antithesis in shameful cowardice. We encounter here a repetition of the closing vision of Browning's *Childe Roland,*
where Roland, like Cuchulain the hero, is blent with his
opposites, the band of brothers who were cowards or
traitors, into one Condition of Fire. There is both a repression and a self-recognition that Browning and Yeats
share, and to this sharing I will devote the rest of this
chapter.

I will center on two phrases, one spoken by the "Shroud that seemed to have authority" in Yeats's poem, and the other by Roland. "Mainly because of what we only *know* / The rattle of those arms makes us afraid," says the Shroud, while Roland cries out, magnificently, "in a sheet of flame / I saw them and I *knew* them all." Both knowings are Gnostic, in that they transcend natural knowing or rational knowing, and also in that the knower becomes one with the known, and that which becomes known is uncanny, daemonic. The Shrouds, in the terms of Yeats's *A Vision*, know what Cuchulain yet must learn, that all must be born again, and they will not cease to fear the hero until they are in the Beatitude. More deeply, they know what Yeats had learned by reading Nietzsche: that all must *recur* again. After their communal ecstasy, they must be reborn as solitary souls, and be cowards again, just as Cuchulain, after his communal ecstasy, must be a hero again. By hinting at this Nietzchean vision, and by implying his own acceptance of it, Yeats indicates the limits of his Gnosticism, for the Eternal Recurrence, however we take it, is hardly a Gnostic ideal. Roland, seeing *all* his precursors, and *knowing* them all, can be said to transcend his own earlier, pragmatic gnosticism that dominated his poem until its climax. Yeats, obliquely, attains to a similar self-recognition at the end. I want to conclude by noting this self-recognition, and by indicating its relationship to a repressive Sublime.

In his *Mixed Opinions and Maxims* (1879), Nietzsche utilized one of the central tropes of the repressive Sublime, the descent to Hades, as a vision of self-recognition in regard to the precursors:

—I, too, have been in the underworld, like Odysseus, and shall be there often yet; and not only rams have I sacrificed to be able to speak with a few of the dead, but I have not spared my own blood. Four pairs it was that did not deny themselves to my sacrifice: Epicurus and Montaigne, Goethe and Spinoza,

Plato and Rousseau, Pascal and Schopenhauer. With these I
must come to terms when I have long wandered alone; they
may call me right and wrong; to them will I listen when in the
process they call each other right and wrong. Whatsoever I say,
resolve, or think up for myself and others—on these eight I fix
my eyes and see their eyes fixed on me.

This fixation of eyes is akin to the primal fixation that
Freud finds at the origins of all repression. Repression, in
Freud, is too rich and varied a concept to be subsumed by
any formula or definition. Indeed, Freudian "repression"
is an astonishing array of possibly incompatible theories,
whereas Freudian "sublimation" is by comparison an un-
derdeveloped and intellectually unsatisfactory notion. I
find useful enough Paul Ricoeur's summary of primal
repression, as meaning "that we are always in the
mediate, in the already expressed, the already said," for
this is the traumatic predicament that results in what I
have termed "the anxiety of influence," the awareness
.that what might be called, analogically, the infantile needs
of the beginning imagination had to be met by the primal
fixation of a Scene of Instruction. Nietzsche, hyperboli-
cally descending to the dead, confronts just such a Scene,
as do Cuchulain and Roland in their purgatorial ordeals.
    I intend to give a fuller account of the problematics
both of Freudian repression, and the poetic analogue of a
repressive Sublime, in my next chapter, when I compare
the even more repressive American Sublime of Emerson
and Whitman to its English precursor in Wordsworth and
his descendants. Here I want to attempt to find the
analogical formula that can give criteria to the degrees of
repression in various instances of a poetic Sublime. In
Freud, the criterion for determining the degree of repression depends upon the extent of estrangement and
distortion that the unconscious displays in its derivative
forms, such as dreams and errors, and also upon the
malformings of repressed instincts in various defensive

maskings. Analogically, we can say that the degree of repression in one poem, as opposed to another, can be judged by a comparison of estrangement, distortion, and malforming, in tropes and images. The formula may well be that catachresis, or abuse of all figurations, attends really intense poetic repression, so that images, in consequence, become not only more grotesque where repression is augmented, but also more outlandishly hyperbolical as depictions of elevated or quasi-divine states of mind or of being. This means, in Freudian terms, that resistance or defense is truly being turned against inward dangers, indeed against dangers that result from an *exaggerated inwardness*. Precursors, as I have remarked in many contexts, become absorbed into the poetic equivalent of the id, and not of the superego. Poems by Shelley are, for Browning and for Yeats, the equivalent of impulses, rather than of events. When such poems are repressed, then negation or disavowal can play little part in the repression, because that would mean mythicizing renunciation or negation, and so coming to worship Ananke or Necessity as one's poetic Word or *davhar*, which would be a terrible worship for a poet who wishes to continue as a poet. Emerson came to such a worship, but ended as a poet, partly in consequence; Whitman repeated this Emersonian pattern, as did Thoreau, and I think Frost. Dickinson and Stevens are very nearly unique in having made such worship the staple of much of their best work, without suffering irreparable poetic loss.

How do Browning and Yeats compare upon our scale of poetic repression, that is, in the catachreses and grotesqueries and hyperbolical visions that we have judged to characterize an even more repressed Sublime? Though Browning is reputed to be primarily a poet of the Grotesque, and Yeats has little such reputation, they will be found to be very nearly equal in the figurations of an acute primal repressiveness. Both turned to dramatizations of the self, Browning in monologues and Yeats in

lyrics and lyrical plays, in order to evade the prime precursor's romances of the self, but the death-drive of
poems like *Alastor* and *Adonais* was detoured by them only
in part. Browning repressed his memories of the kind of
cowardice he had shown in his early confrontation with
his mother and, through her, with the supernaturalist
strictures of Evangelicalism. But the figurations produced
by this poetic repression were the catachreses of self-
ruining, of all those failed questers of whom Roland is the
most Sublime. Yeats's repressed cowardice is more mysterious, biographically speaking, and we will need unau-
thorized biographies before we know enough about it to
understand how it came to undergo the magnificent distortions and haunting estrangements of his greatest
poems. We can see, now, that his Gnostic tendencies
aided Yeats by giving him a wider context in a traditional
ontology, however heterodox, for his own *antithetical*
longings, since the Yeatsian *antithetical,* like the Nietzschean, can be defined as the ultimate resistance against the
almost irresistible force of a primal repression, or as a
fixation upon precursors whose integrity was finally a
little too terrifying. Shelley and Schopenhauer were questers, in their very different ways, who could journey
through the Void without yielding to the temptation of
worshiping the Void as itself being sacred. Yeats, like
Nietzsche, implicitly decided that he too would rather
have the Void as purpose, than be void of purpose.

9

Emerson and Whitman: The American Sublime

> *Parable*—Those thinkers in whom all stars move in cyclic orbits are not the most profound: whoever looks into himself as into vast space and carries galaxies in himself also knows how irregular all galaxies are; they lead into the chaos and labyrinth of existence.
>
> NIETZSCHE

What is the American Sublime, and how does it differ from its European precursor? When Emerson set out to define *The American Scholar*, in 1837, he began with "the old fable" of One Man, taking this vision of a primordial being from Plutarch's Platonizing essay on "Brotherly Love." Characteristically, Emerson saw the division and fall of man as a reification and as an undoing by the trope of metonymy:

> Man is thus metamorphosed into a thing, into many things. The planter, who is Man sent out into the field to gather food, is seldom cheered by any idea of the true dignity of his ministry. He sees his bushel and his cart, and nothing beyond, and sinks into the farmer, instead of Man on the farm. The tradesman scarcely ever gives an ideal worth to his work, but is ridden by the routine of his craft, and the soul is subject to dollars. The priest becomes a form; the attorney a statute-book; the mechanic a machine; the sailor a rope of the ship.

Parallel to these metonymic reductions is the undoing of the scholar as "the delegated intellect" whereas: "In the right state he is *Man Thinking*." To account for the scholar's fall, Emerson first considers the scholar as a problem in influence. The main influences directed upon the scholar—who for Emerson, as for Stevens, comprises also the poet—are (1) Nature, (2) Books, (3) Action. But Nature is revealed to be only the print of the scholar's seal. As for Books: "One must be an inventor to read well." Finally, Action turns out to be "instinct," the world of will and drive. The three precursors of the scholar thus fade away, leaving "self-trust," freedom or wildness. His ground cleared, Emerson attains to the center of his oration: "It is a mischievous notion that we are come late into nature; that the world was finished a long time ago." The wild or free notion is that: "This time, like all times, is a very good one, if we but know what to do with it." From this follows the prophecy that made possible the drastic grandeur of the American Sublime: "A nation of men will for the first time exist, because each believes himself inspired by the Divine Soul which also inspires all men."

Emerson delivered *The American Scholar: An Oration,* at Harvard on August 31, 1837. A few months before, in the spring of 1837, there was a business crash, banks suspended nearly all payments, and a general economic depression dominated society. It is noteworthy, and has been noted, that Emerson's two great outbursts of prophetic vocation coincide with two national moral crises, the Depression of 1837 and the Mexican War of 1846, which Emerson, as an Abolitionist, bitterly opposed. The origins of the American Sublime are connected inextricably to the business collapse of 1837. I want to illustrate this connection by a close reading of relevant entries in Emerson's Journals of 1837, so as to be able to ask and perhaps answer the invariable question that antithetical criticism learns always to ask of each fresh instance of the Sublime. *What is being freshly repressed?* What has been forgotten, on purpose, in the depths, so as to make possible this sudden elevation to the heights? Here is the seer, apparently stimulated to an ascent, by a meditation upon a business depression:

Behold the boasted world has come to nothing. Prudence itself is at her wits' end. Pride, and Thrift, and Expediency, who jeered and chirped and were so well pleased with themselves, and made merry with the dream, as they termed it, of Philosophy and Love,—behold they are all flat, and here is the Soul erect and unconquered still. What answer is it now to say, It has always been so? I acknowledge that, as far back as I can see the widening procession of humanity, the marchers are lame and blind and deaf; but to the soul that whole past is but one finite series in its infinite scope. Deteriorating ever and now desperate. Let me begin anew. Let me teach the finite to know its master. Let me ascend above my fate and work down upon my world.

The Yankee virtues, as internalized by Emerson himself, no longer triumph over the Transcendental vision, which indeed now turns transumptive, projecting all the past as a lame, blind, deaf march, and introjecting a Sublime future, mounted over fate, the finite, the cosmos. What Emerson represses is *Ananke,* the Fate he has learned already to call "compensation." His vision of repetition is a metonymic reduction, an undoing of all other selves, and his restituting *daemonization* renders him solipsistic and free. That a poetic repression brings about the Sublime wildness of freedom is almost the most Emersonian of all Emersonian rhetorical paradoxes, and one that he himself carried to its apocalypse eventually in the grand death-march of the essay *Fate,* in *The Conduct of Life:*

But Fate against Fate is only parrying and defence: there are also the noble creative forces. The revelation of Thought takes man out of servitude into freedom. We rightly say of ourselves, we were born again, and many times. We have successive experiences so important that the new forgets the old, and hence the mythology of the seven or the nine heavens. The day of days, the great day of the feast of life, is that in which the inward eye opens to the Unity in things, to the omnipresence of law:—sees that what is must be and ought to be, or is the best. This beatitude dips from on high down on us and we see. It is not in us so much as we are in it. If the air come to our lungs, we breathe and live; if not, we die. If the light come to our eyes, we see; else not. And if truth come to our mind we suddenly expand to its dimensions, as if we grew to worlds. We are as lawgivers; we speak for Nature; we prophesy and divine.

I want to defer comment on this magnificent instance of the American Sublime by first comparing Emerson, as a moral theorist of interpretation, to Freud and to St. Augustine. Augustine, as Peter Brown says, parallels Freud by speaking of a "Fall" in consciousness:

> Augustine . . . produced a singularly comprehensive explanation of why allegory should have been necessary in the first place. The need for such a language of 'signs' was the result of a specific dislocation of the human consciousness. In this, Augustine takes up a position analogous to that of Freud. In dreams also, a powerful and direct message is said to be deliberately diffracted by some psychic mechanism, into a multiplicity of 'signs' quite as intricate and absurd, yet just as capable of interpretation, as the 'absurd' or 'obscure' passages in the Bible. Both men, therefore, assume that the proliferation of images is due to some precise event, to the development of some geological fault across a hitherto undivided consciousness: for Freud, it is the creation of an unconscious by repression; for Augustine, it is the outcome of the Fall.

Augustine's vision of the Fall, as Brown also shows, had changed from an early, quasi-Plotinian belief, which was that Adam and Eve had "fallen" into physicality: "that the prolific virtues they would have engendered in a purely 'spiritual' existence had declined, with the Fall, into the

mere literal flesh and blood of human families." In the
mature Augustinian doctrine, the dualizing split in human
consciousness is no technical descent to a lower degree of
being, but is the most wilful and terrible of catastrophes.
How does this compare with catastrophe theory in Freud,
and in Emerson? Do all three doctors-of-the-soul, Augustine, Emerson, and Freud agree fundamentally that consciousness, as we know it, cannot inaugurate itself without a catastrophe? The Christian Augustine and the
Empedoclean-Schopenhauerian Freud do not surprise us
in this regard, but why should the Idealizing quasi-
Neoplatonist Emerson insist upon catastrophe as the invariable inaugural act for consciousness?

Here is Emerson's equivalent of the Augustinian or psychoanalytic division into consciousness, from his greatest
essay, *Experience:*

> It is very unhappy, but too late to be helped, the discovery we
> have made that we exist. That discovery is called the Fall of Man.
> Ever afterwards we suspect our instruments. We have learned
> that we do not see directly, but mediately, and that we have no
> means of correcting these colored and distorting lenses which we
> are, or of computing the amount of their errors. Perhaps these
> subject-lenses have a creative power; perhaps there are no ob-
> jects. Once we lived in what we saw; now, the rapaciousness of this
> new power, which threatens to absorb all things, engages us.

This is surely the authentic vision of the daemonic in
Emerson, the apocalyptic frenzy of an American Sublime.
The mystery of this passage, as of the other rhapsodies I
have quoted from Emerson, is in the paradox of repression, of the power brought into being by an enormous
fresh influx of repression. More even than the British
Romantic Sublime, Emerson's American Sublime exposes
what I am tempted to call the deep structure of rhetoric,
by which I mean the defensive nature of rhetoric. I oppose myself here not only to what passes for "Freudian
literary criticism" but to the much more formidable "de-

constructive" literary criticism in which de Man and Derrida follow Rousseau and Nietzsche. De Man, analyzing Nietzsche, concludes that between rhetoric as a system of tropes and rhetoric as persuasion there is an *aporia*, a limit or doubt that cannot be defined. I venture an analysis now of this *aporia*, for what relates one trope to another in a systematic way, and carries each trope from evasion to persuasion, is that trope's function as defense, its imagistic maskings of those detours to death that make up the highway map of the psyche, the drives from anterior fixations to entropic self-destructions.

Emerson followed Vico in declining to confuse meaning with signification, a confusion still evident even in the most advanced models of post-Structuralist thought. For Emerson, meaning is concerned with survival, and signification is only an instrumentality of meaning, this being a distinction in which Peirce followed Emerson. What holds together rhetoric as a system of tropes, and rhetoric as persuasion, is the necessity of defense, defense against everything that threatens survival, and a defense whose aptest name is "meaning." Vico named poetic defense as "divination," which in our vocabulary translates best as "over-determination of meaning." But here I must allow myself a digression into theory-of-misprision.

The poetic defense of repression is always a ratio of representation (the Lurianic *tikkun* or restitution) because in poetic repression *you forget something in order to present something else.* Whereas, poetic sublimation is always a ratio of limitation (*zimzum* or contraction) because by it *you remember something (concentrate it) in order to avoid presenting that something, and you choose to present something else in its place.* Substitution or breaking-of-the-vessels between poetic repression and poetic sublimation is a transformation from the unconscious to consciousness just as the movement from poetic sublimation to poetic introjection or projection restores or returns representations to the unconscious. Tropes, defenses, images, ratios of limitation withdraw representations from the unconscious without replenishing the unconscious, while the counter-movements of representation restitute the unconscious. When Emerson experiences and describes his influxes of the American Sublime, he is at work creating the great trope of the specifically American Unconscious, or what he himself in *Self-Reliance* calls "Spontaneity or Instinct":

The magnetism which all original action exerts is explained when we inquire the reason of self-trust. Who is the Trustee? What is the aboriginal Self, on which a universal reliance may be grounded? What is the nature and power of that science-baffling star, without parallax, without calculable elements, which shoots a ray of beauty even into trivial and impure actions, if the least mark of independence appear? The inquiry leads us to that source, at once the essence of genius, of virtue, and of life, which we call Spontaneity or Instinct. We denote this primary wisdom as Intuition, whilst all later teachings are tuitions. In that deep force, the last fact behind which analysis cannot go, all things find their common origin.

How does the Freudian Unconscious contrast with this Emersonian American Sublime? Freud's concept of the unconscious was first obtained from his theory of repression, and was intended to explain *discontinuities* in the psychic life of every individual. But these were active discontinuities, so that Freud's notion of the unconscious rapidly became a dynamic conception, and not merely a descriptive one. Ideas had been repressed and then continued to be shut out from consciousness, by an ongoing process of repression. Unconscious ideas that could break back through into consciousness, Freud referred to as "preconscious" and distinguished sharply from repressions that could never return, which constituted the unconscious proper. These latter repressions, according to Freud, are ideas and not affects. If they *seem* affects, then they are "potential beginnings which are preventing *by* developing." Yet even these permanently repressed ideas do not make up the whole of the Freudian unconscious. Mysteriously, there is an original unconscious; indeed Freud finally thought that the mind originally was totally unconscious, and that gradually part of the mind became preconscious and part conscious, with yet another part always remaining unconscious. To this unrepressed unconscious, the augmenting ego added materials through fresh repressions.

Emerson's version of the unconscious is a purer instance of poetic or hyperbolical repression. Whatever one may want to say about the structure of the Freudian unconscious (and I do *not* believe it is structured like a language), I think that Emersonian "Spontaneity or Instinct" *is* structured like a rhetoric, that is, is both a system of tropes and also a mode of persuasion. Like Freud's unconscious, it is originary, and again like Freud's giant trope, it is augmented by fresh and purposeful forgettings, by evasions that are performed in order to present something other than the something that is being evaded. But, in Freud, the something evaded is any drive objectionable to ego-ideals, whereas in Emerson the something must take the name of a single drive, the thrust of anteriority, the mystifying strength of the past, which is profoundly objectionable to Emerson's prime ego-ideal, Self-Reliance. Emerson's pugnacity on this theme is in the Optative Mood; as he says: "When we have new perception, we shall gladly disburden the memory of its hoarded treasures as old rubbish." As for what became Nietzsche's "guilt of indebtedness," which is so profoundly analyzed in *Towards the Genealogy of Morals*, Emerson dismisses it with a Sublime shrug, a shrug directed against Coleridge: "In the hour of vision there is nothing that can be called gratitude, or properly joy."

With so daemonic an unconscious as his support, Emerson cheerfully places the spirit wholly in the category that Kierkegaard called only "the aesthetic." I turn again to "The Rotation Method" in *Either* of *Either/Or*, so as to illuminate Emerson's kind of repression:

Forgetting is the shears with which you cut away what you cannot use, doing it under the supreme direction of memory. Forgetting and remembering are thus identical arts, and the artistic achievement of this identity is the Archimedean point from which one lifts the whole world. When we say that we *consign* something to oblivion, we suggest simultaneously that it is to be forgotten and yet also remembered.

Kierkegaard is playing upon his own notion of "repetition," which is his revision of the Hegelian "mediation" into a Christian conception "of the anxious freedom." Emerson's Transcendental equivalent is his famous declaration in the Journal for April 1842: "I am *Defeated* all the time; yet to Victory I am born." Less than a year later, Kierkegaard wrote: "The difficulty facing an existing individual is how to give his existence the continuity without which everything simply vanishes. . . . The goal of movement for an existing individual is to arrive at a decision, and to renew it." I think we can remark on this that Kierkegaard does not want us to be able to distinguish between the desire for repetition, and repetition itself, since it is in the blending of the two that the "anxious freedom" of "becoming a Christian" truly consists. But Emerson was post-Christian; for him that "Great Defeat" belonged totally to the past. What Kierkegaard called "repetition" Emerson called by an endless variety of names until he settled on Fate or Necessity, and he insisted always that we had to distinguish between our desire for such reality, and the reality itself. In the grand passage from the essay *Fate* that I quoted earlier, the emphasis is sublimely upon what Emerson calls successive rebirths, while meaning successive re-begettings of ourselves, during this, our one life. Perpetually, Emerson insists, our new experience forgets the old, so that perhaps

Nietzsche should have remarked of Emerson, not that he
did not know how old he was already or how young he
still was going to be, but only that Emerson did know that
always he was about to become his own father. This, I
now assert, is the distinguishing mark of the specifically
American Sublime, that it begins anew not with restoration or rebirth, in the radically displaced Protestant pattern of the Wordsworthian Sublime, but that it is truly
past even such displacement, despite the line from Ed-
wards to Emerson that scholarship accurately continues to
trace. Not merely rebirth, but the even more hyperbolical
trope of self-rebegetting, is the starting point of the last
Western Sublime, the great sunset of selfhood in the
Evening Land.

But what does this hyperbolical figuration mean, or
rather, how are we to transform its signification into
meaning? We all of us go home each evening, and at
some moment in time, with whatever degree of overt
consciousness, we go back over all the signs that the day
presented to us. In those signs, we seek only what can aid
the continuity of our own discourse, the survival of those
ongoing qualities that will give what is vital in us even
more life. This seeking is the Vichian and Emersonian
making of signification into meaning, by the single test of
aiding our survival. By such a test, the American Sublime
is a trope *intending* to forget the father in order to present
the son or daughter. In this trope, the father is a limitation or what Stevens called a reduction to a First Idea, an
idea of an origin, and the son or daughter intends to be a
restituting representation in which a First Idea is re-
imagined, so as to become the idea of an aim. But what is
a First Idea, unless it be what Freud termed a primal
fixation or an initial repression? And what did that initial
repression forget, or at least intend to forget? Here
Freud touched his *aporia,* and so I turn beyond him to
Kabbalah again, to seek a more ultimate paradigm for the
Scene of Instruction than even Kierkegaard affords me,

since here too Kierkegaard touched his *aporia,* and accepted the Christian limit of the Incarnation. The Orphic Emerson demands an ultimate paradigm which is beyond the pleasure-principle, yet also beyond these competing reality-principles.

Lacan, in his revision of Freud, tells us that the ego is essentially paranoid, that it is a structure founded upon a contradictory or double-bind relationship between a self and an other, or relationship that is at once an opposition and an identity. I reject this as interpretation of Freud, and reject it also as an observation upon the psyche. But Lacan, as I remarked in another context, joins himself to those greater theorists, including Nietzsche and Freud, who talk about people in ways that are more valid even for poems. I do not think that the psyche is a text, but I find it illuminating to discuss texts as though they were psyches, and in doing so I consciously follow the Kabbalists. For, in poems, I take it that the other is always a person, the precursor, however imagined or composite, whereas for Lacan the other is principle, and not person.

The fourth of the six *behinot* or aspects of each *sefirah,* according to Moses Cordovero, is the aspect of a particular *sefirah* that allows the *sefirah* above it to give that particular *sefirah* the strength enabling it, the later *sefirah,* to emanate out further *sefirot.* Or to state it more simply, yet still by a Kabbalistic trope, *it is from a son that a father takes the power, that in turn will enable the son to become a father.* This hyperbolical figuration is a rather complex theory of repression, because the son or later poem initially needs to forget the autonomy of its own power in order to express any *continuity* of power. But this is very close also to the peculiar nature of Sublime representation, where there is an implication always that what is being represented is somehow absent, and so must be restituted by an image. But the image, which in Sublime representation tends to be of a fathering force, as it were, remains distinct from what it represents, at least in the

Continental and British Sublime. This is where I would
locate the *difference* in the Emersonian or American Sublime, which is closer to the Kabbalistic model of Cordovero in its reversal between the roles of the fathering force
and the new self of the son, that is, of the later or belated
poem. In Emerson and in his progeny from Whitman,
Thoreau, Dickinson on through Hart Crane, Stevens, and
our contemporaries, the fathering force and the poetic
self tend to merge together, but the aim of self-presentation
is not defeated, because the fathering force or representative tends to disappear into the poetic self or son, rather
than the self into the image of the fathering force.

I turn to *The Divinity School Address* for a proof-text
here, and offer an Emerson cento of the American Sublime from it:

> That is always best which gives me to myself. The sublime is
> excited in me by the great stoical doctrine, Obey thyself. That
> which shows God in me, fortifies me. That which shows God
> out of me, makes me a wart and a wen. . . .
> Wherever a man comes, there comes revolution. The old is
> for slaves. When a man comes, all books are legible, all things
> transparent, all religions are forms. . . .
> Let me admonish you, first of all, to go alone; to refuse the
> good models. . . .
> I look for the hour when that supreme Beauty which
> ravished the souls of those Eastern men, and chiefly of those
> Hebrews, and through their lips spoke oracles to all time, shall
> speak in the West also. . . . I look for the new Teacher that shall
> follow so far those shining laws that he shall see them come full
> circle. . . .

There are the two central Emersonian images of the
Sublime: "all things transparent" and the Central Man
who shall see the transparency and thus see also the laws
of reality "come full circle." That transparency, to appear
again in Whitman and in Stevens, can be interpreted two
ways, transumptively or reductively. The second would

relate it to Anna Freud's observation, in *The Ego and the Mechanisms of Defense,* that: "The obscurity of a successful repression is only equalled by the transparency of the repressive process when the movement is reversed." The first would relate it to the Hebrew idea of God as avoiding the Greek notions either of immanence or of transcendence. Thorlief Boman, in his *Hebrew Thought Compared with Greek,* shows that the Hebraic image of transparency, as a trope for God, sees the Divine as being neither *in* the world nor *over* the world, but rather *through* the world, not spatially but discontinuously. Let us allow both meanings, this Hebraic transumption and the Freudian reduction, and combine both with Emerson's bringing-forth a father-god out of himself, even as we examine again the two most famous of all American Sublime passages, the epiphanies in the first and last chapters of Emerson's *Nature:*

I become a transparent eyeball; I am nothing; I see all; the currents of the Universal Being circulate through me; I am part or parcel of God.

The problem of restoring to the world original and eternal beauty is solved by the redemption of the soul. The ruin or the blank that we see when we look at nature, is in our own eye. The axis of vision is not coincident with the axis of things, and so they appear not transparent but opaque.

Reductively, the first passage represents a partial return of the repressed, while the second appears to be what Anna Freud calls "the obscurity of a successful repression." But transumptively, the first passage records a successful repression, and the second the failed perspectivism of sublimation. The Emersonian repressiveness attains to a discontinuity with everything that is anterior, and in doing so it accomplishes or prepares for a reversal in which the self is forgotten ("I am nothing") and yet through seeing introjects the fathering force of anteriority. By seeing the

transparency, the poet of the American Sublime *contains* the
father-god, and so augments the poetic self even as he
remembers to forget that self. Wordsworth celebrated the
continuities of hearing, and dreaded the discontinuities of
seeing. Emerson, in the defensive discontinuities of seeing,
found a path to a more drastic, immediate, and total Sublime than European tradition wished or needed to discover.
His greatest disciple, Whitman, an American bard at last,
illustrates better than his master, the seer, both the splendor
and the disaster of so aboriginal a repression.

My proof-text in Whitman is inevitably *Song of Myself*,
but of its fifty-two sections I will concentrate only upon
some Sublime centers, though I want to give a mapping-
out of the revisionary pattern of the entire poem, for
Whitman's romance of the self does follow essentially the
model of the British Romantic crisis-poem, though with
revealing, Emersonian, further distortions of the model.
Employing my own shorthand, this is the pattern of ratios
in *Song of Myself:*

Sections: 1–6   *Clinamen,* irony of presence and absence
            7–27   *Tessera,* synecdoche of part for whole
            28–30 *Kenosis,* metonymy of emptying out
            31–38 *Daemonization,* hyperbole of high and low
            39–49 *Askesis,* metaphor of inside vs. outside
            50–52 *Apophrades,* metalepsis reversing early and
                   late

   To adumbrate this pattern fully would take too long,
but the principal contours can be sketched. The opening
six sections are overtly a celebration, and what they celebrate presumably is a return of the repressed, an ecstatic
union of soul and self, of primary and antithetical, or,
more simply, they celebrate the American Sublime of
influx, of Emersonian self-recognition and consequent
self-reliance. What ought to be overwhelmingly present in
the first six sections is what Whitman, criticizing Keats,
referred to as the great poet's "powerful press of him-

self." But in these opening sections, the reader confronts instead images of absence rather than of presence; indeed, the reader is led inevitably to the bewildered observation that the poet's absence is so sacred a void that his presence never could hope to fill it. Defensively, Whitman opens with a reaction-formation against his precursor Emerson, which rhetorically becomes not the digressiveness or "permanent parabasis" of German Romantic irony, but the sharper, simpler irony of saying one thing while meaning another. Whitman says "I celebrate" and he cunningly means: "I contract and withdraw while asserting that I expand." Thus in section 2, he evades being intoxicated by an outward fragrance, narcissistically preferring "the smoke of my own breath." This characteristic and beautiful evasiveness intensifies in section 4, where the true self, "the Me myself," takes up a stance in total contradiction to the embracings and urgings that the poet only ostensibly celebrates:

Apart from the pulling and hauling stands what I am,
Stands amused, complacent, compassionating, idle, unitary,
Looks down, is erect, or bends an arm on an impalpable certain
    rest,
Looking with side-curved head curious what will come next,
Both in and out of the game and watching and wondering at it.

If this dialectical evasion is a *clinamen* away from Emerson, then precisely what sort of guilt of indebtedness does it seek to void? Is there a crucial enough difference between the Emersonian and Whitmanian versions of an American Sublime so as to allow Whitman enough breathing-space? I need to digress again, upon antithetical theory and the American Sublime, if I am to answer this question and thus be able to get back to mapping *Song of Myself*. What I want to be able to explain is why Whitman, in section 5, resorts to the image of transparency when he describes the embrace between his self and his soul, and why in section 6 he writes so firmly within the materialist tradition of Epicurus and Lucretius. Epicurus said: "The what is unknowable," and Whitman says he cannot answer the child's question: *What is the grass?* Poetically, he does answer, in a magnificent series of tropes, much admired by the hesitant Hopkins, and progressing from the Homeric: "And now it seems to me the beautiful uncut hair of graves" until we are given the astonishing and very American: "This grass is very dark to be from the white heads of old mothers."

In the 1856, Second Edition of *Leaves of Grass*, Whitman addressed Emerson directly, acknowledging that "it is yours to have been the original true Captain who put to sea, intuitive, positive, rendering the first report, to be told less by any report, and more by the mariners of a thousand bays, in each tack of their arriving and departing, many years after this." But Whitman aspired after strength, and so could not abide in this perfectly accurate tribute. In 1863, in a private notation, full of veneration for the precursor, he subtly described Emerson, perhaps better than even Nietzsche was to describe him:

America in the future, in her long train of poets and writers, while knowing more vehement and luxurious ones, will, I think, acknowledge nothing nearer [than] this man, the actual beginner of the whole procession—and certainly nothing purer, cleaner, sweeter, more canny, none, after all, more thoroughly her own and native. The most exquisite taste and caution are in him, always saving his feet from passing beyond the limits, for he is transcendental of limits, and you see underneath the rest a secret proclivity, American maybe, to dare and violate and make escapades.

By the time he wrote *Specimen Days* (1882), the consequences of misprision had triumphed in Whitman. Emerson was then condemned as having only a gentleman's admiration of power, and as having been an influence upon Whitman just "for a month or so." Five years later, Whitman lied outright, saying: "It is of no importance whether I had read Emerson before starting *L. of G.* or not. The fact happens to be positively that I had *not.*" Rather desperately, Whitman went on to say: "*L. of G.*'s word is *the body, including all,* including the intellect and soul; E's word is mind (or intellect or soul)." Though I will return to this last remark of Whitman's later, in studying his opening swerve away from Emerson, I wish to end these citations from Whitman-on-Emerson by quoting the truest of them, again from *Specimen Days:*

> The best part of Emersonianism is, it breeds the giant that destroys itself. Who wants to be any man's mere follower? lurks behind every page. No teacher ever taught, that has so provided for his pupil's setting up independently—no truer evolutionist.

Here, Whitman has provided antithetical theory with the inevitable trope for Emersonianism or the American Sublime: "it breeds the giant that destroys itself." We need not be surprised to discover that the trope was, however, Emerson's own invention, crucial in the essay *Self-Reliance* (which Whitman certainly *had* read before he wrote *Song of Myself*):

> I affect to be intoxicated with sights and suggestions, but I am not intoxicated. My giant goes with me wherever I go.

We can contrast another Emersonian-Whitmanian giant, a double one indeed, that dominates the opening section of the most Emersonian poem in our literature, *An Ordinary Evening in New Haven:*

I

> The eye's plain version is a thing apart,
> The vulgate of experience. Of this,
> A few words, an and yet, and yet, and yet—
>
> As part of the never-ending meditation,
> Part of the question that is a giant himself:
> Of what is this house composed if not of the sun,

These houses, these difficult objects, dilapidate
Appearances of what appearances,
Words, lines, not meanings, not communications,

Dark things without a double, after all,
Unless a second giant kills the first—
A recent imagining of reality,

Much like a new resemblance of the sun,
Down-pouring, up-springing and inevitable,
A larger poem for a larger audience,

As if the crude collops came together as one,
A mythological form, a festival sphere,
A great bosom, beard and being, alive with age.

"The question that is a giant himself" is a late version of
the Stevensian reduction to the First Idea, while the second giant who kills the first is another re-imagining of
the otherwise intolerable First Idea or winter vision. This
second giant is the Emersonian giant or daemonic agent
of the American Sublime, a "giant that destroys itself." A
transumption of these giants, difficult as it was to accomplish, is one of the beautiful achievements of our
contemporary master of this tradition, A. R. Ammons,
when he concludes an early venture into the American
Sublime by saying:

> that is the
>   expression of sea level,
> the talk of giants,
> of ocean, moon, sun, of everything,
> spoken in a dampened grain of sand.

Those giants carry me, at last, into my promised
theoretical digression, after which I intend to make a
return to *Song of Myself* where I left it, in its first six
sections. Giantism, as a trope, whether in Milton, or in
Emerson and his descendants, is related to sightlessness,
or rather to a repressive process that substitutes itself for

tropes and defenses of *re-seeing*, which I take as a synonym for *limitation*, in my particular sense of the Lurianic *zimzum* or "contraction." To recapitulate a distinction made at the start of *A Map of Misreading*, "revisionism" as a word and as a notion contains the triad of re-seeing, re-esteeming or re-estimating, and re-aiming, which in Kabbalistic terms becomes the triad of contraction, breaking-of-the-vessels, and restitution, and in poetic terms the triad of limitation, substitution, and representation. In these terms, sublimation is a *re-seeing* but repression is a *re-aiming*, or, rhetorically, a metaphor re-sees, that is, it changes a perspective, but an hyperbole *re-aims*, that is, redirects a response.

Even so, an irony re-sees, but a synecdoche re-aims; a metonymy reduces a seeing, but a metalepsis redirects a purpose or desire. In re-seeing, you have translated desire into an act, but in re-aiming, you have failed to translate, and so what you re-aim is a desire. In poetic terms, *acting is a limitation, but desiring is a representation.* To get back from an act to a desire, or to translate a desire into an act, you must re-estimate and re-esteem either act or desire, and by preferring one to the other, you substitute and so shatter the vessels, break and remake the forms again. Another way of putting this is that a revisionary ratio (trope, defense, image) of limitation is closer to an act than to a desire, but a ratio of representation is closer to a desire or repurposing. To use Kenneth Burke's rhetorical terms, of his four Master Tropes, three (irony, metonymy, metaphor; or dialectic, reduction, perspective) are acts of re-seeing, or simple revisionism, while the fourth (synecdoche or representation) is a desire that redirects purpose, and so is a more complex revisionism. Hyperbole and transumption, as successively more heightened representations, are even more strongly tropes of desire.

Expanding Burke to my purposes, I would say that the prime poetic acts are to make presence more dialectical,

to reduce differences, and to change our sense of otherness, of being elsewhere, by perspectivizing it. But the
prime poetic desires are to be elsewhere, to be different,
and to represent that otherness, that sense of difference
and of being elsewhere. I would add, as a surmise, that all
of us tend to value poetry more for its desires than for its
acts, more for its re-aimings or purposiveness, than for its
re-seeings. The Sublime, and particularly the American
Sublime, is not a re-seeing but rather is a re-aiming. To
achieve the Sublime is to experience a greater desire than
you have known before, and such an achievement results
from a failure to translate anterior or previous desires
into acts. As the Emersonian, American sense of anteriority was greater, ours being the Evening Land, even so the
Sublime heightened, or repression augmented, if only
because there was more unfulfilled desire to repress.

Emerson forgets English poetic tradition, in his most
Sublime prose passages, because his purpose is to present
something else, an American individuality. This forgetting is not primarily a limitation, that is, a calling attention to a lack both in language and in the self. Rather, this
forgetting aims to reinforce a potentiality for response in
the self, though unfortunately no act of forgetting can do
much to reinforce a potentiality in language. Emerson
therefore founds his Sublime upon a refusal of history,
particularly literary history. But no poetic Sublime can be so
founded without a compensating isolation and even a crip-
pling sublimation of the self, as Wordsworth's Sublime already had demonstrated. Emerson's new desire forgets the
old desire, only at the expense of increasing the distance
between desire and act, which is probably the psychic reason why Emerson's prose style is so discontinuous. More
even than Nietzsche, Emerson's unit of thought and expression tends to be the aphoristic, single sentence. Yet
Emerson, unlike Nietzsche, was primarily an orator, a
proud and knowing continuator of the Oral Tradition.
Nietzsche is consistent with his own deepest purposes in so

emphasizing the aphoristic energy of *writing*, whereas Emerson gives us the endless paradox of a mode of inspired speech that resorts always to aphorisms, which is what we can accept happily in Oscar Wilde, yet bewilders us in the American moralist.

The Emersonian or American Sublime, I am asserting, differs from the British or the Continental model not by a greater or lesser degree of positivity or negativity, but by a greater acceptance or affirmation of discontinuities in the self. Only Emerson could permit himself, within one page of the same essay (*Circles*), first to say: "There is no outside, no inclosing wall, no circumference to us," but then to cry out: "Alas for this infirm faith, this will not strenuous, this vast ebb of a vast flow! I am God in nature; I am a weed by the wall," and then outrageously to add: "The only sin is limitation." At the end of so discontinuous a Sublime, so strong yet so uncertain a repression, there must be also a heightened sense of the void, of the near-identity between the Sublime as a solitary ecstasy and the terrible raptures of nihilism, Nietzsche's *unheimlich* guest hovering by the door. Emerson's odyssey did not end in madness, and yet Emerson burned out, soon after the Civil War. Nietzsche became insane, Emerson became prematurely senile, Wordsworth merely became very boring, and so alas did Whitman, after *Drum-Taps*. In thirty years punctuated by many influxes of sublimity, Emerson went from saying: "It is a mischievous notion that we are come late into nature; that the world was finished a long time ago" to saying, in 1866: "There may be two or three or four steps, according to the genius of each, but for every seeing soul there are two absorbing facts,—*I and the Abyss*." For "the Abyss," we can read: tradition, history, the other, while for "I" we can read "any American." The final price paid for the extreme discontinuities of Emersonian vision is that we are left with a simple, chilling formula: the American Sublime equals *I and the Abyss*.

I return finally to the opening six sections of *Song of
Myself*, with their defensive swerve away from Emerson,
even as they appear to celebrate an Emersonian realization of the self. Whitman, not a poet-of-ideas like Emerson, but more traditionally a poet (however odd that
sounds), seems to have known implicitly that a poetic
representation of a desire tends to be stronger (that is,
less limiting) than a poetic representation of an act. *Song
of Myself*, in its beginnings, therefore substitutes the desires for union between split parts of the self, and between self and soul, for the acts of union proper, whatever those might be. Whitman wishes to originate his own
mode, but he cannot do so without some discontinuity
with Emerson, a prophet of discontinuity, and how do
you cast off an influence that itself denounces all influence? Emersonianism urges itself to breed a giant that
will destroy itself, but this most gigantic of its giants
painfully found himself anticipated in nearly every trope,
and in every movement of the spirit, a pain that Whitman
shared with Thoreau.

It is evident, both from the opening emphases in *Song
of Myself*, and from Whitman's comments in *Specimen
Days*, on the rival words of precursor and ephebe, that
Whitman's intended swerve from Emerson is to deny
Emerson's distinction between the Soul and Nature, in
which Nature includes all of the NOT ME, "both nature
and art, all other men and my own body." Whitman's ME
must include his own body, or so he would persuade us.
He writes what in 1881 he would title at last *Song of
Myself*, and not *Song of the Soul* or even *Song of My Soul*.
But the embrace between his soul and his self in section 5,
which makes the axis of things appear not opaque but
transparent, oddly makes "you my soul" the active part-
ner, and the self, "the other I am," wholly passive in this
courtship. If we translate soul as "character" and self as
"personality," then we would find it difficult to identify so
passive a personality with "Walt Whitman, a kosmos, of

Manhattan the son, / Turbulent, fleshy, sensual, eating, drinking and breeding" of section 24. Clearly, there is a division in Whitman between two elements in the self, as well as between self and soul, and it is the first of these divisions that matters, humanly and poetically. Indeed, it was from the first of these divisions that I believe Emerson initially rescued Whitman, thus making it possible for Whitman to become a poet. The "real me" or "me myself" in Whitman could not bear to be touched, ever, except by the maternal trinity of night, death, and the sea, while Walt Whitman, one of the roughs, learned from Emerson to cry: "Contact!" There is a sublime pathos in Whitman making his Epicurean *clinamen* away from Emerson by overproclaiming the body. Emerson had nothing to say about two subjects and two subjects only, sex and death, because he was too healthy-minded to believe that there was much to say about either. Emerson had no sexual problems, and was a Stoic about death.

I return to mapping *Song of Myself*, with its implicit contrast that Whitman, gloriously and plangently, always had much too much to say about sex and death, being in this the ancestor not only of Hart Crane and, perhaps surprisingly, of Wallace Stevens and, these days, of Ammons and Ashbery, but also of such prose obfuscators of sex and death as Hemingway and his egregious ephebe, Norman Mailer. Whitman, surpassing all his descendants, makes of a linked sex-and-death a noble synecdoche for all of existence, which is the figurative design of sections 7–27 of *Song of Myself*. A universalizing flood tide of re-versals-into-the-opposite reaches a great climax in section 24, which is an antithetical completion of the self without rival in American poetry, astonishing both for its dignity and its pathos, and transcending any other modern poet's attempt to think and represent by synecdoche. The reader cannot know whether to admire this proclamation more for its power or for its precision:

Unscrew the locks from the doors!
Unscrew the doors themselves from their jambs!

Whoever degrades another degrades me,
And whatever is done or said returns at last to me.

Through me the afflatus surging and surging, through me the
    current and index.

I speak the pass-word primeval, I give the sign of democracy,
By God! I will accept nothing which all cannot have their
    counterpart of on the same terms.

Through me many long dumb voices,
Voices of the interminable generations of prisoners and slaves,
Voices of the diseas'd and despairing and of thieves and
    dwarfs,
Voices of the threads that connect the stars, and of wombs and
    of the father-stuff,
And of the rights of them the others are down upon,
Of the deform'd, trivial, flat, foolish, despised,
Fog in the air, beetles rolling balls of dung.

  We can say of this astonishing chant that as completing
synecdoche it verges on emptying-out metonymy, reminding us of the instability of all tropes and of all psychic defenses. Primarily, Whitman's defense in this passage is a fantasy reversal, in which his own fear of contact
with other selves is so turned that no outward overthrow
of his separateness is possible. It is as though he were
denying denial, negating negation, by absorbing every
outward self, every outcast of society, history, and even of
nature. To say that one will accept nothing which all
cannot have their counterpart of on the same terms is
indeed to say that one will accept no overthrow from
outside oneself, no negation or denial. Whitman, with the
genius of his enormous drive towards antithetical completion, can be judged to end the *tessera* phase of his poem in
the remarkable triad of sections 25–27. For in section 25,

nature strikes back against the poet, yet he is strong enough to sustain himself, but in 26–27 he exhaustedly begins to undergo a kind of passive slide-down of spirit that precludes the fierce *kenosis* or emptying-out of his poethood in sections 28–30. At the end of 27, Whitman confesses: "To touch my person to some one else's is about as much as I can stand." The Whitmanian *kenosis*, in 28–30, appears to make of masturbation a metonymic reduction of the self, where touch substitutes for the whole being, and a pathetic salvation is sought through an exaltation of the earth that the poet has moistened:

A minute and a drop of me settle my brain,
I believe the soggy clods shall become lovers and lamps,
And a compend of compends is the meat of a man or woman,
And a summit and flower there is the feeling they have for
　　each other,
And they are to branch boundlessly out of that lesson until it
　　becomes omnific,
And until one and all shall delight us, and we them.

This is the prelude to the most awesome repression in our literature, the greatest instance yet of the American Sublime, sections 31–38. Rather than map the glories of this Sublime, I will examine instead the violent descent into the abyss that culminates it in section 38. Having merged both the fathering force and the universal brotherhood into himself, with terrifying eloquence ("I am the man, I suffer'd, I was there"; and "Agonies are one of my changes of garments"), Whitman pays the fearful price of Emersonian Compensation. Nothing indeed is gotten for nothing:

Enough! enough! enough!
Somehow I have been stunn'd. Stand back!
Give me a little time beyond my cuff'd head, slumbers, dreams,
　　gaping,
I discover myself on the verge of a usual mistake.

That I could forget the mockers and insults!
That I could forget the trickling tears and the blows of the
    bludgeons and hammers!
That I could look with a separate look on my own crucifixion
    and bloody crossing.

I remember now,
I resume the overstaid fraction,
The grave of rock multiplies what has been confided to it, or to
    any graves,
Corpses rise, gashes heal, fastenings roll from me.

Emerson had prophesied a Central Man who would
reverse the "great Defeat" of Christ, insisting that "we
demand Victory." Whitman, more audacious even than
his precursor, dares to present himself both as a repetition of the great Defeat and as the Victory of a Resurrection: "I troop forth replenish'd with supreme power, one
of an average unending procession." What are we to do
with a hyperbolical Sublime this outrageous? Whitman
too is saying: "*I and the Abyss,*" despite the self-deception
of that "average unending procession." But Whitman's
repression is greater, as it has to be, since a crucial part of
its anteriority is a primal fixation upon Emerson, a fixation that I want to explore in the conclusion of this
chapter once I have concluded my sketchy mapping of
the later ratios in *Song of Myself.*

Sections 39–49 are an attempt at a sublimating con-
solidation of the self, in which Whitman presents us with
his version of the most characteristic of High Romantic
metaphors, his self as inside reciprocally addressing the
natural world as a supposedly answering outside. The
final or reductive form of this perspectivizing is summed
up in an appropriately entitled poem of Wallace Stevens,
The American Sublime:

But how does one feel?
One grows used to the weather,

> The landscape and that;
> And the sublime comes down
> To the spirit itself,
>
> The spirit and space,
> The empty spirit
> In vacant space.

That is to say: the Sublime comes down to the Abyss in me inhabiting the Abyss of space. Whitman's version of this coming down completes his great *askesis*, in section 49:

> I hear you whispering there O stars of heaven,
> O suns—O grass of graves—O perpetual transfers and promo-
>   tions,
> If you do not say any thing how can I say any thing?
> . . . .
> Of the turbid pool that lies in the autumn forest,
> Of the moon that descends the steeps of the soughing twilight,
> Toss, sparkles of day and dusk—toss on the black stems that
>   decay in the muck,
> Toss to the moaning gibberish of the dry limbs.
>
> I ascend from the moon, I ascend from the night,
> I perceive that the ghastly glimmer is noonday sunbeams re-
>   flected,
> And debouch to the steady and central from the offspring
>   great or small.

The steadiness of the central is reached here only through the rhetorical equivalent of sublimation, which is metaphor, the metaphor of two lights, sun and moon, with the sun necessarily dominating, and taking as its tenor the Emersonian "steady and central." I return to the formula for poetic sublimation ventured earlier in this discourse. The sublimating ratio is a limitation because what it concentrates is being evaded, that is, is remembered only in order *not* to be presented, with something else substituted in the presentation. Whitman does not present what he is remembering, his dream of divination, of being a dazzling sunrise greater than the merely natural sun. Instead of this autonomous splendor, he accepts now a perspectivizing, a balancing of "sparkles of day and dusk." His restitution for this *askesis* comes in his great poem's close, in sections 50–52, which form a miraculous transumption of all that has gone before. Yet the Whitmanian metaleptic reversal differs crucially from the Wordsworthian-Tennysonian model, in that it places the burden upon the reader, rather than upon the poet. It is the reader, and not the poet, who is challenged directly to make his belatedness into an earliness. Whitman was to perfect this challenge in *Crossing Brooklyn Ferry*, appropriately called *Sun-Down Poem* when it first appeared in the second *Leaves of Grass*, in 1856. Here, in *Song of Myself*, the challenge is made explicit at the close of section 51: "Will you speak before I am gone? will you prove already too late?" Nowhere in Emerson (and I concede to no reader in my fanatical love of Emerson) is there so strong a representation of the Central Man who is coming as there is in Whitman's self-presentation in section 52. I would select this as the greatest of Emerson's prophecies of the Central Man, from the Journals, April 1846:

> He or That which in despair of naming aright, some have called the *Newness*,—as the Hebrews did not like to pronounce the word,—he lurks, he hides, he who is success, reality, joy, power,—that which constitutes Heaven, which reconciles impossibilities, atones for shortcomings, expiates sins or makes them virtues, buries in oblivion the crowded historical past, sinks religions, philosophies, nations, persons to legends; reverses the scale of opinion, of fame; reduces sciences to opinion, and makes the thought of the moment the key to the universe, and the egg of history to come.
>   . . . 'Tis all alike,—astronomy, metaphysics, sword, spade, pencil, or instruments and arts yet to be invented,—this is the

inventor, the worth-giver, the worth. This is He that shall come; or, if He come not, nothing comes: He that disappears in the moment when we go to celebrate Him. If we go to burn those that blame our celebration, He appears in them. The Divine Newness. Hoe and spade, sword and pen, cities, pictures, gardens, laws, bibles, are prized only because they were means He sometimes used. So with astronomy, music, arithmetic, castes, feudalism,—we kiss with devotion these hems of his garment,—we mistake them for Him; they crumble to ashes on our lips.

The Newness is Influx, or fresh repression, lurking and hiding, imaged in depth, in burying and in sinking. This daemonic force then projects the past and introjects the future, and yet *not now*, but only in the realm of what *shall come*: "He . . . disappears in the moment when we go to celebrate Him," and more than his garment would crumble to ashes on our lips. Whitman, as this Newness, is even more splendidly elusive:

The spotted hawk swoops by and accuses me, he complains of
    my gab and my loitering.

I too am not a bit tamed, I too am untranslatable,
I sound my barbaric yawp over the roofs of the world.

The last scud of day holds back for me,
It flings my likeness after the rest and true as any on the
    shadow'd wilds,
It coaxes me to the vapor and the dusk.

I depart as air, I shake my white locks at the runaway sun,
I effuse my flesh in eddies, and drift it in lacy jags.

I bequeath myself to the dirt to grow from the grass I love,
If you want me again look for me under your boot-soles.

You will hardly know who I am or what I mean,
But I shall be good health to you nevertheless,
And filter and fibre your blood.

Failing to fetch me at first keep encouraged,
Missing me one place search another,
I stop somewhere waiting for you.

The hawk accuses Whitman of belatedness, of "loiter-
ing," but the poet is one with the hawk, "untranslatable"
in that his desire is perpetual, always transcending act.
There, in the twilight, Whitman arrests the lateness of the
day, dissolving the presentness of the present, and effus-
ing his own presence until it is air and earth. As the
atmosphere we are to breathe, the ground we are to walk,
the poet introjects our future, and is somewhere up
ahead, waiting for us to catch up. So far ahead is he on
our mutual quest, that he can afford to stop, though he
will not tell us precisely where. His dominant trope remains the grass, but this trope is now transumptive, for it
is grass not yet grown but "to grow." Implicit in such a
trope is the more-than-Emersonian promise that *this* Central Man will not disappear "in the moment when we go
to celebrate him."

I end by returning to Whitman's American Sublime of
sections 31–38, with specific reference to the grand march
of section 33, where the poet says: "I am afoot with my
vision." Here is a part of this audacious mounting into the
Sublime:

Solitary at midnight in my back yard, my thoughts gone from
     me a long while.
Walking the old hills of Judaea with the beautiful, gentle God
     by my side,
Speeding through space, speeding through heaven and the
     stars,
Speeding amid the seven satellites and the broad ring, and the
     diameter of eighty thousands miles,
Speeding with tail'd meteors, throwing fire-balls like the rest,
Carrying the crescent child that carries its own full mother in
     its belly,

Storming, enjoying, planning, loving, cautioning,
Backing and filling, appearing and disappearing,
I tread day and night such roads.

I visit the orchards of spheres and look at the product,
And look at quintillions ripen'd and look at quintillions green.

I fly those flights of a fluid and swallowing soul,
My course runs below the soundings of plummets.

I help myself to material and immaterial,
No guard can shut me off, no law prevent me.

As an hyperbolical progression, this sequence is matched only by its misprision or sublime parody, the flight of the Canon Aspirin in *Notes toward a Supreme Fiction*. Whitman's angelic flight breaks down the distinction between material and immaterial, because his soul, as he precisely says, is "fluid and swallowing." Similarly, the Canon's angelic flight breaks down the limits between fact and thought, but the Canon's soul being more limited, the later angelic flight fails exactly where Whitman's cannot fail. The Canon imposes orders upon reality, but Whitman discovers or uncovers orders, because he is discovering himself (even though he does not uncover himself, despite his constant assertions that he is about to do so). I vary an earlier question in order to conclude this discourse. Why is Whitman's American Sublime larger and stronger than either the Sublime of his precursor, Emerson, or the Sublime of his ephebe, Stevens? In the language of misprision, this means: why and how is Whitman's poetic repression greater and more forceful than that of the other major figures in his own tradition?

Whitman's ego, in his most Sublime transformations, wholly absorbs and thus pragmatically forgets the fathering force, and presents instead the force of the son, of his own self or, in Whitman's case, perhaps we should say of his own selves. Where Emerson *urges* forgetfulness of anteriority, Whitman more strenuously *does* forget it, though at a considerable cost. Emerson says: *"I and the Abyss"*; Whitman says: *"The Abyss of My Self."* The second statement is necessarily more Sublime and, alas, even more American.

10

Wallace Stevens: The Transcendental Strain

> The ancients are no transcendentalists; they rest always
> in the spontaneous consciousness.
>
> EMERSON

In the frequently bizarre *Ecce Homo*, Nietzsche has a stimulating essay called "Why I Am So Clever," sandwiched in between "Why I Am So Wise" and "Why I Write Such Good Books." "Cleverness," in this sense, turns out to be the self-preservation through self-defense that allows Nietzsche to express his wisdom in his own writing without being blocked out by precursors:

Not to see many things, not to hear many things, not to permit many things to come close—first imperative of prudence, first proof that one is no mere accident but a necessity. The usual word for this instinct of self-defense is *taste*. It commands us not only to say No when Yes would be "selfless" but also to say *No as rarely as possible*. . . . Scholars spend all of their energies on saying Yes and No, on criticism of what others have thought— they themselves no longer think.

Nietzsche's prime concern, as he says in his subtitle, is "How One Becomes What One Is." His answer risks the paradox or double-bind, so frequent in Romanticism, of anti-self-consciousness uneasily allied to the drive for an expanding consciousness:

To become what one is, one must not have the faintest notion *what* one is. From this point of view even the *blunders* of life have their own meaning and value—the occasional side roads and

267

wrong roads, the delays, "modesties," seriousness wasted on tasks
that are remote from *the* task. . . .
    The whole surface of consciousness—consciousness *is* a
surface—must be kept clear of all great imperatives.

Stevens was as deliberately reticent as Nietzsche was
deliberately self-revelatory, but he followed Nietzsche in
this subtle mode of self-defense, so that he too at last
might prove that he was no accident, but a necessity (if
not quite a destiny, as Nietzsche accurately proclaimed
himself to be). In *The Comedian as the Letter C* (1922), a
desperate dead-end poem despite all its exuberant
grotesquerie, Stevens seems to have both praised and
blamed himself for his Nietzschean and prudential evasions, his defenses against the pressures of Romantic tradition:

> How many poems he denied himself
> In his observant progress, lesser things
> Than the relentless contact he desired;
> How many sea-masks he ignored; what sounds
> He shut out from his tempering ear; what thoughts,
> Like jades affecting the sequestered bride;
> And what descants, he sent to banishment!

"Relentless contact" is the Emersonian and Whitmanian
ideal, but hardly the Transcendental reality. Yet it is the
ideal that Stevens set himself to quest beyond, and as we will
see, to quest beyond in vain:

> What was the purpose of his pilgrimage,
> Whatever shape it took in Crispin's mind,
> If not, when all is said, to drive away
> The shadow of his fellows from the skies,
> And, from their stale intelligence released,
> To make a new intelligence prevail?

The final or transumptive form of that shadow in Stevens
is the "great shadow's last embellishment" of *The Auroras of*

Autumn. Rather than again map that marvelous poem, I turn to a lyric of 1954, close to the end, the subtle *On the Way to the Bus:*

> A light snow, like frost, has fallen during the night.
> Gloomily, the journalist confronts
>
> Transparent man in a translated world,
> In which he feeds on a new known,
>
> In a season, a climate of morning, of elucidation,
> A refreshment of cold air, cold breath,
>
> A perception of cold breath, more revealing than
> A perception of sleep, more powerful
>
> Than a power of sleep, a clearness emerging
> From cold, slightly irised, slightly bedazzled,
>
> But a perfection emerging from a new known,
> An understanding beyond journalism,
>
> A way of pronouncing the word inside one's tongue
> Under the wintry trees of the terrace.

The "journalist" is the aspect of the old Stevens still in continuity with the reductionist of a lifetime's meditations and poems, a "journalist" largely in the sense of a person who keeps a journal, a daily record of reflections, which in Stevens's case has become his poetry. There is a reductive play, certainly, upon mere "journalism" as opposed to literature, but there is a link also to journalists like Emerson and Thoreau, who confronted daily "Transparent man in a translated world," where "translated" means "troped." Fundamentally *On the Way to the Bus,* like so many of Stevens's last poems written from 1949 on to the end in 1955, is a revision of *The Snow Man,* a text that *On the Way to the Bus* very nearly reverses. But I will come to this near-reversal after an account of *The Snow Man.*

The Snow Man is a lyric monument to belatedness, and can be considered Stevens's most crucial poem. There is

an unhappy irony, clearly, in the situation of the belated
strong poet, since as much as in any poet ever, the spirit
in him insists upon priority and autonomy, yet the text he
produces is condemned to offer itself for interpretation
as being already an interpretation of other interpretations, rather than as what it asserts itself to be, an
interpretation of life. No illusion about his status and
function is more difficult to shed, as I have learned
through being denounced by virtually every poet I meet.
Yet I am puzzled by one aspect of these denunciations,
energizing as it is to be denounced. The function of
criticism at the present time, as I conceive it, is to find a
middle way between the paths of demystification of meaning, and of recollection or restoration of meaning, or
between limitation and representation. But the only
aesthetic path between limitation and representation is
substitution, and so all that criticism can hope to teach,
whether to the common reader or to the poet, is a series
of stronger modes of substitution. Substitution, in this
sense, is a mode of creation-through-catastrophe. The
vessels or fixed forms break in every act of reading or of
writing, but *how* they break is to a considerable extent in
the power of each reader and of each writer. Yet there
are patterns in the breaking that resist the power, however strong, of any reader and of every writer. These
patterns—evident as sequences of images, or of tropes, or
of psychic defenses—are as definite as those of any dance,
and as varied as there are various dances. But poets do
not invent the dances they dance, and we *can tell* the
dancer from the dance. The stronger poet not only per-
forms the dance more skillfully than the weaker poet, but
he modifies it as well, and yet it does remain the same
dance. I am afraid that there does tend to be one fairly
definite dance pattern in post-Enlightenment poetry,
which can be altered by strong substitution, but still it
does remain the same dance.

I give Stevens's *The Snow Man* as an instance, my choice

being not arbitrary, since the poem seems both central and quite thoroughly original, and yet it too reveals itself as another version of the apotropaic litany that poetry has become. It begins with the injunction of absence, for a man formed of snow is one emblem of absence, and a mind of winter is necessarily another. The mind, as Stevens says elsewhere, is itself the great poem of winter, but this is the mind as one defense only, as the metonymic reduction that isolates and undoes the object-world. Such a mind, moving from its initial *illusio* of saying "mind" while intending a loss of cognition, through the isolations of a reified nature, would be content to abide in the metaphor that finally perspectivizes an observing nothingness against a nothingness observed. But this apparently least restitutive of poems moves also to heighten its initial synecdoche of the beholder, to the hyperbole of pathos in the misery of the Shelleyan wind, on to the introjective metalepsis of the final "beholds," where the "nothing" that is there and the "nothing himself" of the beholder both are effectually equated with the greatest of American epiphanies: "I am nothing; I see all." *That* beholder, no Snow Man, yet "crossing a bare common, in snow puddles, at twilight, under a clouded sky," could end *his* reverie by affirming: "I am part or parcel of God." Stevens will go quite as far at the climax of *Notes toward a Supreme Fiction:* "I have not but I am and as I am, I am." *The Snow Man*, back in 1921, abandons us to its title: to live with the trope of pathos, without the fallacy of attributing life to the object world, is to live only as and how a body of winter would live.

Plotinus liked to call the Gnostics "deceived deceivers," which seems to me also a good description of strong poets. To be a Snow Man is not to be deceived, but of course it is also not to be a strong poet, but only a "journalist." A strong poet is strong by virtue of "a perfection emerging from a new known," indeed from "an understanding beyond journalism." On his way to the

bus, the very old Stevens not only beholds but *knows* a
new perception, and this knowledge, as befits a poet, is "a
way of pronouncing the word." This is not the orator's
word, the transparency as proclaimed by Emerson, but is
rather a private perfection, "inside of one's tongue." Yet
it is on the way to the Emersonian word of oral tradition,
a way that is charted in many of the final poems, as here
in *The Sail of Ulysses:*

> The great Omnium descends on us
> As a free race. We know it, one
> By one, in the right of all. Each man
> Is an approach to the vigilance
> In which the litter of truths becomes
> A whole, the day on which the last star
> Has been counted, the genealogy
> Of gods and men destroyed, the right
> To know established as the right to be.

This is Stevens returning, a century later, to the primary, early Emerson of 1839 who could assert that
"Adam in the garden, I am to new name all the beasts in
the field and all the gods in the sky." The motive for
destroying the genealogy of gods and men is the same in
both the seers, the more extravagant *maggid* of Concord
and his more circumspect speculator of Hartford. We
have seen how strained the Transcendental strain was
even in Emerson and Whitman; of the three I would
judge it to be the least strained in the very old Stevens, as
here again in *The Sail of Ulysses:*

> In the generations of thought, man's sons
> And heirs are powers of the mind,
> His only testament and estate.
> He has nothing but the truth to leave.
> How then shall the mind be less than free
> Since only to know is to be free?

That is noble verse, and of course it is a Transcendental
idealization, and of course it is a lie, not just against time but

even more audaciously against the condition of our existence as knowers. In the generations of thought, man's sons and heirs are men and women, *other* men and women, men and women who come after. The testament and estate handed on is tradition, and man leaves not the truth, certainly not in literature, but cumulative error, a legacy of tropes. Only to know is hardly to be free, but is indeed an acknowledgment of contingency. Stevens, necessarily, is never more Emersonian than when he declares the freedom or wildness of his own knowing, for here too Emersonianism breeds the giant that destroys itself.

What shall we call this strain in Stevens, unless it be a Transcendental one? It was there always, but from about 1949 on it dwarfs every other element in the poems. The canonical misreading of Stevens has its prophetess in the brilliant Helen Vendler, for whom Stevens is wholly an ironist, whose one true subject is dessication. I do not recognize this Stevens in the poetry. Mrs. Vendler calls her analysis of *An Ordinary Evening in New Haven* "the total leaflessness," thus seeking to reduce the entire poem to its least characteristic section, the lament for old age that fails to dominate even section xvi, where it occurs. More characteristic, I would say, is section xxiii:

> The sun is half the world, half everything,
> The bodiless half. There is always this bodiless half,
> This illumination, this elevation, this future
>
> Or say, the late going colors of that past,
> Effete green, the woman in black cassimere.
> If, then, New Haven is half sun, what remains,
>
> At evening, after dark, is the other half,
> Lighted by space, big over those that sleep,
> Of the single future of night, the single sleep,
>
> As of a long, inevitable sound,
> A kind of cozening and coaxing sound,
> And the goodness of lying in a maternal sound,

Unfretted by day's separate, several selves,
Being part of everything come together as one.
In this identity, disembodiments

Still keep occurring. What is, uncertainly,
Desire prolongs its adventure to create
Forms of farewell, furtive among green ferns.

It should be said of Stevens that, throughout his poetic
career, he could not trope without the sun. His First Idea
is an idea of man, but for him "we are men of sun," and
so the First Idea in Stevens is always also an idea of the
sun, and the sun re-imagined is therefore the central
image of his poetry. I suspect that Zarathustra's solar
trajectory, in Nietzsche, was a large component in Stevens's re-imaginings of the sun, from *Sunday Morning* in
1915 on to *Not Ideas about the Thing but the Thing Itself,*
nearly forty years later. But the anteriority of the image is
very nearly endless, since Nietzsche, Emerson, Whitman
themselves exploited an immense tradition of solar revisionism. In Stevens, the image of the sun is so comprehensive as to defy summary, but if a single passage
can be selected as being representative, it might be this,
from *Waving Adieu, Adieu, Adieu:*

>   . . . Ever-jubilant,
> What is there here but weather, what spirit
> Have I except it comes from the sun?

If this rhetorical question intends to be answered: "No
spirit, except it comes from the sun," as I think it is, then
section xxiii of *An Ordinary Evening in New Haven* begins
with a *clinamen* from transcendence, from Emerson in
Nature insisting:

To speak truly, few adult persons can see nature. Most persons do not see the sun. At least they have a very superficial
seeing. The sun illuminates only the eye and the heart of the
child.

The Stevensian swerve from origins reacts also against Whitman at his most defiant, in *Song of Myself,* section 25:

Dazzling and tremendous how quick the sun-rise would kill me,
If I could not now and always send sun-rise out of me,

We also ascend dazzling and tremendous as the sun,
We found our own O my soul in the calm and cool of the
  daybreak.

Seeing the sun, for Emerson, was a composite trope in which the Emersonian eye and the sun blent into one value. Seeing the sun, for Whitman, was to foster the rising of a counter-sun, in himself. Stevens begins section xxiii with a repressed desire for wholeness and transcendence, while overtly indulging in a rhetorical irony: "The sun is half the world, half everything, / The bodiless half." He says "half" but means "all the world," means that the sun is everything. The "bodiless" figuration recalls the opening of *The Auroras of Autumn,* and here as there is a dialectical image of absence and presence. The sun is present as "illumination" and "elevation" but absent because it is always "future." In the next tercet, Stevens defensively turns-against-the-self, by attacking the past as an "effete green," the *Harmonium* world now being viewed as colored belatedly. New Haven becomes the restituting synecdoche or antithetical completion, the whole of which the sun and night are only parts. If one half of New Haven is sun, and is Stevens's invention or discovery, the night-half belongs to Whitman's *The Sleepers,* the world where night is an identity with the mother and so with death and birth, and where the long, inevitable sound must be the sound of the sea, calling its castaways home:

                    . . . what remains,
  At evening, after dark, is the other half,
  Lighted by space, big over those that sleep,
  Of the single future of night, the single sleep,

> As of a long, inevitable sound,
> A kind of cozening and coaxing sound,
> And the goodness of lying in a maternal sound . . .

In these central tercets of section XXIII, the alternation follows Whitman's characteristic pattern. The word "single," by a catachresis of metonymy, becomes a figurative reduction to emptiness, a regressive return to origins. The fullness of space, big over the childlike sleepers, empties out into the single future of night and sleep, which is necessarily death. But the daemonic response, in an extraordinary repression into a Counter-Sublime, is a forgetting of death and a remembering, substituting representation of the mother and of her goodness, which poetically means an assumption of the powers of the Transcendental muse. The precise apotropaic pattern of the Romantic crisis-poem then repeats itself as an inside/ outside metaphor of "identity" does the work of sublimation, exquisitely conveyed by the image of fretting, of shadowing or latticing a pattern of displacement, between separate selves and a composite being, night or the mother:

> Unfretted by day's separate, several selves,
> Being part of everything come together as one.

But such a metaphorical identity is epistemologically unreliable, and Stevens moves instead to a transumptive trope, poised with deliberate uncertainty between freshness and belatedness:

> In this identity, disembodiments
>
> Still keep occurring. What is, uncertainly,
> Desire prolongs its adventure to create
> Forms of farewell, furtive among green ferns.

Here farewell has been projected, if only into the variety of forms, and desire has been introjected, if only into a prolongation rather than into an apotheosis. As an adventure, desire shades off furtively into the "effete green, the woman in black cassimere," which were "the late going colors of that past." Desire hardly could be praised more ambiguously, and yet it does remain desire. There is a dark link in the hyperbolic trope of the "long, inevitable sound" of night and the mother, and the prolonging of the furtive adventure, hinting that desire is finally a desire for death. But I do not think it accidental that this and so many other sections of *An Ordinary Evening in New Haven* follow the patterns of imagery of the High Romantic paradigm, and it is to the almost continual presence of such patterns in Stevens that I now direct this discourse.

I have discussed elsewhere Stevens's contemptuous attitude towards poetic influence. Was there ever another poet of his achievement who could write this blindly and self-deceivingly about the relation of a new poet to anteriority?

If we were all alike; if we were millions of people saying do, re, mi in unison, one poet would be enough and Hesiod himself would do very well. Everything he said would be in no need of expounding or would have been expounded long ago. But we are not all alike and everything needs expounding all the time because, as people live and die, each one perceiving life and death for himself, and mostly by and in himself, there develops a curiosity about the perceptions of others. This is what makes it possible to go on saying new things about old things. The fact is that the saying of new things in new ways is grateful to us. If a bootblack says that he was so tired that he lay down like a dog under a tree, he is saying a new thing about an old thing, in a new way. His new way is not a literary novelty; it is an unaffected statement of his perception of the thing.

When I read this passage, I am moved by the quality of Stevens's exasperation, yet I am reminded also of Emerson's insight, in his essay "History," when he remarks: "But it is the fault of our rhetoric that we cannot strongly

state one fact without seeming to belie some other." I
remember also Nietzsche's aphorism: "One is not finished
with one's passion because one represents it: rather, one
is finished with it *when* one represents it:" Stevens, insisting upon the perceptiveness of his fictive bootblack, is
representing his own anxieties about anteriority, and his
own rhetoric belies the fact of a belated poet's deepest
fear, which is that increasingly we do become all too
much alike. Stevens can say, pugnaciously and effectively,
that "one poet would be enough and Hesiod himself
would do very well," but how would it have seemed, to
Stevens or to us, if he had said that "one poet would be
enough and Whitman himself would do very well," let
alone a contemporary rival like Eliot or Pound or Wil-
liams?

In the same introduction to a new poet that I have just
cited, Stevens proceeded to obfuscate American Transcen-
dentalism, with the same zest for misprision that he frequently manifested towards Romanticism. To be anti-
Transcendental, Stevens said, is to take as your subject "the
particulars of experience." Without bothering to cite
Thoreau or Whitman against this uninteresting falsification, I am content to cite Emerson from the not irrelevant
essay called *The Transcendentalist:*

> The idealist, in speaking of events, sees them as spirits. He
> does not deny the sensuous fact: by no means; but he will not
> see that alone. He does not deny the presence of this table, this
> chair, and the walls of this room, but he looks at these things as
> the reverse side of the tapestry, as the *other end,* each being a
> sequel or completion of a spiritual fact which nearly concerns
> him. This manner of looking at things transfers every object in
> nature from an independent and anomalous position without
> there, into the consciousness.

Or as Stevens's returned mariners say in *An Ordinary
Evening in New Haven,* "We are back once more in the
land of the elm trees, / But folded over, turned round," a

turning or "alteration / Of words that was a change of nature." Grand fulfiller as he was of the Emersonian program, yet less grandly fulfilling than Whitman had been, Stevens suffered more even than Whitman the intolerable Transcendental version of the anxiety of influence. Rather than continue to wander between Stevensian texts, I will concentrate the rest of this discourse upon one strong text, the attempt by Stevens to appropriate for himself the Emersonian-Whitmanian center, *Notes toward a Supreme Fiction*. What is the fate of the Transcendental strain in this most strenuous of Stevensian apotropaic litanies?

Like Peer Gynt, we must go round about, to get behind Stevens's defenses here, and this circuitous route leads through the most important of twentieth-century influences upon Stevens, Paul Valéry, by which I mean Valéry as prose speculator upon poetry, rather than Valéry as poet. Here, in the dialogue *Dance and the Soul,* as noted by Frank Kermode, are the first two phases of Stevens's dialectic: the reduction to the First Idea, and the realization that the human cannot long survive such reduction:

Socrates. . . . tell me then, do you not know some specific remedy, or some exact antidote, for that evil amongst all evils, that poison of poisons, that venom inimical to all nature? . . .

Phaedrus. What venom?

Socrates. . . . Which is called: *the weariness of living?*—I mean, understand me, not the passing weariness, the tedium which comes of fatigue, or that of which we see the germ or the limits; but that perfect tedium, that pure tedium which does not come from misfortune or infirmity, and which is compatible with the happiest of all conditions that we may contemplate—that tedium, in fine, whose substance is none other than life itself, and which has no other second cause than the clear-sightedness of the man who is alive. This absolute tedium is in itself nothing other than life in its nakedness, when it sees itself clearly.

Eryximachus. It is most true that if our soul purges itself of all
falseness, and deprives itself of every fraudulent addition to
what is, our existence is at once endangered by this cold, exact,
reasonable, and moderate consideration of human life as it
is. . . .
Why cure so reasonable an ill? No doubt there is nothing
more morbid in itself, nothing more inimical to nature, than to
see things as they are. A cold and perfect clarity is a poison
impossible to combat. The real, in its pure state, stops the heart
instantaneously. . . . One drop of that icy lymph suffices to
relax in a soul the springs and palpitations of desire, ex-
terminate all hopes, ruin all the gods present in our blood. The
Virtues and the most noble colors pale before it, and are little
by little consumed. To a handful of ashes is the past reduced,.
and the future to a tiny icicle. The soul appears to itself as an
empty and measurable form.—Here, then, things as they are
come together, limit one another, and are thus chained together in the most rigorous and mortal fashion. . . . O Socrates,
the universe cannot for one instant endure to be only what it
is. . . .
The mistakes, the appearances, the play of the dioptrics of
the mind deepen and quicken the world's miserable mass. . . .
The idea introduces into what is, the leaven of what is not. . . .
But truth sometimes shows its hand after all, and jars in the
harmonious system of phantasmagorias and errors.

We can observe that the Eryximachus of Valéry is himself strongly influenced by Schopenhauer and by
Nietzsche, and particularly by the latter. Stevens's winter
or snow man vision, the reduction to the First Idea, thus
reaches back to Nietzsche through Valéry. The third
phase of Stevens's dialectic, the re-imagining of the intolerable First Idea through the fabrication of a Supreme
Fiction, also seems to reach back to Nietzsche, in this case
through Vaihinger's *The Philosophy of 'As If'*, with its last
chapter on "Nietzsche's Will to Illusion" which Frank
Doggett establishes Stevens as having pondered. From

Vaihinger-on-Nietzsche, Stevens took "the idea / Of this invention, this invented world" and, more crucially even, the notion that the world in which we lived was itself a fiction, just as our autonomous self or identity was only a fiction or a "supreme illusion."

Valéry, for all his debt to Nietzsche, was a subtler genealogist of influence than Nietzsche was, if only because Valéry had pondered his relation to his prime precursor, Mallarmé, less blindly than Nietzsche had considered his own relation to Schopenhauer. In his *Letter about Mallarmé*, Valéry verges upon the realization that poetic influence is essentially misprision and revisionism:

Whether in science or the arts, if we look for the source of an achievement, we can observe that *what a man does* either repeats or refutes *what someone else has done*—repeats it in other tones, refines or amplifies or simplifies it, loads or overloads it with meaning; or else rebuts, overturns, destroys and denies it, but thereby assumes it and has invisibly used it. Opposites are born from opposites.

Stevens, as a theorist of poetry, is little more than a self-deceiver, while Valéry is certainly as profound a speculator upon poetry as our century has produced. Yet Stevens, more than Valéry, Rilke, Yeats, well may have been what Eliot judged Valéry to have been, the century's truly indispensable poet. How can such an assertion be vindicated? Stevens does not begin to match Valéry in subtlety of mind or clarity of consciousness. Stevens, compared to Rilke, has an inadequate sense of vocation, and a fearful poverty of invention. Set against Yeats, Stevens lacks dramatic intensity and nearly all color and flamboyance of self-presentation. What *does* Stevens have, besides endless persistence and preternatural eloquence, the qualities he had inherited from the Emerson-Whitman tradition? Does he have his poverty and nothing more? Is it only his terrible American imaginative need, his enormous sense of belatedness, that distinguishes him among his major contemporaries?

The curious answer is that Stevens is the authentic twentieth-century poet of the Sublime, surpassing even Rilke in that highest of modes. I call this answer curious only because it contradicts all merely canonical misreading that continues to give us Stevens as an ironist, as a wry celebrant of a diminished version of Romantic or Transcendental selfhood. Perhaps no other modern poet was as unlikely to revindicate the Sublime as Stevens was, and yet the actual burden of his major poetry is the movement both towards a possible wisdom and towards a possible ecstasy, between which Stevens refuses to choose, though Yeats had insisted that an individual could hope to move only towards one or the other. The Stevens I am sketching can be conveyed in a rapid and arbitrary cento of a few Arnoldian or Blackmurian touchstones. If there is a modern Sublime at all, then this is it, and you need but hear it to recognize its giant authority:

. . . Evening, when the measure skips a beat
And then another, one by one, and all
To a seething minor swiftly modulate.
Bare night is best. Bare earth is best. Bare, bare,
Except for our own houses, huddled low
Beneath the arches and their spangled air,
Beneath the rhapsodies of fire and fire,
Where the voice that is in us makes a true response,
Where the voice that is great within us rises up,
As we stand gazing at the rounded moon.

In the far South the sun of autumn is passing
Like Walt Whitman walking along a ruddy shore.
He is singing and chanting the things that are part of him,
The worlds that were and will be, death and day.
Nothing is final, he chants. No man shall see the end.
His beard is of fire and his staff is a leaping flame.

                        If earth dissolves
Its evil after death, it dissolves it while
We live. Thence come the final chants, the chants
Of the brooder seeking the acutest end
Of speech: to pierce the heart's residuum
And there to find music for a single line,
Equal to memory, one line in which
The vital music formulates the words.

Behold the men in helmets borne on steel,
Discolored, how they are going to defeat.

This is nothing until in a single man contained,
Nothing until this named thing nameless is
And is destroyed. He opens the door of his house

On flames. The scholar of one candle sees
An Arctic effulgence flaring on the frame
Of everything he is. And he feels afraid.

In a confusion on bed and books, a portent
On the chair, a moving transparence on the nuns,
A light on the candle tearing against the wick
To join a hovering excellence, to escape
From fire and be part only of that of which

Fire is the symbol: the celestial possible.
Speak to your pillow as if it was yourself.
Be orator but with an accurate tongue . . .

    What does it mean to recognize in these passages, and scores like them in Stevens, the culmination of the American Sublime, or even of the Sublime in modern poetry? All through these chapters, I have been arguing that the poetic Sublime is identical with a particular kind of repression, or rather repressive troping, and I have been attempting to define that kind in relation to some of Freud's ideas about repression. There is a very difficult sense, still to be studied, in which Freud's concepts of

repression are misprisions of Schopenhauer's theories of
the Sublime. Stevens is very much in the tradition of
Schopenhauer and of Freud; how deeply he read either,
we cannot know, but he is the most overtly Freudian of
modern strong poets, and Schopenhauer and Nietzsche
are his European philosophical precursors, even as William James and Santayana are his American forebears.
Stevens was a more acute poetic psychologist than he was
a profound philosophical poet; Frank Kermode rightly
warns us that "it is better to feel the peculiar lines of force
that dominate *Notes* than to fit it into a philosophy
founded on all the other poems." But scholars like
Richard P. Adams are right also in being reminded continually of Schopenhauer while they feel the force that
dominates Stevens's *Notes*. I risk sounding ironic when I
affirm that Stevens's greatness rose out of the scandalous
force of his repressiveness, but I mean only to be descriptive, and I find Schopenhauer's description of the Sublime to be the best aid I know in understanding what
Stevens was able to do with his powers of repression.

Schopenhauer grounds his Sublime upon *forgetting*.
One must give the whole power of one's mind to perception, and then sink into that perception. Then one
"forgets even his individuality, his will, and only continues to exist as the pure subject, the clear mirror of the
object." In this self-losing, one becomes "*pure*, will-less,
painless, timeless *subject of knowledge*." And, lost to self, we
attain the Sublime:

> If we lose ourselves in the contemplation of the infinite
> greatness of the universe in space and time, meditate on the
> thousands of years that are past or to come, or if the heavens at
> night actually bring before our eyes innumerable worlds and so
> force upon our consciousness the immensity of the universe, we
> feel ourselves dwindle to nothing; as individuals, as living
> bodies, as transient phenomena of will, we feel ourselves pass
> away and vanish into nothing like drops in the ocean. But at

once there rises against this ghost of our own nothingness, against such lying impossibility, the immediate consciousness that all these worlds exist only as our idea, only as modifications of the eternal subject of pure knowing, which we find ourselves to be as soon as we forget our individuality, and which is the necessary supporter of all worlds and at all times the condition of their possibility. The vastness of the world which disquieted us before, rests now in us; our dependence upon it is annulled by its dependence upon us.

Schopenhauer's Sublime rises, we can surmise, only when the objects of contemplation have a hostile relation to the will, when the power of objects menaces the will. I want to transpose Schopenhauer into the domain of poetic influence, because I think Stevens accomplished such a transposition through his apotropaic dialectic of: reducing to a First Idea, finding the reduction intolerable, and then re-imagining the First Idea. The *what* that Stevens reduces is equivalent to Schopenhauer's object of contemplation in its hostile relation to the will. For a poet, however, this *what* is not a natural sublimity, but is the achievement of the precursor. The object of contemplation that has a hostile relation to the will is *the precursor's poem*; it is the power of the precursor's poem that menaces the ephebe's will.

Transposing Schopenhauer into the situation of poetic influence, we would get something like this: The significant forms of the earlier poem invite the new poet to pure contemplation of a possible poetic act. Yet these forms are hostile to the will as the will exhibits itself in its poetic objectivity, which would be the poems of the new poet. These poems are menaced by the greater power of the older poems or, as Schopenhauer says, "sink into insignificance before their immeasurable greatness." On this Schopenhauerian or idealizing view, if the new poet recognizes and perceives this danger, and consciously turns away from it, forcibly detaching himself from his will and its relations, then the new poet could surrender himself to knowledge. The ephebe quietly would contemplate those parent-poems that are so terrible to his own will, and he would comprehend only their deepest meaning (though such a meaning, being as he conceives it, necessarily would be a misprision). This meaning would be foreign to all relation (including, presumably, the influence relation), and as the ephebe gladly lingered over its contemplation, he would be raised above all will into the state of the Sublime. Or, as I would say, the ephebe would have made the Sublime in the precursor's poem.

I believe that some such transposition of Schopenhauer on the Sublime was a vital element in Stevens's major attempt to surmount the anxiety of influence, the attempt being that cluster of ideas about the First Idea which is at the center of much of Stevens's work. I turn to *Notes toward a Supreme Fiction* as text, where no reading can go far without an interpretation of the First Idea.

In Stevens, the necessity for poetry—the "poverty"—rises out of a spirit that denies "the poetic," construed as the unconscious illusive element that yet gives us the poison of social happiness. Poetry is thus the gift of the perversity of the spirit, because poetry rises out of the reductive impulse, or the profound desire not to be deceived. The desire goes too far, and strips subject and object to the intolerable, to the First Idea. What is most important about the First Idea *is* that it *is* intolerable; we cannot live with it. Re-imagining the First Idea is for Stevens the *only* act of the poet, and since we are men of sun, the First Idea is both an unacceptable idea of Man and an unacceptable idea of the sun. The major error in Stevens-criticism is to follow Stevens too closely in his *working assumption* (*not* his deepest conviction) that the First Idea is the Truth, albeit intolerable. The First Idea *cannot* be the Truth, for if it were, then we would be content to live with nature as the animals live with nature.

For Stevens, the truth necessarily is a fiction, the fiction that results from feeling, or the re-imagining of the First Idea. Even the First Idea is an *imagined* thing, and not a thing only. I would summarize this difficult matter in Stevens by saying that the reductive act of wintry vision, the Snow Man stance, is not imaginative in its *impulse* and yet is imaginative in its effect. This is the odd balance Stevens sought to maintain when he remarked of his own achievement that: "The author's work suggests the possibility of a supreme fiction, recognized as a fiction, in which men could propose to themselves a fulfilment."

What does Stevens forget, in his poetic repression, in order for him to be able to present his dialectic of the First Idea in the place of what is being forgotten? I would say that he forgets the darkest insight achieved by our native strain, by the Transcendental tradition of American Romanticism: *In the beginning was the Lie.* All later lies are made against this giant Lie at the origin, and so all strong American poems whatsoever, being later lies, lie against time. But what was the Primal Lie, in an American imaginative context? Surely, it was the Emersonian denial of *Nachträglichkeit,* of being as a nation "after the event." This denial is our national revisionism, that made of all previous cultural history only a deferred action that prepared for our new stage of development. But I am entering here upon yet another aspect of Freud's bewilderingly complex concept of repression, and I will try to clarify the notion of *Nachträglichkeit* before analyzing its denial and repression in *Notes toward a Supreme Fiction.*

Nachträglichkeit, in Freud, rhetorically considered is a metaleptic or transumptive notion. The memory-trace is revised belatedly so as to adjust either to new experience or to a new vision of experience. Freud's crucial statement here comes in an 1896 letter to Fliess: "I am working on the assumption that our psychical mechanism has come into being by a process of stratification: the material present in the form of memory-traces being subjected

from time to time to a *re-arrangement* in accordance with
fresh circumstances—to a *re-transcription*."

This appears to mean that memory-traces that have
undergone the defense of *isolation* tend to be revised
after-the-event. Presumably, the motive for the revision is
that isolation yields to another defense, which I assume
must be a greater repression. Since sexual development
tends to provide the model for Freud's idea of *Nachträglichkeit*, we can surmise that it is the temporal oddity of
sexual maturation that suggests the temporal oddities of
cultural and intellectual maturation, or the temporal vag-
aries of all insight.

The defense of isolation is, rhetorically considered, a
reifying kind of metonymy, which tropes against context,
and Freud seems to imply that *Nachträglichkeit* rises in
response to situations where impulses and impressions
sense that they must reserve themselves for another time,
"loftier and more secluded," as Stevens remarks in his
late, rather Paterian essay called *Two or Three Ideas*. *Notes*
chants the same burden of being after-the-event, of being
out of context:

> From this the poem springs: that we live in a place
> That is not our own and, much more, not ourselves
> And hard it is in spite of blazoned days.

I am not going to offer a complete commentary upon
Notes here, reserving that for a long-gestating book on
Stevens. But I want to dissent, as before, from earlier
canonical readings and, again, my own included. The
critics of Stevens have misread his intricate evasions as his
version of Modernism, yet the study of misprision will
reveal how traditional and overdetermined are the patterns of his defensive tropings. It is the peculiar triumph
of Stevens's poetry that he constructed, out of his very
intense anxiety of belatedness, the Sublime of his
strongest poetry. His isolating metonymies are restituted
by the personally constructed pattern (largely following

Valéry) in which he re-imagines his ironically conceived First Idea, a re-imagining that brings back again the Transcendental strain of American poetry. In section v of *It Must Be Abstract,* the first movement of *Notes,* Stevens contrasts lion, elephant, and bear with his ephebe, to the dialectical advantage *and* disadvantage of the human. It is splendid to be defiant, to roar at the desert with the lion, to blare at the darkness with the elephant, to snarl at the thunder with the bear. To be a human poet is rather less defiantly splendid:

> But you, ephebe, look from your attic window,
> Your mansard with a rented piano. You lie
>
> In silence upon your bed. You clutch the corner
> Of the pillow in your hand. You writhe and press
> A bitter utterance from your writhing, dumb
>
> Yet voluble dumb violence. You look
> Across the roofs as sigil and as ward
> And in your centre mark them and are cowed . . .
>
> These are the heroic children whom time breeds
> Against the first idea—to lash the lion,
> Caparison elephants, teach bears to juggle.

The roofs are seen as by a sigil, hence a seal or signet, a magical image of what it means to be an ephebe, an indoor being. Seen also as by a ward, the roofs mark the saving limitation of the ephebe, who does not confront nature directly, as the animals do. In the next section, the weather is "Not to / Be spoken to, without a roof," again the mark of "the dumbfoundering abyss / Between us and the object," as Stevens's later *Saint John and the Back-Ache* will phrase it. The ephebe lives in poverty, in a rented roof, and with an instrument neither his own nor himself. His utterance comes hard, yet is at least "voluble," since like the song of the girl at Key West it *is* uttered "word by word." Time breeds no more heroic children than its

belated poets, however ridiculous they may seem, for the
poets do not merely cry out *at*, but more strongly *against*
the First Idea. The re-imagined fictions are no more than
circus acts, granted, yet rhetorically this is transumption
rather than irony, projecting the past, introjecting a future, while admitting the loss of a grotesque present. But
how is this a transcendence, a new attainment of the
American Sublime? That is surely the question that the
canonical, ironizing critics of Stevens would venture, in
challenge to this apparently dubious heroism.

For a first answer, I would give the poem's next section,
with its great revival of the Transcendental fiction, the
giant of the American Sublime:

> Without a name and nothing to be desired,
> If only imagined but imagined well.
>
> My house has changed a little in the sun.
> The fragrance of the magnolias comes close,
> False flick, false form, but falseness close to kin.
>
> It must be visible or invisible,
> Invisible or visible or both:
> A seeing and unseeing in the eye.
>
> The weather and the giant of the weather,
> Say the weather, the mere weather, the mere air:
> An abstraction blooded, as a man by thought.

Kermode points to the resemblance between this section and a passage in Stevens's prose book, *The Necessary
Angel:*

> It is as if a man who lived indoors should go outdoors on a day
> of sympathetic weather. His realization of the weather would
> exceed that of a man who lives outdoors. It might, in fact, be
> intense enough to convert the real world about him into an
> imagined world. In short, a sense of reality keen enough to be in
> excess of the normal sense of reality creates a reality of its own.

The prose is more equivocal than the verse, for the poem speaks of more than a "sense of reality" yielding to "an imagined world" or "reality of its own." In the poem, the house *has* changed a little, and the falseness of the flick of change is a Nietzschean or necessary falseness. The "false form" is thus indeed a trope, and there is no weather without the giant, because there is no poetic meaning without the trope, here the repressive trope of hyperbole or the giant of transparency. The giant is the only thinker of, and so the only begetter of, the First Idea. Or, to requote Valéry, the giant saves "the universe [that] cannot for one instant endure to be only what it is." The "false flick, false form" is identical with Valéry's "the mistakes, the appearances, the play of the dioptrics of the mind." For it is the Emersonian giant who, like Valéry's idea, "introduces into what is, the leaven of what is not."

Emerson's names for that giant included "spontaneity," "instinct," and "Self-Reliance," and any other name that would deny being after-the-event. The giant of transparency is identical with the repression of *Nachträglichkeit*, the repression of the necessity for deferred revisionism. But to repress the American sense of cultural belatedness demanded a more primal repression than earlier poetic repressions or achievements of the Sublime had required. And primal repression returns us to the fixation of a primal Scene of Instruction, which means to an inaugural act of consciousness in which the poet overtly makes his own covenant with the god-in-himself. That, I think now, is why Stevens had to bring *Notes* to an apotheosis in which the poet himself displaces Jehovah:

> What am I to believe? If the angel in his cloud,
> Serenely gazing at the violent abyss,
> Plucks on his strings to pluck abysmal glory,
>
> Leaps downward through evening's revelations, and
> On his spredden wings, needs nothing but deep space,
> Forgets the gold centre, the golden destiny,

Grows warm in the motionless motion of his flight,
Am I that imagine this angel less satisfied?
Are the wings his, the lapis-haunted air?

Is it he or is it I that experience this?
Is it I then that keep saying there is an hour
Filled with expressible bliss, in which I have

No need, am happy, forget need's golden hand,
Am satisfied without solacing majesty,
And if there is an hour there is a day,

There is a month, a year, there is a time
In which majesty is a mirror of the self:
I have not but I am and as I am, I am.

The repressed anteriority here partly belongs to
Wordsworth, whose climactic passage in *The Prelude*,
Book xiv, lines 93–114, is being echoed, quite unconsciously I think. There is definite allusion not only to
God's naming of Himself to Moses, but also to Coleridge's
formulation of the Primary Imagination. But all this anteriority is subsumed by Transcendental influx, by that
Sublime re-begetting of the poetic self that is uniquely
and desperately American. Hyperbole, in a post-Christian
context, could not go much beyond the poet's saying: "I
have not but I am and as I am, I am." To have not is also
to have no past, and to have no future. It is TO BE in the
supposed presence of the present. Like Emerson and
Whitman before him, Stevens persuades himself by his
own rhetoric that momentarily, in his poem, his ontological self and his empirical self have come together.
Nietzsche, until he went mad, did not confuse himself
with his own Zarathustra. The Transcendental strain in
Stevens is the native strain in our poetry, and it exacted
of Stevens a rich philosophical confusion upon which
everything that is strongest in American poetic tradition
is founded. Nothing is got for nothing, and it need not
surprise us that Stevens's last poem sublimely celebrates a

"Mere Being" that is beyond not only reason but also beyond all "human meaning" and even "human feeling." The American Sublime ends as the abyss, as the void beckoning just beyond the palm at the end of the mind. There is a great chill in Emerson, and in his children voluntary and involuntary—in Whitman, Thoreau, Dickinson, as in Hawthorne, Melville, James. But there is no chill in all of these so absolute and so Sublime as in the final vision of the Transcendental strain in Wallace Stevens:

> The bird sings. Its feathers shine.
>
> The palm stands on the edge of space.
> The wind moves slowly in the branches.
> The bird's fire-fangled feathers dangle down.